CONTENTS

I0406731

ACKNOWLEDGMENTS

Commencing a project of this magnitude was very similar to the old adage of eating an elephant. Although daunting, the task was possible, but needed to be done one bite at a time. Both of us were very fortunate to have access to years of original Chrysler authentication and are indebted to the many who precede us and share in the passion of documenting these amazing machines.

We want to thank Wes Eisenschenk and Bob Wilson of CarTech for the opportunity to undertake this project, and their patience in guiding us through the necessary hoops to bring this together.

Additionally, we would be at a loss without Rick Kreuziger from Restorations by Rick; Jefferson Bryant of Red Dirt Rods; Mike Saless of Legendary Auto Interiors; Jeff Leonard and Ray Yager of Classic Industries; Kevin King of YearOne; Jason Tessler of Just Dashes; Steve, Chris, and Jeremiah at Spicer Automotive and Four Wheel Drive; Ryan Brutt; and Diego Rosenberg.

Kevin Shaw

I would like to thank my wife, Heather, for her support, encouragement, and patience throughout this past year; my daughters, Morgan and Natalie; my father, Kerry, for passing down his passion for absurdly expensive toys; and my brother Cameron for encouraging me to buy my first Dodge more than a dozen years ago.

Special thanks go to Randy Bolig for giving me my start, to Dave Young for his insight, to Dave Everhart of HP Performance, to Bobby Kimbrough for keeping me sane when I needed help the most, and to Mike Wilkins for joining me on this journey.

Thanks to all the people who specifically contributed to the book: Duane Cates, Chet Biggers, Gary Faulkner, Mitch Spicer, and others who love these cars enough to share everything about them for those who are trying to bring these cars back to life.

Mike Wilkins

I would like to thank the following people for fostering love and knowledge of these wonderful cars over the years. First, my hometown pastor Bob Post, who had a friendly connection to a small town Chrysler dealer, Bynum Chrysler dealership in Siloam Springs, Arkansas. Because he was interested in helping everyone get a "good deal" on a new car the parking lot was always full of great Mopars. So I grew up with many Chrysler, Plymouth, and Dodge cars in my life over the years of 1960–1975. Next were all my buds with Mopars, including Mike Bush, Darrel "Buzz" McGuire, Wes Burton, Todd Kidd, Jimmy Johnson, and my brother Rogzilla, who always had these cool cars.

I also want to thank all the people I came in contact with over the years who knew way more than I did about these awesome cars: Roger Gibson, Cliff Gromer, Kevin Diossi, Paul Jacobs, Robert Wolf, Richard Ehrenberg, Frank Badalson, Ken Mosier, Dave Walden, Gary Faulkner, and Galen Govier; they answered all of my questions when none of this information was available to the average guy. To all my buds in the Music City Mopar Club in Nashville, Tennessee, and my special Mopar judge bud, brother Ron.

To my wonderful wife, Sulyn, who had no idea how dedicated to these cars I was when she married me, and to my way cool kids, Valerie and Blake.

Thank you to Kevin Shaw who has been more than a brother to me over the years of writing this book.

ABOUT THE AUTHORS

Authors Kevin Shaw (left) and Mike Wilkins (right) install a heavily modified Chrysler RB 440 engine into a 1969 Dodge Charger.

Kevin Shaw is a decade-long powersports and automotive journalist whose love for things that go too fast has led him from his earliest days as the associate editor at *Mopar Muscle* and *Corvette Fever*, to a senior editor for *Power Automedia*, helming the digital magazine titles *Street Legal TV, LSX TV, Chevy Hardcore*, and *Rod Authority*. Today, he operates his own digital publishing company, Shaw Group Media. Almost always found with stained hands and dirt under his fingernails, Kevin has an eye for the technical while keeping an eye out for beautiful photography and a great story.

Mike Wilkins is a lifelong Mopar owner, restorer, and car enthusiast, as well as a respected judge of original Plymouth and Dodge B-Bodies both nationally and locally. Self-taught from his early teens, Wilkins has spent nearly half a century driving, racing, and restoring some of the finest Mopars in the United States, earning several Antique Automobile of America Grand National Senior awards, Mopar National Best of Show and first place awards, 16 magazine appearances, and a feature in the *Chrysler, Dodge, and Plymouth Muscle* book. He has dedicated thousands of hours examining original untouched cars, providing and gathering research from many Mopar experts over the years of restoring every nut and bolt of these vehicles.

PREFACE

When the opportunity was first presented to produce a restoration guide for B-Body Mopars, we condensed the model years to 1968–1970 for several reasons: the overall popularity of the models introduced during these short three years of production, the quantity of units sold, and the abundance of aftermarket support for these model years. Although our thinking was sound, the clearer minds at CarTech advised against such a narrow target, citing that many of the popular models we addressed had been introduced prior to 1968, particularly the Dodge Charger, Coronet R/T, and Plymouth GTX.

In delving into the research, we thankfully found a fair amount of crossover between the two groups (1966–1967 and 1968–1970), which eased our process tremendously. Obviously, plenty of "one off" modifications, tweaks, and improvements were made from model year to model year, as Chrysler was embroiled in the height of the muscle car wars against General Motors and Ford. Many bristle at the idea of models changing so rapidly from year to year, but such was the fashion of American automakers during these tentative years.

Today, model changes are spaced out over three to five years (if not longer), with minor changes between them.

Nevertheless, with the charge in front of us, we immediately went to our own private libraries for assistance. Undoubtedly, Paul A. Herd's *Charger, Road Runner & Super Bee Restoration Guide* was a central resource. And many others have proved to be instrumental in the development of this book as they've assisted in the restorations of countless vintage Mopars on the road today living a second life. In essence, this book is a companion to these works; we have striven to provide content not otherwise found or equally organized. In taking the assignment quite literally, we sought not to make this a "here's what it takes to get your project Mopar out on the street" breeze-through, but a revelatory tutorial in how these machines were assembled from the factory and how that process can be adequately replicated.

Although many guides, technical articles, and books are dedicated to the minutia of assembling B and RB Chrysler engines, 727 and A-833 manual transmission, and 8¾ and Dana 60 rear ends, we do offer details on properly re-creating the assembly of these very important parts. Other instructions that we've included, such as replacing floorboards and quarter panels, which might be well outside of the realm of the layman restorer, also show the detail and care necessary to resurrect a car seemingly "too far gone." Again, we didn't want to merely skim the surface, but wished instead to truly delve in deep where and when we could (page count and time allowing). We felt that other topics, such as wiring, rebuilding engines/transmissions, and welding, are handily covered in other resources and therefore omitted.

We also strove as diligently as possible to eradicate as much fluff as possible. Often, books such as this are rife with filler pages, offering personal opinion, conjecture, and content simply inapplicable to restoring a car to OEM level.

This was our charge, and we took it seriously. This restoration guide does not contain aftermarket superchargers, 18-inch wheels, or custom flame paint jobs. Although we wish for all readers to get the utmost enjoyment out of their cars, we are not content to offer input that would simply "get her rolling." Our aim is to elevate your understanding of the true meaning of "restoration."

Whether you choose to drive or trailer your finished Chrysler B-Body is left entirely up to you.

INTRODUCTION

Although this book focuses on the 1966–1970 Dodge and Plymouth vehicles based upon the Chrysler B platform, the B-Body chassis was the basis for rear-wheel-drive Chrysler cars dating as far back as 1962 and as late as 1979. Interestingly, despite the B-Body chassis debuting in 1962, Chrysler's practice of naming models by letter did not begin until 1964–1965. Each of the B-Body cars in this period, for either make, was built upon the same chassis. However, the outward appearance varied greatly among makes and models.

From 1966 to 1970, Plymouth used the B-Body chassis for four cars with nearly identical design aesthetics, differing of course, in trim packages, drivetrain options, and accessories: Belvedere, Satellite, GTX, and Road Runner. The Superbird set itself apart from this lineup with its extended nose and a high-mounted rear wing, making it clearly the only Plymouth B-Body to appear radically different from the others.

For Dodge's B-Bodies, the external design cues varied more. Although Dodge's Coronet, Coronet R/T, and Super Bee followed Plymouth's philosophy of mild differentiation through the trim package, the fastback Charger was significantly more stylized in its appearance, particularly after its redesign in 1968. Add to that the Daytona and its extended nose and towering rear wing, and the Dodge lineup looked far more diverse than its Plymouth siblings.

Designed as Chrysler's "intermediate" platform, the B-Body chassis provided the automaker a versatile chassis from which to build 18 different models. Over the years, the B-Body's 116-inch wheelbase was shortened and lengthened to accommodate new models and longer wagons. Nevertheless, the platform proved to be a true performer in nearly every imaginable sphere: from street driving to the quarter-mile to the high banks of NASCAR racetracks.

Debuting halfway through the model year, the "M" code Super Bee featured an inline tri-power setup atop a 440. Common for display at shows, the hood rods supporting the liftoff hood were not offered by Chrysler.

Chrysler debuted a new body style for the B-Body Coronet in 1968. Engine packages ranged from the 225 6-cylinder "slant-6" up to the dual-quad–fueled 426 Hemi.

Available Powertrains

Power was never in short supply, if chirping the tires (or worse) was on your to-do list. Of course, Chrysler offered plenty of economical power-plants as well, including a variety of slant-6 (170, 198, and 225-cci) engines, several variations of the 273 and 318 small-block V-8s, and even 2-barrel carbureted low-deck big-block 383s.

For those wanting to make a true impact at the stoplight, high-output versions of the 361 and the 383 (with a 4-barrel carburetor) V-8, the venerable RB 440 engine available in a handful of carburetion packages (from the stout 4-barrel setup to the heavy-breathing 6-barrel triple car-buretor package), and of course, the legendary 426 Hemi engine with dual 4-barrel carburetors, became available for the street in the B-Body chassis in 1966.

The purpose of this book is to help you identify, authenticate, disassemble, restore, and reassemble your GTX or other B-Body machine. We strove to include as much detail as possible so that you could best replicate the process Chrysler itself used in assembling these muscle cars.

Chrysler B-Body Platform Cars

1962 Dodge Dart	1965–1976 Dodge Coronet
1962–1964 Dodge Polara	1966–1978 Dodge Charger
1962–1964 Plymouth Fury	1967–1971 Plymouth GTX
1962–1964 Plymouth Savoy	1968–1975 Plymouth Road Runner
1962–1970 Plymouth Belvedere	1975–1978 Plymouth Fury
1963–1964 Dodge 220 (Canadian)	1975–1979 Chrysler Cordoba
1963–1964 Dodge 330	1977–1978 Dodge Monaco
1963–1964 Dodge 440	1978–1979 Dodge Magnum
1965–1974 Plymouth Satellite	1979 Chrysler 300

By 1969, the Chrysler B-Body chassis was already five years old. This image of the second-generation Dodge Charger (featuring the iconic Coke-bottle shape by Richard Sias and Harvey J. Winn) shows the aggressive bodylines created on this iconic car. (Photo Courtesy Historic Restorations)

As competition from Ford and General Motors escalated the horsepower wars, evolution of the powertrains continued throughout this four-year period, with improvements in camshaft grinds, connecting rod, piston and piston pin design and materials, vibration dampening, internal balancing, valvetrain, cylinder head, and exhaust and intake manifold design.

Likewise, improvements to torque converters (or flywheels, when equipped with a manual transmission) were balanced to match the ever-increasing engine performance. When power outputs increased, so did the demand on the rest of the drivetrain. The once-standard 3-speed manual (with its column-mounted shifter) that backed most B-Body cars equipped with an engine beneath the 4-barrel 273, gave way to the A-833 4-speed manual.

Designed to contend with the forces delivered by the brutish 440 and 426 Hemis, the 4-speed featured all synchronized forward speeds and a positive reverse-lockout feature (new for 1966). Additionally, the 4-speed was console shifted, and was optional when powered by a 383 (4-barrel) V-8 or 440. Production records show that the 4-speed was standard for the higher performance engines unless an automatic was optioned.

The automatic in question was Chrysler's 3-speed TorqueFlite transmission. Featuring an aluminum housing, the automatic featured an optional internally actuated parking sprag and could be shifted either on the column or center console.

Considering all of the available powertrain combinations, rear gear offerings, and engine packages that Chrysler offered from the factory, and what you can dream up, your selection for your particular project car is as limited as your imagination and budget. Thankfully, Ma Mopar allowed for a wide variety of powertrain and engine combinations for the B-Body lineup, freeing up your restoration project to be as mild or wild as you choose.

The fabled Air Grabber assembly, operated from a control in the cockpit, sucked cold air in through the hood and into the carburetor below, feeding a steady flow to mix with the fuel.

The iconic Hemi. Never before or since have three numbers on the exterior panel of a car struck so much fear in a foe at a stoplight.

GETTING STARTED

Purchasing a Chrysler B-Body is a great project that is immensely rewarding in a variety of ways. Not only does the finished outcome provide you with a classic muscle car that you are proud of, enjoy driving, or can turn around for a return on your investment, but along the way you acquire new abilities, skill, and patience.

But be warned: In most cases you spend much more time and money than you expected or budgeted for. Only the most experienced resto-

ration shop or builder can expertly estimate the hours and dollars necessary to bring any project car back to running condition.

So prior to purchasing your first Mopar project, it is imperative to take into account several factors; key among them is assessing your budget, your skill level, the tools and equipment needed, and your ultimate project goals. In this chapter we help you evaluate these considerations so that you can find the right project to suit your means, abilities, and budget.

Not All Cars Are Created Equal

All too often, would-be restorers come across a car that piques their interest and become excited before truly assessing the situation. Although the money they've squirreled away might be enough to lightly clean up a rough driver, sometimes the opportunity to purchase an original big-block R/T in significantly worse shape arises and blinds their judgment.

Thinking that the R/T is a once-in-a-lifetime opportunity, they jump headfirst into what could potentially become a money pit. As difficult as it may be to accept, some cars are just "too far gone." Yes, the idea of a significantly rare and original Hemi 4-speed rotting away in a backfield is a terrible one to consider, but sometimes they're just too rotted away to save.

Many Chrysler vehicles left the factory with either raw or only lightly treated metal components. Cars that have spent too many freezing winters outside are likely candidates to be passed over. Too much of the car might have succumbed to cancerous rust to salvage, the victim of drastic

Choosing to rescue a forgotten muscle car might save you money up front but can be costly when you begin to unravel all of the damage caused by years of neglect.

swings in temperature, the corrosive properties of salt used to melt iced-over roads, and moisture.

Likewise, a project can be far too complicated for your skill set. Vehicles such as Chargers, Daytonas, and Superbirds featured complex vacuum-operated hideaway headlight doors. Similar systems are found on cars equipped with Air Grabber cold-air induction. Cars equipped with air conditioning, multiple carburetors, or even cruise control can leave you scratching your head or worse yet, chasing incredibly rare, and thereby expensive, parts.

Additionally, incredibly collectible or rare vehicles can prove to be far too difficult to restore correctly. Chrysler offered a litany of options to the buyer during these years, ensuring the possibility of seemingly endless combinations. Unfortunately, decades of use (or misuse), modifications made by previous owners, and general wear-and-tear can make reassembling such a machine a veritable treasure hunt.

That is why it is important for you to have an open mind when selecting the "perfect project" to restore. Be brutally honest with yourself. Do not be afraid to pass up the

It is very likely that some parts on your Mopar muscle car have already been spirited away, particularly if the car came equipped with rare parts or a desirable engine.

first potential project you find, or the second or even the fifth. Don't let your eyes get too big. You're going to be spending a lot of time and effort on this car.

Dollars and Sense

Unlike rebuilding a Ford Mustang or Chevrolet Camaro, undertaking a Mopar project vehicle poses some unique and expensive challenges. Even the most mass-produced Chrysler B-Bodies' numbers pale when compared to the sheer quantities of the other manufacturers. Although rarity and obscurity lends

itself to greater demand for a finished restoration, so too does it elevate the cost of parts necessary to complete your project. Even the most run-of-the-mill 318-powered Dodge or Plymouth B-Body can surprise you by depleting your checkbook in little time. Budgeting for a project vehicle requires considering how much money you are willing to spend to purchase the car, and then weighing all of the work necessary to bring the project to driving condition.

It's a widely understood maxim that spending more money upfront for a more complete car can actually save you quite a bit in the long run. Although an original 440+6 Road Runner might sound like a fun car to have, a stripped-bare hulk sitting on its frame rails is missing much more than meets the eye.

Missing linkages, air cleaner components, and other oddities that you might not immediately consider can add up very quickly. Obviously, the closer the project is to being a functioning automobile the better; you spend less time scouring message boards and online vendors for the rare oddities that are no longer available.

Buying a Car: Is It Original?

We have all seen ads using the key words and phrases "numbers matching," "all original," "survivor," and "NOS parts," only to discover a car that may or may not be all it was said to be. Armed with knowledge, documented numbers, and a desire to check all the most important identifiers, you can verify the claims.

The old adage "You can fool some of the people some of the time, but not all of the people all of time" applies to the many sellers who try to fool potential buyers. However, even the best cannot hide reality when a knowledgeable buyer inspects the car. The value of a true numbers-matching car far outweighs the value of a car that has none of its original equipment. Whether you are buying the car to drive or as an investment, documenting the car before you purchase it can mean fewer headaches, more value, and increased peace of mind when and if you do decide to sell the car.

Again, because of the low production numbers of Chrysler B-Bodies compared to their across-town rivals, the size of the aftermarket is equally slim. Don't expect to walk into your local speed shop or classic car swap meet and walk out with what you need, or not pay a premium.

Likewise, as we've mentioned above, some extremely desirable and therefore expensive Chryslers are out there. This might tempt you to perform a "re-creation" or passable "clone," converting a low-optioned vehicle into a high-optioned one. This can be and is regularly done throughout the industry, but it isn't as easy as you might think.

Even converting a lowly small-block–powered Dodge Charger into a winged Daytona is a massive undertaking that can cost well over $20,000 in just the nosecone, wing, and rear window plug. Unless you have the initial capital to invest, do not enter into a project that will deplete your savings before you get the chance to enjoy the finished product.

Know Your Skills

Next, consider how much of the work you're willing to do yourself. Truly assessing your skill level is one of the hardest things to do. We all want to believe we're capable of anything, but now is the time to admit where your shortcomings are in regard to restoring a classic Mopar. It's okay. Nobody will think any less of you for being honest.

This step is equally as valuable in your project budgeting as selecting the right car. How? Only when fairly weighing what portions of the build you're willing to do yourself versus outsourcing are you able to better approximate your expenses.

Consider whether you will handle the disassembly, labeling, and cataloging. How about the bodywork and rust removal? Do you have a welder and metal tools? Do you trust yourself to do all of the preparation prior to painting your project? How about rebuilding the engine and drivetrain? Wiring and plumbing?

These are a small selection of larger tasks that complete the restoration of the project. In this book, we provide an outline to help you break down the many steps necessary in disassembling, restoring, and reassembling a classic Mopar B-Body muscle car. But it's up to you to decide what steps you take yourself, and those that you farm out.

If you want to prep and paint the car yourself, you need to compile a comprehensive list of tools, equipment, and materials as well as schedule the time and budget. In both cases round up. There's never any harm in coming in under budget. We outline everything you need to prep, paint, and finish an OEM-level restoration that you can use as a guide. If you opt

instead to send your car out for paint and bodywork, now is the time to start researching local and reputable body shops, ideally those that have classic automotive experience.

Even before purchasing a project car, consider spending some much needed "due diligence" by acquiring catalogs of the major aftermarket suppliers that specialize in Mopars (YearOne, Classic Industries, B/E&A Restoration Parts, Dante's Parts, etc.). This provides a very general understanding of the costs of highly consumable parts such as interior components, brake and suspension parts, trim, emblems, and much more.

Start Shopping for a Shop

After you've read the chapters about how to strip, do bodywork, paint, and polish your project car, you may say, "I can't do all that. I need to find a good shop to get my car in paint."

Finding a good shop to restore your vintage Mopar is not as easy as

Having your engine balanced and blueprinted gives your powerplant the best viability for survival and is highly recommended. It certainly helps when your restoration shop has a dyno in-house as well.

Internet Sources

In the age of the Internet you can find literally thousands of places to buy a 1966–1970 B-Body Plymouth or Dodge. The days of looking in the local newspaper classified section are long gone. But that is a good thing. It is a very good thing. In the classifieds you could only get a short description and a phone number to call.

With the "classified" ads on the Internet you can see detailed pictures or view a video of the car. You can even find out exactly where the car is located. You can also investigate online auctions.

But with all of this information as close as your computer screen or phone display you still must be careful and take all necessary steps to avoid getting burned. The saying "Buyer Beware" is just as true today as it was 25 years ago.

Websites

Three of the most popular sites to search are eBay.com, CarsOnLine.com, and craigslist.org. Also many Mopar clubs sites have a "cars for sale" section.

Each of these sites has pros and cons and it is best to use the ones that have some kind of buyer protection built into the buying process. When using these sites to buy a car or parts for your project it is good to use a PayPal.com account; it has a built-in protection process in case the purchase does not go as planned.

Always remember, "if it is too good to be true," it probably is. The Internet is a great place to find the car of your dreams but it also has some pitfalls to be aware of when making a purchase. Do your homework, and if at all possible, view the car in person and follow the guidelines listed later in this chapter for documenting a car.

eBay.com

This site is by far the most popular and the safest place to go for cars and parts. When you link a PayPal.com account to your eBay account and you purchase a car through the two sites you have buyer protection and a recourse process to protect the transaction. You can see the seller's history, read feedback from all of the people who have purchased from the seller, and ask questions through your account that give you documentation of all of the communication about the purchase.

Purchasing a car through eBay has a few negative aspects. It is an auction site where you are bidding against many other buyers, and you can get caught up in the last-minute bidding and pay much more than the car is worth. Another shortfall is that the car may be on the East Coast while you are on the West Coast and the auction is only five days long. So unless you are able to inspect the car in person before the auction ends you are basically buying the car sight unseen. Pictures are good, but nothing is as good as seeing it for yourself. When you do buy the car you have to arrange for shipping through a trucking company, then pay for the car before you can even see it.

This site works very hard to protect those who use it, but there have been instances where someone's account has been hacked and a non-existent car is listed. An uninformed buyer wires the payment for the car up front and the hackers have your money and you have nothing. Never wire funds until you are sure the car is what you think it is and the seller is legit!

CarsOnLine.com

This site is a modern classified ad section. You can see cars listed for sale from all over the country. It is not an auction site but a site where a car can be listed "for sale" with a full-length description, at least three or four good pictures, an asking price, and the seller's information. The seller has the option to post many more pictures and even a video of the car running. This site is well organized so you can search for the exact model you are looking for without the pressure of having to make a decision whether or not to purchase in a short amount of time.

The transaction is between the seller and the buyer so there isn't any information about the seller or his/her selling history, and there isn't any recourse if the car is not as advertised. The purchase price, arrangements for delivery, and all aspects of the transaction are up to the buyer just as when you look in the local paper for your project, but on a national level.

Craigslist.org

This is a very popular site simply because it is free. It is a bare-bones classified ad site with sellers from all over the country. It is a good online venue and for finding a really good deal on a car that has been tucked away in a garage and hasn't seen the light of day in many years. You can also find a freshly restored $100,000 car. Buying parts and cars through this site is just like using the classified ads. All of the transaction is between the buyer and the seller and there isn't any real protection for a deal gone bad.

Online Auctions

Outlining the parameters for finding the right car can literally constitute its own book, so we're going to only touch on this subject here with more hints and suggestions throughout the entirety of this book.

As stated earlier, spending more money upfront for a more complete car, even one in running or near-running condition, can save you immense time and labor. Of course, not everyone has the capital to purchase such a car, so a vehicle in rougher condition or in need of substantially more repair lowers the initial asking price.

Suitable Chrysler B-Bodies for restoration can be found nearly everywhere, although in lesser numbers. The observant eye can still find the occasional 1970 Super Bee tucked away in a rural backyard, a 1967 Plymouth Satellite down an urban alleyway, or the familiar C-pillar of a 1968 Dodge Charger in the back of a crowded supermarket parking lot.

Before resorting to online auction sites, I strongly suggest combing your local trades for listings, swap meets, and even large car shows. Many bring their unfinished projects to the shows to sell, and many a good deal have been made there. Obviously, online sites including Craigslist or major Mopar forums (Moparts.com, Allpar.com, etc.) as well as a variety of Facebook pages also host large swap meet sections where cars are listed on a daily basis.

I even suggest joining your local Mopar club, as many of these members are avid collectors and enthusiasts who in addition to knowing where a potential project car might be, can also lend a hand and some much appreciated expertise in helping your restoration.

I only suggest resorting to online shopping if the local scene appears to be thoroughly picked over, as purchasing a car "sight unseen" is less than ideal and shipping a car across the country is expensive, particularly if it doesn't run. ∎

going to the closest repair shop and asking for an estimate. What do you ask first, or for that matter what do you ask last? Finding a quality shop that knows Mopars and how to restore them, and that can turn your car around in a timely manner and not jack up the price along the way, is one of your most important decisions.

The best place to begin your search for a good shop is the local car show or cruise-in. Also check with local Mopar club members about who they have used. Look at as many nice cars as possible and talk to the owners. By talking to the car's owner you can find out if he recommends the shop, how long it took to get the car finished, and even how much it cost. Word of mouth is always better than a blind search on the Internet. By doing this you can form a good opinion of that shop's work and overall experience from other customers.

When you do find someone with a car you admire, find out how exten-

sive the repairs were. If the quarter was replaced ask the owner if you can look in the trunk and see how well the shop did on the welds. Check the car overall for good fitment of doors, fenders, and correct body panel gaps. Look for waves down the side of the car and examine the finish of the paint. With luck you will find a shop that speaks Mopar. If not remember that you may have to educate the shop on the differences that make a Mopar correct and stand your ground if you want them to do the work like Ma Mopar did.

If the shop assembled the car after painting, check all the windows, glass, interior, and engine compartment for correct appearance. Look at the car as if you were judging it at a car show. Also check other projects by the same shop and find out if the shop is consistently turning out good cars.

After you have talked to several owners, narrowed down the prospec-

tive candidates, and have answers you are comfortable with, drop in and get to know the shop up close and personal. For example, when you arrive, do you see 10 or more cars sitting in a row waiting for work to begin? Your car has to get in line and that could mean a lot of time before the work even begins. Check out the condition of the shop. Watch for good workflow, notice how many employees work there, whether the tools are in order, etc. A body shop is often a dirty place but you can tell if professionals run the shop. Some of the best restorations come out of one-man, one-car shops, so don't let the size of the shop be the deciding factor.

Review the Budget

Before you sit down with the shop, make sure that you know your available budget. You need to know the level and quality of paint job you can afford, and it's best to have your spouse on board. More than one marriage has had problems over a restoration project.

The individual shop determines how you pay for and monitor the progress of your car's paint and bodywork. If they are going to perform a full restoration and deliver a turnkey car, it becomes even more complicated. Never, and I mean *never*, pay the entire amount up front. Always get a written contract of work to be performed, payment schedule, time frame, and specific supplies to be used. More than one owner has had his or her car in "Paint Shop Jail." So a written contract is a must.

After you reach an agreement visit the shop, take pictures of the progress, and keep a good working relationship with the people who are doing the work. The last thing you want to do is make an enemy of the guy who ultimately determines the final outcome of your investment. Keep a written journal with dates and progress pictures.

Getting your car in paint is one of, if not *the* most important and difficult step of a restoration. Whether you build the car after paint, or have the shop complete the car, the paint

is the first thing you and everyone else notice. It should be a source of pride and satisfaction, not irritation and frustration!

Work Area

The final step prior to actually purchasing your new project car is preparing a place to keep it and work on it (preferably these two places are the same). An enclosed and weatherproof garage with plenty of room to move around the car is best. Understand that much of the time during the build your project remains immobile. So wherever you're planning to store your car, make sure that you're not blocking foot traffic or an area that is accessed regularly.

In addition, make sure that the garage is uncluttered and free of shelves stacked with items that could fall on your car. It sounds unlikely, but you'd be surprised how often a box of Christmas decorations has fallen on a project car. Try to avoid anything hanging above your car as well. Simply make your new car's garage as clean, organized, and safe as possible.

Make sure you have ample storage space for all of the parts you pull off, documenting, and storing until it's time to restore and reinstall them on your car. A workbench is worth its weight in gold, as is an organized tool box or chest. Rooting through disheveled drawers of wrenches or searching through a pile of sockets for the right tool is time wasted.

Other tools necessary to any build include a bench or table vise, a quality air compressor (I suggest a 50-gallon minimum), an impact gun, a handheld as well as a bench grinder, a rivet gun, an electric drill and spot-weld cutter, a variable speed buffer, wool pads, foam pads, sanding discs, four heavy-duty jack stands, and a floor jack.

Although you don't have to own them, having access to an engine hoist ("cherry picker"); a four-leg engine stand; a MIG welder, mask, and gloves; media or "blast" cabinet; and a quality gravity-fed spray gun and touch-up gun is good, particularly if you plan to do much of the restoration yourself.

Thankfully, many tools are available for rent or loan from large

A clean and tidy work area is a must when restoring a Mopar B-Body. Here gaskets are in one area, nuts/bolts/ fasteners in another, and fluids and cleaning supplies rest atop the cabinets.

Although 50 years of exposure to the elements might leave a lot of potential projects "too far gone" (particularly for the novice restorer), many enthusiasts contend that plenty of cars are still to be found and brought back.

Tools

You need many tools and pieces of equipment to restore a car; here is a quick list of what I call "must haves."

- Garage (two-car minimum)
- Air compressor (50-gallon minimum)
- Good set of wrenches, sockets, screwdrivers, Allen wrenches, pliers, channel locks, breaker bar
- Bench grinder
- Handheld grinder
- Drill and bits
- Impact wrench
- Heavy-duty jack stands (4)
- Torque wrench
- Ohmmeter
- Test light
- Droplight
- Floor jack
- Sawzall
- Eye protection
- Facemask
- Trim remover tool
- Rubber mallet
- Vacuum gauge and pump
- Ball-peen hammer
- Wire cutters
- Razor knife
- Bench vise
- Workbench
- Creeper

The following tools and equipment are recommended and can be borrowed or rented:

- Cherry picker
- MIG welder, welder's mask, gloves
- Gravity-fed spray gun, touch-up gun
- Engine stand
- Trailer (18 feet minimum)
- Vehicle to tow trailer and car
- Hog ring pliers
- Blast cabinet
- Under-coating gun
- Ring compressor
- Rivet gun
- Spot-weld cutter
- Variable-speed buffer, wool pads, foam pads, sanding discs
- Die grinder with cutting wheels
- Corbin clamp pliers
- Air file
- Hammer and dolly set
- Dual-action (DA) sander
- Sanding blocks of various sizes
- Palm sander short throw ◼

automotive part chain stores and from friends. Items including wheel pullers, timing lights, and torque wrenches can be at the ready when you need them, and save you hundreds of dollars over buying them, particularly if you plan to build just one car.

Do Your Research

Upon seeing your potential project in person, some major identifiers must be confirmed before making a final purchase. First, verify if the title is clear and registered to the person who is selling it. Is it registered?

Even if the car is a steal, the potential for exorbitant DMV fees could be a detractor.

How about the vehicle identification number (VIN); do the numbers match? Thankfully, Mopars are known for their marking of nearly every part with a stamp or part number, as well as a detailed fender tag and "build sheet" that can be referenced for verification.

The build sheet (or broadcast sheet as it is officially called) was the options list that followed the car down the assembly line, documenting the entirety of the options installed on the car, the paint and

interior colors, accessories, powertrain, and much more. The broadcast sheet can completely reveal what your Mopar looked like when it

Gather as much information as possible to unlock the options, paint code, and powertrain on a particular Chrysler B-Body when it left the factory.

The Dutchman panel, or window valance as it is commonly called, is often corroded because the factory rear window featured very poor drainage. This left water to collect and ultimately corrode the metal. (Photo Courtesy Ryan Brutt)

rolled off the assembly line, though not all cars had one and some even had the wrong one. Always make sure to match the VIN on the broadcast sheet with that of the car.

Unlike fender tags, which attached with screws to the inner wheelwell inside the engine bay, build sheets were either tucked in the underside of a seat or beneath the carpet. Both the fender tag and broadcast sheet (as well as the VIN) are easily identified.

Next, verify if the engine, transmission, and rear end are original to the car. Although the prospect of an aftermarket big-block swap into a small-block or 6-cylinder might be attractive, it's important to know whether the person doing the swap would need to upgrade the suspension to accommodate the dramatic change in weight, the engine cradle (K-member), and electrical systems.

How about the auxiliaries? What power options did the car originally come with and are they intact? Air conditioning, power brakes, and power steering are common options that can be disconnected, removed, or replaced if not kept in good running condition.

Inspection Details

Although body panels vary from model to model, below is a collection of "trouble spots" commonly found on 1966–1970 Chrysler B-Bodies that are susceptible to rust.

Body and Panel Alignment

Next, and most obvious, is the condition of the body. Depending on the completion of the car itself, this may take some time. I suggest bringing a magnet to run along the body, as a magnet loses its pull when it encounters body filler. Look for bubbling, pitting, or discoloring in the paint, as these are sure signs of rust rising up to the surface. Major areas to observe are in the rear quarters, around the rear window, at the bottom rear of the front fenders, and along the running boards.

Open the doors and inspect the jambs, doorsill, and hinges. If possible, peel back a portion of carpet to get a good look at the floorpan. Inside of the trunk is imperative too. Unfortunately, Chryslers have some "trouble areas" that were notorious for rust, one being the "Dutchman panel," the portion of sheet metal between the rear window and the deck lid.

Next, get down on your hands and knees and look at the condition of the frame rails, trunk, and floorboards. A topical or "quickie" paint job can cover up surface rust but often doesn't address the undercarriage. It's also a good opportunity to

The lower ends of the front fenders suffered greatly from rust because of two key factors: (1) drainage from the roof's A-pillar ran down between the fender and doorjamb, and (2) rain and moisture collected where the fender bolted to the running boards. Thankfully, the inside of each fender was sprayed with an undercoating, but often the application was incredibly shoddy and uneven.

Although the lower quarter panels were dipped in a rust-preventive primer, cars that lived in severely cold and wet climates or where roads were salted during the winter are often found with rust bubbling up through the paint.

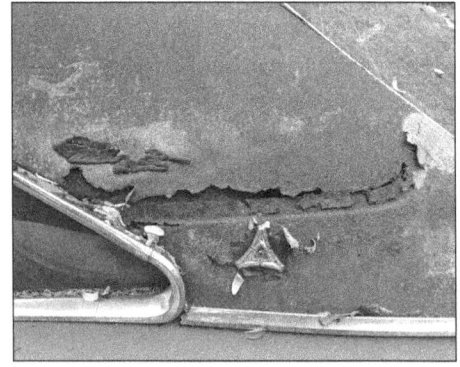

It's commonly understood that cars optioned with vinyl tops fared the worst, as the vinyl top, albeit an attractive option, retained quite a bit of moisture. Roofs were left unpainted, sealed with only a thin coat of primer from the factory, and thereby vulnerable to cancerous rust.

Years of moisture and sunshine can deteriorate a dash and cluster to nearly unsalvageable condition. Be prepared for discolored gauges and cracked steering wheels that need attention. Many of these parts need reconditioning, as replacements are not available in the reproduction market.

observe the condition of the brake and fuel lines for breaks, missing clips or hangars, and damage.

Finally, look closely at the body panel alignment. Using a coin or even your fingertip to check seam gaps, look for unevenness or warping. Again, chips in the paint around the edges of the doorsills, trunk, and hood can be signs of misalignment. Other telltale signs include whether the factory seam sealer is in place and whether new welds can be observed either inside the trunk or in the undercarriage. You can use the old trick of rolling a marble to see if it rolls smoothly. Ultimately, you're looking to see if all the panels were hung correctly and if the car suffered severe damage in a wreck that distorted the car's frame.

Interior Components

Finally, find out how modified the interior of the car is. How original is the car? Are the gauges original? The steering wheel or column? How about the radio? The presence of an aftermarket radio and speakers, and how cleanly the installation was, often gives a good indication about other modifications made to the car. Chasing hundreds of feet of wiring can be a tiring exercise when trying to find a broken signal; it can be avoided with a careful review of the car in question.

Running and Stopping

Although it's unlikely that your project car is running, if you're looking at a "driver" take it for a 20-minute test. Listen for squeaks, rattles, chatter, clunks, or any other sounds. These might be indicators of loose, misaligned, or broken parts. Pay close attention to how the car handles, accelerates, and stops. All of these can reveal what kind of project you're walking into.

Restoration Levels

Finally, and quite possibly the most important of all of these steps to consider prior to purchasing a Mopar project car, is deciding your goals for this build. There are many ways to build these cars, as they excel in so many different areas. As an OEM-level restoration, possibly no other chassis of domestic muscle

car retains greater value, demand, and general appeal than the B-Body Chryslers: Dodge Chargers, Plymouth Road Runners, Super Bees, Daytonas, and the like.

If you're interested in building a street/strip performer, Mopar B-Bodies have an excellent track record, and when built right, are nearly unstoppable. Mopar B-Body project cars are well represented in major enthusiast magazines. Likewise, the B-Body chassis has become a favored platform for many autocross and G-Machine builders, if top-level handling and street performance is your goal.

Even if you're hoping just to enjoy a slightly warmed-over street-worthy driver, it's important to make that decision now. This allows you ample time to plan for expenses such as aftermarket performance parts, time at an engine dyno, and so on.

We cannot emphasize enough how crucial it is to your project to fully realize the ultimate goal of your build and, this is key, not deviate from it. Executing a build to its fullest and final extent requires a great deal of commitment, discipline, and patience. Changing thematic direction mid-build is almost fatal to a project car. Now is the time to decide what kind of car you want your project to be and plan accordingly.

The journey from discovery to full recovery can be an arduous one, but equally fulfilling. Personally undertaking such a task can appear daunting at first but is a major source of personal pride when completed.

IDENTITY DOCUMENTS

If you are fortunate enough to have any original factory documents with your car you are in the minority. If a car has even one of these documents it raises the desirability and even the value of the car. Only a very small percentage of 1966–1970 Plymouth and Dodge B-Bodies are lucky enough to have some of these documents and even fewer have all of these important papers.

The broadcast sheet, Certicard, window sticker, dealer invoice, owner's manual, warranty manual, and original receipts are all forms of documentation for these classic cars. Their importance cannot be underestimated when establishing the pedigree and history of your car.

This original fender tag is from a Butterscotch 1969½ 440 6-barrel Plymouth Road Runner. (To the right is the factory tuning decal.)

Always inquire about the original paperwork before purchasing your dream machine. When your car left the dealership the original owner probably had a packet of original paperwork. How many of these documents survived over the years varies. This chapter helps you understand and decode these documents.

Broadcast Sheet

The broadcast sheet, or build sheet, can be the most important document for your car. The data listed on these sheets is very similar. Every part used to manufacture the car is on the broadcast sheet. The fender tag has some of the options listed depending on the plant that built your car, but without the original broadcast sheet many options cannot be proven to be original.

Assembly line workers used these sheets to determine which parts to install on a specific car. Build sheets changed from year to year and have minor and even major differences in appearance. Make sure you are referencing the correct codes for your car's specific year. The codes could indicate different parts in different years.

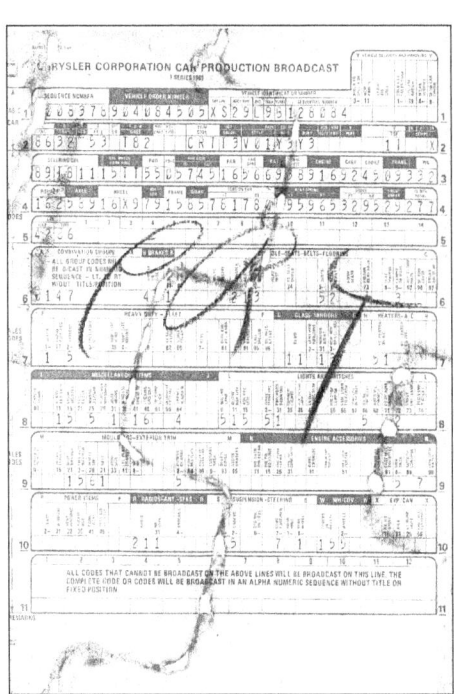

This particular example of a Chrysler broadcast sheet is from a 1969 Dodge Charger R/T equipped with a RB 440, assembled at the main Dodge facility in Hamtramck, Michigan. Locating a broadcast sheet can be a major windfall to unearthing the pedigree of an otherwise unknown or unidentified project car.

Every option is listed on this sheet. The codes under each option tells everything about the car and needs to be examined. You can find lists of these codes in the widely known "White Books" produced by Galen Govier, which can be purchased at a variety of places, including eBay and Mopar shows. Even the earliest assembly lines used a build sheet to assemble each car. They were not left in the cars until somewhere around the late 1950s or early 1960s. The line workers placed these sheets in the car in various locations. The first place to look for your broadcast sheet is under the backseat tucked into the springs. In Mopars they can also be found in the springs of any front or rear seat back or seat bottom, under the carpet, in the headliner, taped to the top of the glove box, and sometimes taped to the top of the heater core.

Many cars left the factory without a broadcast sheet and others might have left with a build sheet from another car. Some cars even have more than one broadcast sheet. Numerous other explanations can be made as to why your car doesn't have a broadcast sheet. Someone may have found it and discarded it years ago when no one really cared about these sheets. A previous owner may have removed the sheet for safe keeping and then lost it. Mice love to eat these sheets and owners have often found a nest made of a pile of little numbers on pieces of paper.

All is not lost, however, if you do not have the original broadcast sheet for your car. You may be tempted to have one made from someone who reproduces these sheets. We strongly recommend you do not do this because no matter how good it may look, it is still only a copy. Fake broadcast sheets, Certicards, and fender tags lead to doubt and suspicion, and devalue your car.

Certicard

Another important part of your car's documentation is whether or not it has the original Certicard. These cards were issued on the Plymouth and Dodge B-Bodies only during the years 1965–1968. The Certicard, or as other manufacturers called it, a warrantee card, had the VIN, select option codes, the owner's specific information, and date of delivery of the vehicle to the dealer. The dealer used this card to help identify the car when it came in for service. They were easily lost and very few cars actually have their original card.

The Certicard came in different forms over these short four years. It evolved from being a plastic card in the glove box, to an aluminum card stored in the engine compartment in a black plastic holder, to a pocket in the back of the owner's manual for 1968 models. In 1969 this information was hand written in the owner's manual by the dealer.

As you can imagine a loose card that was mounted in the hot engine compartment in a plastic holder and finally in the glove in the owner's manual didn't last very long. You are very fortunate if this card comes with your car.

Window Sticker or Dealer Invoice

In 1959 a window sticker was required by law to be prominently displayed in the car's window for the customer to see. This sticker included information about the dealership and prices of the base model equipment and options. It also included the very important Manufacturer's Suggested Retail Price. Even today when a potential customer walks into a new-car showroom, the first thing they look for is the window sticker.

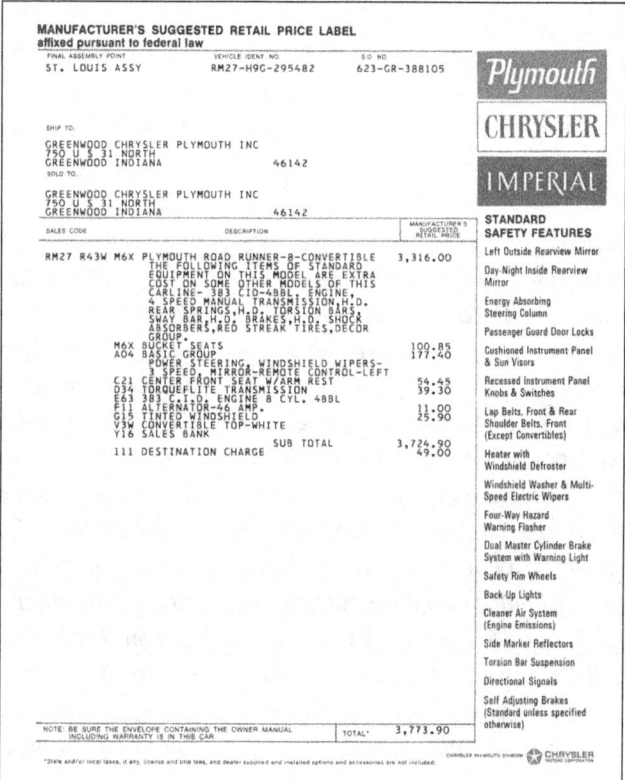

These re-creations of original Chrysler window stickers can be made using your vehicle's original information. A reasonable facsimile is easily fabricated using Chrysler archives and the data provided by your B-Body's VIN and Certicard.

Your vehicle's VIN tag should also coincide with your broadcast sheet, and several other locations throughout your Chrysler. Shown is the VIN from a 1969 Plymouth Road Runner convertible 383 car.

Information Sources

The Marti Report, a document that Marti Auto Works produced for collectible cars, provides almost all the details for a Ford, Mercury, or Lincoln car. General Motors owners also find information about the details of their cars from various groups, including the manufacturer.

If your Mopar is 1967 or older, you can request the build record from Chrysler at Chrysler Historical Collection, 12501 Chrysler Frwy., CIMS 41-011-21, Detroit, MI 48288 (Fax 313-252-2928), chryslerheritage.com.

Unfortunately all these records were lost for 1968–1970 Plymouths and Dodge B-Bodies.

If you are interested in learning more about decoding your broadcast sheet, several websites go into greater detail about this important document: mopar1.us/build.html, moparland.tripod.com/id63.html, mymopar.com, mmcdetroit.com.

The window sticker is often lost. Even if the original owner received the window sticker with the car, often it was lost or discarded as the car changed owners. You can have a window sticker created for your car, but again, it can be spotted as a reproduction.

If you are fortunate enough to have the original dealer invoice for your car you can learn important dealer information from it.

Fender Tag Decoding

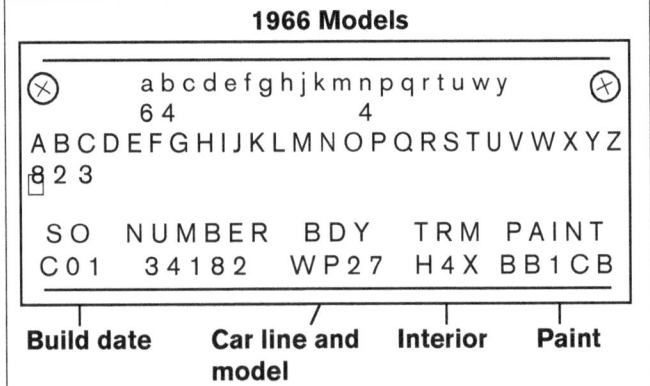

1966 Models

Build date | **Car line and model** | **Interior** | **Paint**

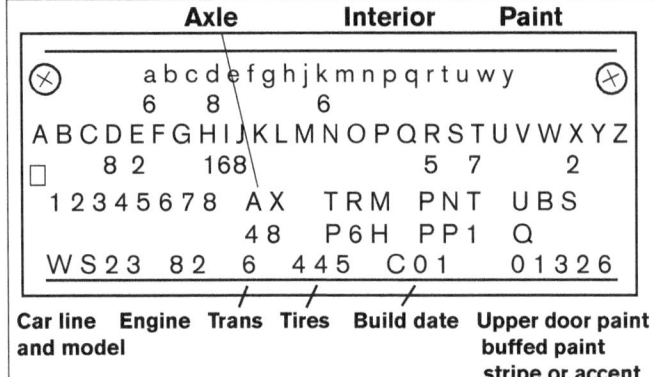

Axle **Interior** **Paint**

Car line and model **Engine** **Trans** **Tires** **Build date** **Upper door paint buffed paint stripe or accent**

1966 Models: The fender tags for 1962–1966 B-Bodies are laid out in a linear, easy-to-read fashion. The scheduled build date is found below left of the "SO Number." The number under "BDY" marks the chassis designation, which happens to be the same as the first three letters of the VIN. The number below "TRM" is the interior trim code. The exterior trim codes are found under "PNT." Some examples may have these numbers transposed.

The uppercase letters (fourth line from the bottom) are the option categories; a number under any of these letters designates an option in that letter's category. The row of lowercase letters at the top of the tag is another row of option categories. A number below any of these letters represents an option in that letter's category.

1967–1968 Models: For 1967 and 1968 the fender tag arrangement was modified, with the bottom three lines changed. The bottom left began with two letters and two numbers identifying the car line and model, the same as the first four characters in the VIN. Following these is a two-digit engine code, a one-digit transmission code, and a three-digit tire code. Next is a three-digit build date and order number. The third line from the bottom, numbers 1 through 8, denote categories. To the right is an "AX" or axle designation, with "TRM" and "PNT" marking interior trim and exterior colors, respectively. Continuing, the letters "UBS" stand for upper interior door color, buffed paint, and stripe or accent color. Option categories are listed on the fifth row and the top of the tag.

After some practice you can look at a fender tag and decode the whole car in a couple of seconds. This car was delivered in Q5 Seafoam Turquoise Metallic with the A14 Plymouth Spring Special. The V21 Performance Hood paint and V6R Red Longitude Stripe were standard in the Plymouth Spring Special package. (Michelle Kiffmeyer Photo)

What Is Numbers Matching?

Many ads state: "This car is numbers matching." Just what exactly does that mean and why is it so important? Opinions vary regarding how much of the car has to be original to make it "numbers matching." When a car comes off the assembly line it is truly numbers matching. Or is it really? Chrysler, especially, built these cars with many parts that do not fall into logical expected date ranges or correct part numbers.

There is always room for "exceptions to the rule," but, to be accepted, these exceptions must be documented and proven. The majority of the cars came with all of their numbers matching. That includes VIN, data plate, build sheet, Monroney label (window sticker), date codes, part numbers, bolt markings, correct finishes, and plating. The closer a car is to having all of its "original" as-delivered parts, the more valuable it is. That is why an original 5,600-mile 1969½ Super Bee is worth something in the six-figure range.

The title of the car includes the complete VIN, and must match the car you are purchasing. It is attached with two special black rosette rivets. These rivets are available today if you need replacements. The dry Chrysler corporation logo found on the plate is also available.

It is a federal offense to transfer the VIN from one car to another, so

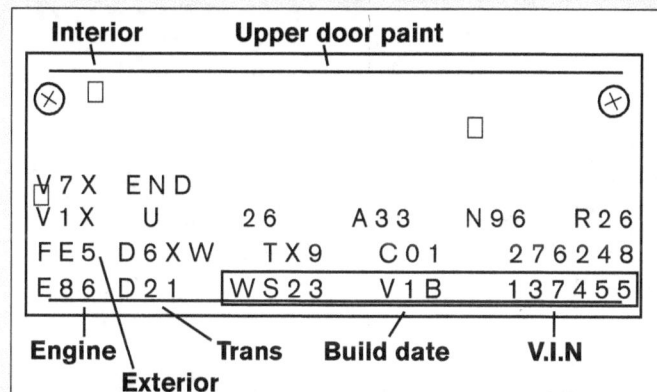

1969–1974 (except Lynch Road Plant): The fender tags were restyled for 1969 and survived this way until 1974 (that is for all cars not produced in the Lynch Road Plant). The bottom line, at the left, is a three-digit code for the engine and a three-digit code for the transmission followed by the VIN. The second line starts with a two- or three-digit paint code and three- or four-digit interior upper door color or type code (two for 1969, three for 1970 and later). A three-digit build date and vehicle order number follows. All codes above these are order option codes. Characters "END," "EN1," or "EN2" appear if the code listing ends, and if the factory ran out of room on the tag, a "CTD" may appear, noting that a second fender tag may appear.

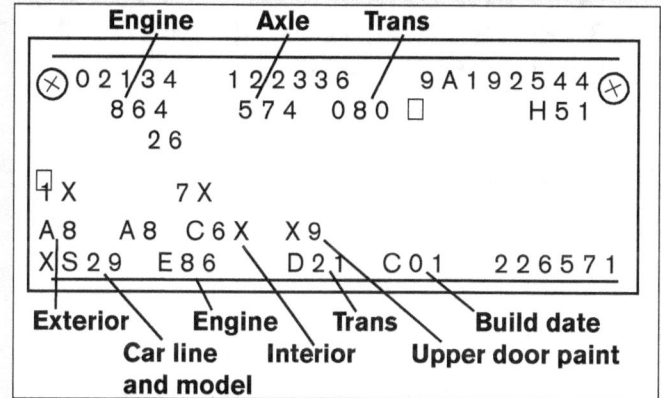

1969–1970 Lynch Road Plant: During production at the Lynch Road Plant in 1969, fender tags were unlike other tags. The bottom row begins with a four-digit car line and model code (same as the four digits in the VIN), followed by a three-digit engine code, a two-digit transmission code, a three-digit build date, and a vehicle order number. The second line starts with the exterior color (two-digit code), a three-digit interior code, and a two-character upper interior door color code. Above these are usually abbreviated actual option codes. Lynch Road tags typically list very few options regardless of how heavily optioned the car was.

Decoding a VIN plate

One of the most common questions is "How do I decode my VIN?" It's actually very simple to do. You only have two versions to consider: 1966–1967 and 1968–1974.

1966–1967 Mopar VINs

1st Digit: Car Make
B = Barracuda (1967)   V = Valiant
L = Dart   W = Coronet
R = Belvedere/Satellite X = Charger

2nd Digit: Series
E = Belvedere Fleet, Coronet Fleet
L = Valiant 100, Dart 170, Belvedere I, Coronet Deluxe
H = Valiant 200 (1966), Valiant Signet, Dart 270, Belvedere II, Coronet 440, Barracuda (1967)
K = Belvedere Police, Coronet Police Belvedere II Super Stock (1967), Coronet 440 Super Stock (1967)
P = Barracuda (1966), Dart GT, Satellite, Coronet 500, Charger
S = Belvedere GTX (1967), Coronet R/T (1967)
T = Belvedere Taxi, Coronet Taxi

3rd and 4th Digits: Body Style
21 = 2-door sedan
23 = 2-door coupe
27 = 2-door convertible
29 = 2-door sports coupe
41 = 4-door sedan
45 = 4-door station wagon (6-passenger)
46 = 4-door station wagon (9-passenger)

5th Digit: Engine
A = 170-ci 101-hp (1966), or 115-hp (1967) 1-barrel slant-6
B = 225-ci 145-hp 1-barrel slant-6
C = Special order slant-6
D = 273-ci 180-hp (19xx) 2-barrel V-8
D = 273-ci 235-hp or 275-hp (1966) 4-barrel V-8
E = 273-ci 235-hp 4-barrel V-8 (1967)
E = 318-ci 230-hp 2-barrel V-8 (1966)
F = 318-ci 230-hp 2-barrel V-8 (1967)
F = 361-ci 265-hp 2-barrel V-8 (1966)
G = 383-ci 270-hp 2-barrel V-8 (1967)
G = 383-ci 325-hp 4-barrel V-8 (1966)
H = 383-ci 325-hp 4-barrel V-8 (1967)

H = 426-ci 425-hp 2 x 4-barrel V-8 Hemi (1966)
J = 426-ci 425-hp 2 x 4-barrel V-8 Hemi (1967)
L = 440-ci 375-hp 4-barrel V-8 (1967)

6th Digit: Model Year
6 = 1966
7 = 1967

7th Digit: Assembly Plant
1 = Lynch Road, Detroit, Michigan
2 = Dodge Main, Hamtramck, Michigan
3 = Jefferson Avenue, Detroit, Michigan
4 = Belvidere, Illinois
5 = Los Angeles, California
6 = Newark, Deleware
7 = St. Louis, Missouri
8 = Export
9 = Windsor, Ontario, Canada
8th through 13th Digits: Sequential production number starting with 100001

1968–1974 Mopar VINs

1st Digit: Car Make
B = Barracuda   V = Valiant/Duster
J = Challenger   W = Coronet/1971–1974
L = Dart   Charger
R = Belvedere/Satellite X = 1966–1970 Charger

2nd Digit: Series
G = Coronet New York Taxi (1972–1974)
H = Valiant Signet (1968–1969), Barracuda (1968–1969), Barracuda 'Cuda (1969), Scamp (1971–1974), Dart 270 (1968), Dart Custom (1969–1974), Dart Swinger (1971–1974), Satellite (1968–1970), Satellite Sebring (1971–1974), Satellite Custom (1971–1974), Coronet 440 (1968–1970), Charger (1970), Charger coupe (1971–1974), Coronet Custom (1971–1974), Barracuda (1970–1974), Challenger (1970–1974), Challenger T/A (1970)
K = Belvedere Police (1968–1970), Satellite Police (1971–1974), Coronet Police (1968–1974)
L = Valiant (1968–1974), Duster (1970–1974), Dart (1968–1974), Dart Swinger (1968–1970), Dart Swinger Special (1971–1974), Demon (1971–1972), Dart Sport (1973–1974), Belvedere (1968–1970), Satellite coupe (1971–

1974), Coronet (1968–1974), Charger coupe (1971–1974)

M = Dart Swinger 340 (1969–1970), Demon 340 (1971–1972), Dart Sport 340 (1973), Dart Sport 360 (1974), Road Runner (1968–1974), Road Runner Superbird (1970), Road Runner GTX (1972–1974), Coronet Super Bee (1968–1970), Charger Super Bee (1971)

N = Coronet New York Taxi (1970–1971)

O = Barracuda Super Stock (1968), Dart Super Stock (1968)

P = Valiant Brougham (1974), Dart GT (1968–1969), Dart SE (1974), Sport Satellite (1968–1970), Satellite Sebring Plus (1971–1974), Satellite Brougham (1971), Regent, Coronet 500, Charger (1968–1969), Charger 500 (1970–1971), Charger SE (1971–1974), Coronet Brougham (1971), Crestwood (1971–1974), Barracuda Gran Coupe (1970–1971)

S = Duster 340 (1970–1973), Duster 360 (1974), Dart GTS (1968–1969), Dart GSS (1968), Challenger R/T (1970), GTX (1968–1971), Coronet R/T (1968–1970), Charger R/T (1968–1971), Charger 500 (early 1969), Barracuda 'Cuda (1970–1974), Barracuda AAR 'Cuda (1970), Challenger R/T (1970–1971), Challenger Rallye (1972)

T = Belvedere Taxi (1968–1970), Satellite Taxi (1971–1974), Coronet Taxi (1968–1974)

X = Charger 500 (late 1969), Charger Daytona (1969)

3rd and 4th Digits: Body Style

21 = 2-door sedan
23 = 2-door coupe
27 = 2-door convertible
29 = 2-door sports coupe
41 = 4-door sedan
45 = 4-door station wagon (6-passenger)
46 = 4-door station wagon (9-passenger)

5th Digit: Engine

A = 170-ci 115-hp 1-barrel slant-6 (1968–1969)
B = 225-ci 145-hp 1-barrel slant-6 (1968–1969)
B = 198-ci 125-hp (1970–1971), 100-hp (1972), or 95-hp (1973–1974) 1-barrel slant-6
C = Special order slant-6 (1968–1969)
C = 225-ci 145-hp (1970–1971), 110-hp (1972), or 105-hp (1973–1974) 1-barrel slant-6
D = 273-ci 190-hp 2-barrel V-8 (1968–1969)
E = Special order slant-6 (1970–1974)
F = 318-ci 230-hp 2-barrel V-8 (1968–1969)

G = 383-ci 290-hp 2-barrel V-8 (1968–1969)
G = 318-ci 230-hp (1970–1971), 150-hp (1972–1974), 155-hp (1972), or 170-hp (1973–1974 Road Runner) 2-barrel V-8
H = 383-ci 330-hp or 335-hp 4-barrel V-8 (1968–1969)
H = 340-ci 275-hp (1970–1971) or 240-hp (1972–1973) 4-barrel V-8
J = 426-ci 425-hp 2 x 4–barrel V-8 Hemi (1968–1969)
J = 340-ci 290-hp 3 x 2–barrel V-8 (1970) (AAR & T/A)
L = 440-ci 375-hp 4-barrel V-8 (1968–1969)
L = 383-ci 290-hp (1970) or 275-hp (1971) 2-barrel V-8
L = 360-ci 200-hp or 245-hp 4-barrel V-8 (1974)
M = Special order V-8 (1968–1969)
M = 440-ci 390-hp 3 x 2–barrel V-8 (1969) (Six Pack/6-barrel)
M = 400-ci 190-hp (1972), 175-hp or 185-hp (1973) 2-barrel V-8
N = 383-ci 330-hp or 335-hp (1970) or 300-hp (1971) 4-barrel V-8
N = 400-ci 205-hp 4-barrel V-8 (1974)
P = 340-ci 275-hp 4-barrel V-8 (1968–1969)
P = 400-ci 255-hp (1972), 260-hp (1973), or 250-hp (1974) 4-barrel V-8
R = 426-ci 425-hp 2 x 4–barrel V-8 Hemi (1970–1971)
U = 440-ci 375-hp (1970), 370-hp (1971), 280-hp (1972–1973), 290-hp (1972), or 275-hp (1974) 4-barrel V-8
V = 440 3 2-barrel, 390-hp (1970), 440 3 2-barrel 385-hp (1971), or 440 3 2-barrel 330-hp (1972)
Z = Special order V-8 (1970–1974)

6th Digit: Model Year

8 = 1968	2 = 1972
9 = 1969	3 = 1973
0 = 1970	4 = 1974
1 = 1971	

7th Digit: Assembly Plant

A = Lynch Road, Detroit, Michigan
B = Dodge Main, Hamtramck, Michigan
C = Jefferson Avenue, Detroit, Michigan
D = Belvidere, Ilinois
E = Los Angeles, California
F = Newark, Deleware
G = St. Louis, Missouri
H = New Stanton, Pennsylvania
P = Export
R = Windsor, Ontario, Canada ■

Here are the casting identifications for a particular block. The casting number is shown above, "D N" indicates whether it was cast during the day or night, and the dial indicates the hour.

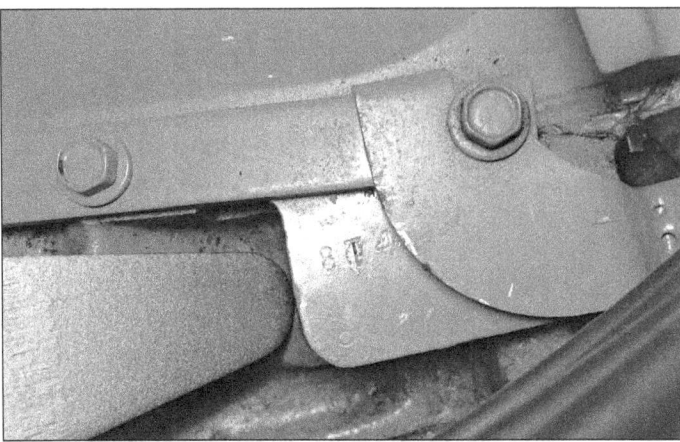

The assembly pad indicates when the engine was assembled and whether it was equipped with high-performance parts.

don't do it. Some say that it is an offense to remove the plate from the dash for restoration purposes.

Fender Tag

This tag is critical in documenting a numbers-matching car. It served as production information for the assembly line and was attached on most cars before they were even painted. At most assembly plants this tag was attached to the inside driver-side fender shelf with one screw and then bent up so paint reached under the tag. It was then screwed down with the rear screw. This is the reason the front screw is painted the body color and the rear screw is natural. This factory bend as well as various punched-out inspector marks and additional stamped markings from the top down are found on original tags. There are major differences between the pre-1969 fender tags and the 1969 and 1970 tags.

The Lynch Road assembly plant fender tags included the least information and had a different layout of the codes. They are usually not painted and are natural in appearance because they hung inside the car during painting instead of being attached to the fender. Consequently, they are not bent on the corner and neither attachment screw is painted.

If a car has a very rusty fender tag you can find a company to remake the tag with enough documentation. If a car does not have a fender tag one can be re-created if you have the car's build sheet. Without the build sheet a correct tag cannot be produced. "Fake" tags can be spotted, and a bogus tag usually makes the entire car suspect. If the tag is missing it is preferable to just leave the car without one. *But* a missing fender tag makes the car worth at least 25 to 40 percent less than the same car with the original tag.

On pre-1969 fender tags the VIN does not appear on the tag, but the Shipping Order (SO) number does. This number is on the body of the car instead of on the VIN such as those on the 1969–1970 cars.

VIN Locations

The VIN is found on the dash on the driver's side stamped into a metal plate on 1968–1970 models. For 1966–1967, the VIN is attached to the front of the doorjamb. The VIN is found on the dash of all 1966–1970 B-Bodies.

Where else are the vehicles' VINs located? On Plymouth and Dodge B-Bodies you find them stamped in the following places: engine, transmission, radiator support, and trunk rail lip. Pre-1969 cars have a Shipping Order number instead of a VIN.

Engine and Transmission

On the 1966 and 1967 B-Bodies you don't find VIN stamps on the engines or transmissions; only cast numbers and date codes. It is important to know the history of the car to ensure original equipment.

On 1968 cars the SO number is stamped on the top of the engine where the engine and bellhousing or transmission case meet. It is also stamped on the passenger-side pad of the transmission. These two numbers need to match because the same stamp was used on both.

On 1969 cars produced before January 1969, the entire VIN is stamped on the engine pan rail. After January 1969 and through 1970 cars, the partial VIN of the car is stamped on the engine's pan rail on the passenger's side of the car. It is also stamped on the passenger-side pad of the transmission. These numbers match because they were stamped at the same time with the same stamping mechanism. You can compare these numbers by taking a piece of paper and a pencil and rubbing the pencil over the paper while it is placed on top of the stamped number.

Cast date codes are also found on all transmissions and all engines on the passenger's side of the block. You also find stamped date codes indicating the assembly date of the engine, on a machined pad, located on the front of the engine. The pad for the 440 is on the driver's side; for the 383 it is on the passenger's side.

Radiator Support and Trunk Rail Lip

The numbers here are of a differ-

ent font than the numbers stamped on the engine and transmission. Usually stamped upside down on the radiator support you find either the SO number or the partial VIN, depending on the year of the car.

Chrysler stamped the VIN onto the radiator core support on 1969-and-later B-Bodies. This number must coincide with the in-dash VIN tag to be numbers matching.

Component Codes

Major components have date codes and are important to check before purchase. They should not be viewed as deal breakers if they are missing but a bonus if present and functional.

Much detail went into the system of component coding. Here is a list of coded and dated items found on all A12-coded 1969½ Plymouth Road Runners and Dodge Super Bees.

- Rear axle
- Radiator
- Wiper motor
- Glass
- Wheels
- Seat belts
- Jack
- Horn
- Alternator
- Carburetor
- Torsion bars
- Lower control arms

- Exhaust manifolds
- Hoses
- Fuel pump
- Starter
- Coil
- Relays
- Motor mounts
- Brake parts
- Headlights
- Power steering pump and cooler
- U joint clamps

- Alternator (PN 2642537)
- Master cylinder (PN 2808577)
- Starter relay (PN 4638260)
- Plug wires (date: H 1Q 69)
- Distributor tag (PN 2875982 IBS 4014D 7 9)
- Front carburetor (PN 3412050 R4391)
- Center carburetor (PN 3412053 R4392)
- Rear carburetor (PN 3412051 R 4394)
- Viscous drive (PN 2806070)
- Fan blade (PN 2863216)
- Coil, short (PN 2444242)
- Coil, long (PN 2444241)
- Paper tags on carbs (50 on front, 51 on rear)
- Paper tag on center carburetor (52 on driver's side)
- Front and rear carburetors (stamped with 24 on driver's side)
- Choke pull-down, Holley 54
- Idle stop solenoid, hex-head (PN DR1114420)
- Spark plugs (Champion J11Y)
- Oil plug, indented
- Ballast resistor (PN 2095501)
- Axle strap and stamp (build sheet 108; 999)
- Radiator (PN 054) ∎

Several types of date-code markings were used on most parts. For example, 509 stands for May 9 and B23 stands for November 23. Here is a breakdown of the month codes.

1 = January	7 = July
2 = February	8 = August
3 = March	9 = September
4 = April	A = October
5 = May	B = November
6 = June	C = December

Federal VIN Label or Door Sticker

In 1969 only on the Charger Daytona, and in 1970 on all cars, an additional sticker that has the full VIN was attached to the driver-side door. On 1966–1967 cars a chrome plate is attached to the front driver-side door frame. These can be reproduced so check the tag for signs of wear to determine if it is original.

Numbers Matching?

Now the question is, Do you have a numbers-matching car if all of these numbers match your car's VIN or SO number? The answer is yes! But, you must also verify that the cast and stamped date codes of each of these areas precede the build date of the car. Watch for engine and transmission pads that have grind marks different from the factory machine marks, and make sure the stamps use the correct font.

Some people say that the date codes for the rear end, radiator, wiper motor, etc. must match for the car to be "numbers matching." It is our opinion that these other parts may be date-code correct, but could come from other cars. They did not have the vehicle's unique identification number issued at the factory and therefore are not required to make the car "numbers matching."

Date codes and part numbers provide an opportunity to determine just how original the car is and further establish its value. Almost every component of these cars is date coded and/or has its original part number. These date codes always precede the car's build date and can also help when you do need to replace non-original parts during the restoration.

In the case of the engine and transmission it is normal for the casting date to precede the build date by 60 days and the assembly date by 30 days. Other parts can precede the build date by as much as six months. The major exception to this rule is with the 1969½ 6-barrel and 6-Pack Road Runners and Super Bees. They only have two build dates on their fender tags, either 3 29 or 4 26. However, these cars were built as late as July and, therefore, to the inexperienced the date codes of their parts are in fact after the build date on the tag, but still correct for that car depending on when it was actually produced.

Conclusion

You may know many things about a vehicle before you buy it. But you must inspect the car in person. Many cars exchange hands over the Internet and across many miles. If you cannot inspect the car in person before you buy it hire a professional to inspect it for you. If that is not financially feasible ask for as many detailed pictures as possible from the seller. Specifically request the items you want to see and focus on the numbers-matching areas first. The closer to original the car and its parts, the easier the restoration.

The word *restoration* is used very broadly in the classic car hobby. It means to return a car to its original condition when it left the dealer. Unfortunately, not many enthusiasts take that to heart with their project.

Variations to the original condition that are acceptable to you are usually based on finances and what you really want to do with the car to fully enjoy it. By applying the information in this chapter you know what you are buying up front, and its value, so that a fair price can be agreed upon.

DISASSEMBLY

Now that you have your project car purchased, documented, and safely stored in your garage the task of restoration can seem overwhelming. From this point forward it is tempting to simply start taking everything apart and tossing it in the corner just like the guys on TV. But that is the last thing you should do. Take your time and take as many pictures as possible throughout the disassembly process. They will help you when it's time to put the car back together.

Remove all the trim, headlights, taillights, glass, interior, and steering column. Remove the doors, hood, and trunk lid. Examine whether the parts can be used, document and bag the small parts, tag the large ones, and box and store them in a dry, secure place.

You quickly realize that a car that is assembled takes up much less room than all of its parts. That means organization is one of the keys to success for a restoration project.

Organize Your Parts

The first thing to do is purchase several sizes of Ziploc bags, permanent markers, boxes of different sizes, and paper tags with a wire that can be attached to large components.

Each part that is removed should be bagged or tagged, sorted, and organized by the specific area the parts came from. If this is your first full restoration it is very easy to label the parts that make sense at the moment, but in two years you find yourself scratching your head and completely lost as to what the part is and where it goes. This is especially true when it comes to bolts, nuts, clips, and fasteners. Do not toss them into a coffee can and think you can put it all back the same way it came off. The description you write on the bag or tag must clearly identify the part.

Next, put the small Ziploc bags in boxes for storage. On the outside of the box write a list of the contents and place it on a shelf. As you bag and tag each part document it as to whether it is an original or a replacement.

The disassembly phase is a good time to start a list of parts that need to be replaced. A spread sheet of part

Choosing to rescue a forgotten muscle car might save you money up front but can be costly when you begin to unravel all of the damage caused by years of neglect. (Photo Courtesy Ryan Brutt)

Bagging and labeling your parts as they are removed is crucial for reassembling the car. Organize each series of bags noting what area of the car they came from.

needs is a great way to note where you bought the part, how much you paid for it, and what you still need to find. Do not throw away anything, even if it is not usable. You may need it for reference, or maybe it has a clip that you use later.

The disassembly process depends on how you plan to restore the car. If you have a shop and you are going to do a total rotisserie restoration, everything comes off the car all at once. This means that you must have all the parts labeled and stored according to the specific area of the

car. If you are planning a rolling restoration where you take the car to someone else's shop, you only disassemble the car to the point where it can still be moved.

Therefore, the suspension remains on the car. And if you plan on driving the car while you are working on it you only do one area at a time. An example is to restore the drivetrain first and then tackle the trunk, followed by the interior, and finally the paint. If you are planning on competing at a high level such as the Mopar Nationals or the Antique Automobile

Club of America you have to do a complete rotisserie restoration.

Some Materials Require Special Handling

During disassembly you handle different types of materials. Each one requires techniques specific to the part.

For example, the windshield seal is rubber and has a tuck-in flap that secures the glass. Use an anti-corrosion, penetrating spray lubricant such as WD-40 or PB Blaster to soak the seal and let it set for several hours. Never pry on the glass, especially with anything made of metal. You can use a blade screwdriver to pry away from the glass so that the flap is released. Then you can cut the old seal with a box knife and remove the glass.

If the windshield is in good enough shape to reuse, store it standing on its edge and never lay it out flat. This goes for all the glass no matter where it is in the car. If the glass is cloudy around the edges or has scratches that can be seen, replace it. Some kits claim that you can polish out scratches. This really does not work. Completely clean the glass to see if you can reuse it. If not you can purchase replacement glass that can be date coded so it is correct for your car. Soft materials, such as rubber seals and interior panels, are almost always in need of replacement. If you are fortunate enough to have interior

Trying to pull the engine up and out of the engine compartment can result in quite a bit of damage. Most find it significantly easier to "drop" the drivetrain in a similar but opposite fashion from the way the engine was originally installed at the factory.

With the suspension out it's much easier to work on and assess what needs replacing and what needs refurbishing.

and rubber parts that can be reused clean them thoroughly before storing them. You can freshen interior panels by re-dying them with paint by SEM Products, which is specifically made to return the appearance to original.

Dash pads, glove-box doors, kick panels, and interior trim often can be restored and reused. Every original part from your car that can be saved should be used. However, often they are too far-gone and have to be replaced. Even if you do not use a part don't throw it away or try to sell it. Keep it until the restoration is finished and then decide if it has any value or can be sold. You might even keep it for a future driver project.

Remove all the trim, headlights and taillights, glass, and interior. This includes the removal of the steering column. Remove the doors, hood, and trunk lids. Examine whether the parts can be used and document and bag the small parts, tag the large ones, and box and store them in a dry, secure place. You quickly realize that an assembled car takes up much

less room than all of its parts. If you have taken your time and carefully organized and labeled the parts you are ready to proceed to disassembling all the big stuff.

Powertrain and Suspension

If you are doing a total rotisserie restoration you can remove the powertrain completely. The best way to remove the engine, transmission, and front suspension is to take it all out as one assembly from the bottom of the car. When you have disconnected all the wiring, brake lines, fuel lines, and driveshaft, you can support the K-member with a rolling cradle.

Then you can pull the torsion bars. Remove the torsion bar clips that keep the bars securely in the frame rail. They are found at the rear of the bar. Completely release all the tension on the lower control arms adjusters. Use a special torsion bar tool that clamps on the bar and has a long handle, then use a hammer to knock the bar toward the rear of the car. *Do not* use a vise grips or

anything that scars or scratches the bar. The bar can fail if it is marred.

Remove the front tires and wheels and then disconnect the upper A-arms.

Support the transmission with another floor jack and remove the transmission crossmember.

Then, using a cherry picker, attach a strap to the front bumper and secure the car by removing any slack in the strap. Because you still have the rear suspension in place the car can pivot while you raise the front end enough to clear the front suspension, engine, and transmission. Remove the four K-member bolts and lift the car off of the K-member, engine, transmission, and front suspension.

Roll the entire assembly away from the body. Then lower the body onto two jack stands positioned under the front frame rails approximately where the K-member was.

Next put the car up on jack stands on the rear frame rails just in front of the spring hanger. If your car has rear torque boxes they are substantial enough to support the rear of the car.

Although disassembly is almost always easier than putting things back together, it's absolutely paramount to an OEM-level restoration to keep studious notes and pictures and properly bag and label all of the various clips, hardware, and pieces you remove from your B-Body.

Remove the rear tires and wheels and store them. Then you can remove the rear end and springs as one unit.

Position the floor jack under the center section of the rear end and remove the eight nuts that hold the front spring hanger to the frame. Remove the rear shackle bolts, freeing up the springs. Be sure to remove the shocks and any brake lines. When you lower the rear end and spring assembly you can pull it out from under the car. Although the car is supported on the four jack stands and the front and rear assemblies are removed you can remove the gas tank and bumpers and anything left on the body.

Use heavy-duty jack stands and always make sure the car is supported properly. If you do not it can lead to serious harm (or death to you and anyone else around the car). If you have a lift in your shop you can easily do all of this in a fraction of the time it takes without a lift.

When the body is secured on the rotisserie you can separate the transmission from the engine, then the engine and the front suspension from the K-member. Remove the springs from the rear end.

Whether you are able to rebuild every part from the car yourself or you farm out many of these main assemblies, you need to make a plan of attack. Without a plan you can easily become discouraged, and, as the saying goes, "If you fail to plan, you plan to fail."

Parts Cleaning

At this point you have complete assemblies and many, many, parts in various stages of disassembly. The car is on the rotisserie; the engine, transmission, and front and rear suspension are apart and probably very dirty and greasy from years of use. This is the perfect time to rent a high-pressure steam washer. It cleans everything, including the undercoating from the car and parts. It makes a mess so be sure to clean everything outside on your driveway. Wear protective clothes and get busy cleaning all those years of road grime and dirt away.

When you finish you will be glad to have clean parts. You can now identify any inspection marks and document their location and color with pictures.

DIY or Farm Out?

Remember that it often takes 2 to 10 times longer to have something such as an engine rebuilt than the shop or professional doing the work tells you.

If you are having your car painted by someone else you can plan on at least a year if they say they can do it in six months.

Determine how and who will do the metal work, prep work, and paint on your car.

It is best to take the steps to get your car painted before attacking the mechanicals of the car. It doesn't hurt a car to sit painted for a year or two while you build the engine, transmission, or suspension. Getting the car in paint is the biggest and most important step in your restoration process. Focus on that goal first and the rest is assembly and bolt-on of the completed assemblies.

How to Remove Trim and Clips

Your Mopar's trim is nearly as important as the body-work (and paint), as it adds so much personality to the car. The following are some helpful tips to properly removing a B-Body's brightwork. ■

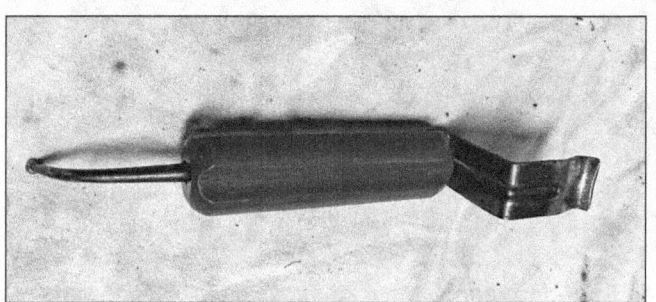

Several tools work to release these clips. The wind-shield clip removal tool is ideal for removing the stain-less trim, and the other end can be used to install the front windshield rubber seal tuckable flap.

All the stainless on the window trim of all of these cars, whether vinyl top or not, is of the same design. It is held on around the windows with a clip that snaps into the trim's rolled edge. These clips are often rusted and difficult to release without damaging the stainless trim.

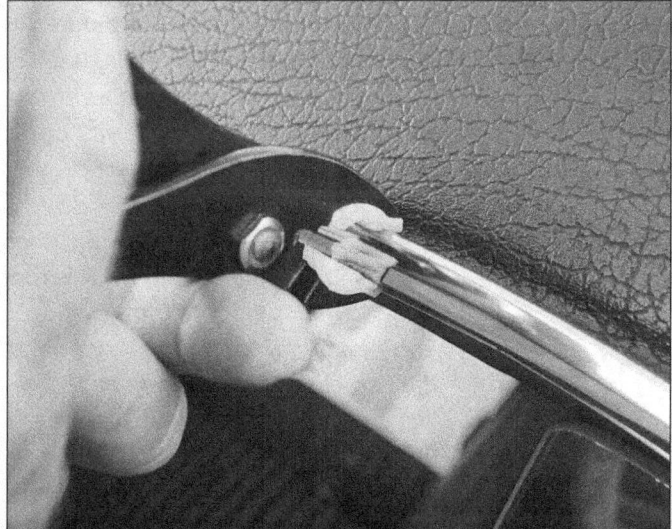

Corners and drip rail moldings require careful removal techniques. Use pliers with plastic inserts so you do not damage the trim. Pry from the bottom up a little at a time and it comes off. A screw that is under the top window seal's stainless trim secures the corner. This piece of trim must be removed to access the screw.

This corner trim piece is used on cars with or without vinyl tops but without belt line moldings. On the Dodge models the belt line molding actually attaches to the drip-rail molding.

How to Remove Trim and Clips

All of the stainless trim shown on this post B-Body must be carefully removed and polished. Very thin seal retainers screw into the roof rail and must be removed before you can remove the drip-rail molding. It must be installed in the reverse order.

The front and rear window stainless clips are different and cannot be interchanged. Notice the spacing of the front window clips, which starts at intervals of about 1¾ inches from the corner of the channel. When you are ready to re-install the stainless, mark the position of each clip with masking tape on the body so you know where to apply the pressure to snap the trim into the clip.

After the car has been painted attach the front and rear stainless clips with a small screw. The old clip screw has often been enlarged and cannot be reused. You simply re-drill the hole moving it over an inch or two but at the same depth as the original.

The drip rail molding and all of the door seals can be installed before the front and rear glass stainless. Leave the installation of the windshield until last just in case you have problems with the dash electrical components.

It is important to place the corner clip in the original position. If it is too close to the corner the trim does not lay flat and if it is too far away from the corner it does not snap all the way down. Space it about 1¾ inches from the corner of the channel.

Add the clips after you install the vinyl top. Then install the glass with the rubber seal. You must mark the clip locations and pop the polished stainless into place. To help the trim pop into place much easier put a small amount of grease on each clip where it will touch the trim.

BODYWORK

Removing rust, straightening body panels, and correcting body-lines and gaps are difficult and important steps to restoring a car. This aspect of the restoration can be the longest, most expensive, and most frustrating. It can also be the most rewarding.

Before you begin the bodywork, you have to know what kind of budget you have, your skills, and what facilities and equipment are available. You can choose to have a shop complete all the work, or you can do some of the work yourself and have someone else paint, or you might be able to do it all yourself.

Whatever path you choose begin by taking time to evaluate the rust areas that need to be addressed and either decide on a shop or make plans to complete the work yourself.

This chapter helps you think through the bodywork process and make a solid, wise decision about what avenue is best for your situation and how to get to the finished, painted car that you will love and show with great pride.

Rust! It's a Dirty Word!

The only B-Body that does not have any rust issues is one that has been kept in a garage and never been driven or has already been restored. Replacing rusted metal panels and patching rusted sections must be done. Good, original body panels and NOS (new original stock) panels are difficult to find and very expensive when you do find the right ones for your specific application. Fortunately more good metal replacement panels are being produced now than ever before.

Auto Metal Direct (AMD) is a great place to acquire panels to replace all those rusted floorboards, trunk, quarter, and Dutchman panels. Often it is faster and much better to replace an entire panel rather than cutting out and replacing a section of an existing panel. It is a worthy goal to keep as much of your original sheet metal as

Unfortunately, it's difficult to fully assess the extent of 50 years of weather and water damage until a car is fully stripped to its barest core. Also, there is no truer "square one" to begin your restoration. (Photo Courtesy Historic Restorations)

possible. So even if you are not going to do the work yourself, you need to evaluate and document all of the rust problems that need attention and how much of these areas need to be replaced.

The extent of rust you find on one of these cars varies depending on the life it led and whether it came from the "rust belt" or the "desert." The areas where rust occurs are common on almost all models and years of the Plymouth and Dodge B-Body lines. Before buying a car you must completely examine it, paying the most attention to the structural integrity of the car. Even though a car can actually be re-created using the technology and advanced skills of a very few shops, you should steer clear of cars that have frame rails, firewall, and extensive metal that must be replaced. But do not be afraid to replace the areas that almost always need attention on a good, solid, project car.

Common Rust Locations

Always check the trunk and floorboards. These cars were driven and these areas received a lot of wear and tear because they were directly exposed to many elements, including water, salt, dirt, and even oil and transmission fluid. While checking the trunk also check the rear panel behind the rear bumper. Just like the floors the rear sections of the quarter panels and fenders were also exposed continually to these elements. Check them to see if they can be patched or if they must be replaced.

The glass channels in the front lower corners and especially the lower rear corners allowed water to sit and often are rusted. These rear corners can be rusted into the Dutchman panel and it may also have to be replaced.

Additional places to look for rust are under the battery tray, including the inner fender under the tray. Examine all the doors, their front and rear corners, and the rocker panels.

What if the car has a vinyl roof? Even the best-kept cars rusted under the vinyl roof, especially at the seam from the quarter panel to the roof. These tops were notorious for trapping moisture. Many people are resigned to putting the vinyl roof back on a car because of the fear of rust. If your car came with a vinyl roof, replace it with the correct one. You probably will not use your restored car as a daily driver without any regard for protecting it from the elements.

Stripping to Bare Metal

Each of the several ways to strip your car down to the bare metal has its advantages. The method you select depends upon the resources available to you. A rotisserie makes all of this much easier and in the end produces good results. But using a rotisserie is not the only way to be successful. I have spent many, many hours on a creeper stripping off undercoating with a torch and putty knife with the car supported on jack stands.

Media Blasting

Positive: It can be used to strip the entire car to bare metal. Do not use sand; it warps the car's metal. You must take the car to a professional so the car's suspension remains in place, or fabricated dollies must be used to transport the car.

Negative: Cost and transporting to and from the shop. Also, you may find residual media in the car for months and months.

Chemical Stripper

Positive: Available at local parts stores. I recommend the "airplane" stripper. After applying it you can scrape off the layers of paint with a putty knife. Then, while wearing chemical-resistant gloves, use coarse steel wool and a stripper to reveal the bare metal. Rinse with water and dry with towels. This works well and does not require you to transport the car.

Negative: Very labor intensive and the stripper can burn your skin. Be sure to use eye and skin protection. Also, you must remove and neutralize all residual stripper before paint.

Sanding Disc and Variable-Speed Buffer

Positive: Can strip the car in one afternoon using 80-grit discs and a buffer. The scratches in the metal promote good adhesion of filler and primer but are not so deep that they are visible after proper primer coverage.

Negative: Creates a huge amount of dust and if not careful can warp the metal if held in one place too long. Also, care must be used around edges and along bodylines.

High-Pressure Steam Washer

Positive: With a rotisserie this method is fantastic for the undercarriage. The results are wonderful. If not using a rotisserie the old-fashioned way of heating the undercoating with a heat gun or torch and scraping it off works too.

Negative: Makes a huge mess.

Condition Assessment

When you have completely stripped your car to the bare metal and disassembled all the body parts, you can see the true condition of everything and effectively evaluate what can be repaired, replaced, or simply refinished. If you come to the conclusion that you are in over your head go back to "Start Shopping for a Shop" in Chapter 1; you may want to modify your strategy.

Having stripped and disassembled the car yourself you have saved a lot of money in labor costs. When you take the pieces of the car into a shop you will know first-hand what needs to be done to finish them. Then you and the shop owner can come up with a fair evaluation of the amount of work remaining and how much it will cost.

A good rule of thumb in a restoration is that you should only replace the parts that need to be replaced. Remove and repair all rust with patch panels when you can, but never patch something if the final result would be much better if you had replaced it.

For example, if you need to replace a quarter panel but the other side is good, don't simply replace the good side. Why would anyone replace a factory quarter panel with a reproduction that might not fit as well as the original? However, you must not stop short by only replacing the exterior rust without dealing with the hidden rust.

If patch panels and dent repairs are the only work needed, just about anyone can achieve good results. With minimal investment in tools and a basic understanding of the principles of metal repair, metal straightening, and body filler application and finishing, the average enthusiast can successfully prepare a car for paint.

Patch Installation

A die grinder with a cutting wheel and a plasma cutter are two very efficient tools for removing rusted areas.

If you plan on doing a lot of rust repair in the future invest in a plasma cutter. The first step is to cut out the rust. Make sure you remove enough so that you have good-quality metal to weld the patch to and create a lasting repair. You can use the following general procedure.

When you have removed the rust, make a pattern so you know the shape of the new patch. If the rusted area is uniform, you can simply measure it. Cut the patch from either good metal on a donor parts car or from metal stock.

If the patch has any factory bends or contours replace it with the exact same area from a donor or purchase a panel from AMD or another manufacturer that makes replacement panels.

Make sure the mating surfaces are clean and free from paint. Use the die grinder or an electric handheld grinder and slightly bevel the edges so that the weld can be ground down and not lose its integrity.

Clamp the patch in place and spot-weld each corner. Then stitch-weld, alternating areas, so that you do not warp the metal, until the patch is completely welded.

Grind down the welds and finish with a skim coat of filler. You may need a hammer and a dolly to shape the metal before, during, or after welding the patch panel in place.

Subframe Repair

By Jefferson Bryant of Red Dirt Rods

The classic Mopar B-Body has some of the best lines of the muscle car era. Unfortunately, the B-Body also has some of the worst potential damage areas. Some of them can remain hidden for many years only to be found when the damage is too

severe for simple repair. The front subframe is one such area.

The top of the subframe is open along several places on the body, allowing dirt and water to collect inside. Eventually the steel rusts through, leaving the uni-body structure in bad shape. Contributing risk factors for rust are: The K-member bolts to the subframe and B-Bodied cars have often led hard lives that subjected them to cracks. These are potentially deadly situations, so it pays to be careful.

Repairing this type of damage depends on what and where the damage is. Replacement subframes are available, but they are expensive and the installation process requires massive surgery on your car. Often you can get away with simply rebuilding the affected area with a homemade patch.

This 1969 Road Runner led a hard life before it was chosen for a major rebuild. The subframe seemed to be in excellent shape, until the K-member was removed. That was when the passenger-side rear mount fell out of the subframe. The subframe had been stressed from hard driving and the metal was so weak that the backup plate for the K-member bolt ripped free from the rest of the subframe. I found eight cracks in the side of the subframe channel. The rest of the subframe was in perfect shape, but this was an unsafe situation. Rather than cut out the entire subframe, I decided to repair it.

I reinforced the subframe using a piece of 3 x 4 box tubing. I reused the original backing plate to secure the K-member, as it was in good shape. By the time the repair was finished, the subframe was substantially stronger than it was when it left the factory. This is a serious repair that requires quality welding and fabricating skills.

The repair continues with the removal of anything in the way. For the K-member mount, this meant the bumpstop brackets that are spot welded to the frame. Using a drill bit (or Rota-broach cutter), I cut out the spot welds and removed the bracket in one piece. The bracket will be reused, so I didn't trash it or grind it off.

Using a grinder with a flap wheel (or a die-grinder with a Scotch-Brite pad), I cleaned off the frame and trimmed any jagged edges on the damaged area.

I removed all of the undercoating and paint so that I could find all of the cracks on the steel. I located each crack, found where it stopped, and drilled the end with a small drill bit. A 1/8-inch bit is usually large enough to do the job. The goal here was to remove the stress fracture so that the crack does not continue.

Next, I cut a piece of 3 x 4 tubing to fit inside the subframe. I had to add a second piece of 1/8-inch steel to the sides of the tubing because the actual subframe is 3¼ inches wide on the inside. I welded the plates to the tubing along the edges with three plug welds in the center of each plate. I cut the tubing along the 4-inch side to match the depth of the factory subframe.

I measured the location of the driver-side mount using several locating points front and rear of the bolt hole, and then duplicated these measurements on the passenger's side. I inserted the repair channel into the subframe and marked the location of the bolt hole. I added some reference marks to ensure the channel went back to where it needed to be, as it was test-fit several times.

With the location for the K-member bolt noted, I removed the repair channel and drilled the bolt hole, along with two holes for the spots welds that secured the backing plate and nut to the channel.

The backing plate had a small section of the original subframe welded to it. I removed these spot welds using a Rota-broach cutter. I centered the backing plate in the repair channel, clamped it in place, and welded it with a MIG welder.

I marked and drilled the sides of the subframe for three spot welds. I installed the repair channel, measuring it carefully for placement. I painted the frame with some weld-through primer to protect the metal from rusting. When it was determined to be in the exact spot, I used two welding clamps to lock it in place. I threaded a bolt into the K-member nut to keep welding spatter out of the threads.

I spot-welded the channel to the subframe along the three holes on each side. Using the clamps, I pulled the edges of the subframe tight to the repair channel and welded the repair using a series of inch-long stitch welds. This deters warping. The factory subframe is only 14-gauge, so warpage is a real concern.

When the repair was welded in place, I welded up the cracks. Keeping the welds to 1-inch increments is a good idea. This reduces warping and the potential for burn-through on the relatively thin sheet metal.

Next, I dressed the welds with a right-angle grinder using a flap wheel. Unlike a standard grinding disc, the flap wheel makes quick work of the excess weld without leaving large scars on the metal. Flap wheels also don't put as much heat into the metal. When the welds were smooth, I sprayed the frame with some weld-through primer and reinstalled the bumpstop bracket in the original location.

To finish the repair, I wiped fiberglass-reinforced body filler onto the subframe and sanded it smooth. The result is a clean repair that looks like nothing was ever done. The K-member lined up perfectly, and the repaired section is much stronger than it was from the factory.

This project took about two days to complete from start to finish.

Tools Required

- MIG welder
- Chop saw\Sawzall
- Grinder with flap wheel
- Drill
- Spot-weld cutter and drill bits

Subframe Repair

1 When the K-member was removed, the backing plate literally fell out of the frame. This is not a good sign.

2 *I used a Rota-broach spot-weld cutter to remove the spot welds on the bumpstop bracket, which is in the way of the cracks.*

3 *You can see how high the cracks go up on the subframe; this one is essentially to the top of the channel.*

4 *I used a grinder to clean up the spot welds and jagged edges of the subframe opening.*

5 *I built the repair channel from a piece of 3 x 4 tubing, with 1/8-inch plate added to the sides to make it wide enough. It was perimeter welded and plug welded in the center so that there is no chance of a future failure.*

6 *I took lots of measurements on the frame to locate the bolt hole on the passenger's side, fore, aft, and side to side. These were noted on the frame and transferred to the driver's side.*

7 *The repair channel slides up into the subframe and I marked it with a punch for the bolt location.*

8 *Using a large Rota-broach cutter, I cut the channel for the bolt hole. This mimics the look of the factory subframe. I also drilled two holes for the spot welds, just as the factory did.*

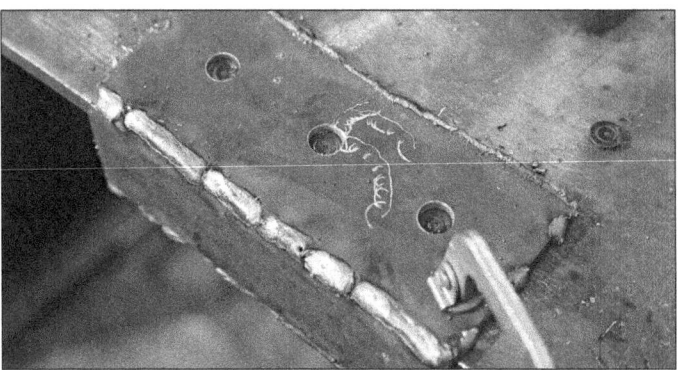

9 *I cut away the remaining section of the factory subframe using the Rota-broach spot-weld cutter. A center-punch makes this task much easier, as the alignment pin rides in a divot; otherwise, the cutter walks all over the place.*

10 *I then welded the backing plate into the repair channel.*

11 *I drilled the cracks, along with several spot welds for the side of the repair channel. I want this repair to be solid with no chance of moving or cracking again.*

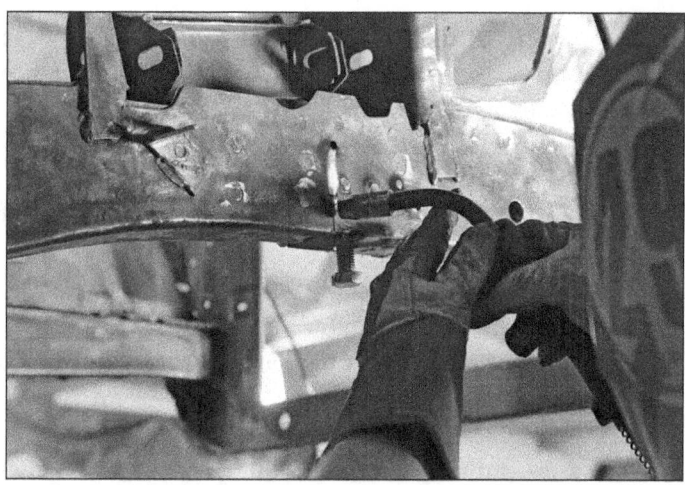

12 *After I installed the channel and aligned it to the measurements, I clamped the frame tight to the channel and welded it up. The factory subframe is only 14-gauge, so too much heat warps the channel. I only welded an inch at a time.*

13 *With the clamps removed, I welded up the cracks.*

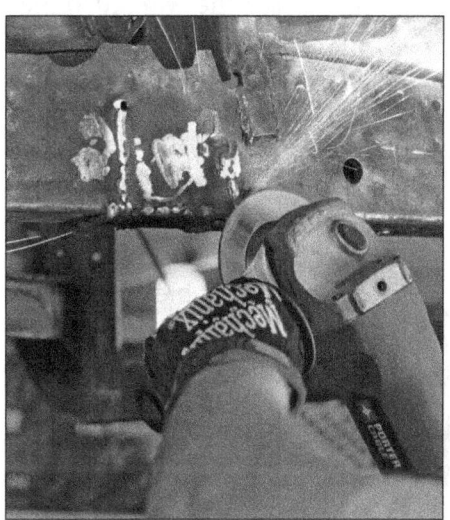

14 *I used the flap wheel to smooth out the welds, leaving a clean surface, ready for the finish work.*

15 *I applied a high-zinc weld-through primer and welded the original bumpstop bracket back into position.*

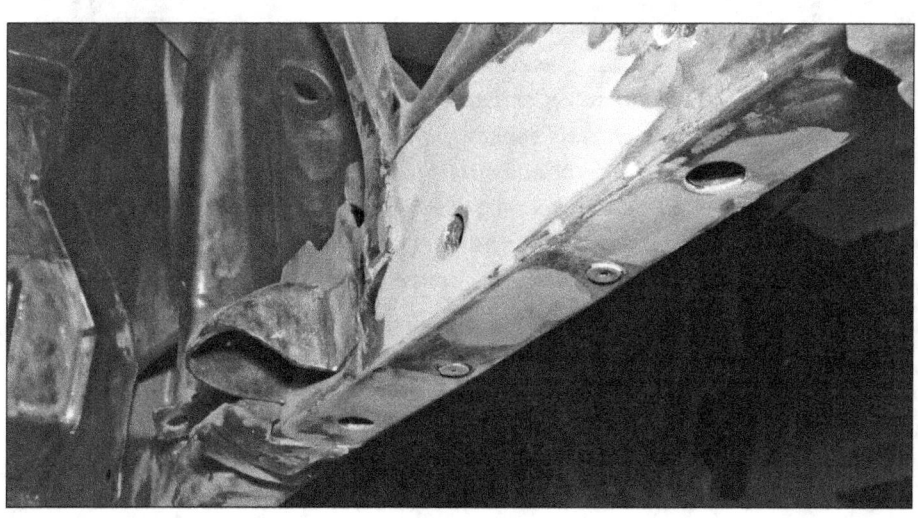

16 *The last step was the addition of a coat of Duraglas fiberglass-reinforced body filler. This filler is water resistant, fills pinholes, and is more durable than standard body fillers available off the shelf today.*

Floorpan Patch

By Jefferson Bryant of Red Dirt Rods

B-Bodies have several common rust issues, and the front floorpans are near the top of the list. The driver's side is usually the worst, but both front pans are highly susceptible to the ravages of rust. When you have it, the only option is to cut it out; otherwise the cancer spreads.

This 1969 Road Runner was purchased as a mild restoration, but upon further inspection, the floors had merely been covered up in an attempt to mask the rust issues. Most of the holes could have been patched with partial sections, but this method often takes more effort and the results are not as good as replacing the entire floorpan.

Before jumping feet first into a project of this magnitude think through the key components to this task: materials, available tools, and most important, your skills.

Materials

Both old and new materials should closely match; mismatched gauges of sheet metal lead to burn-through and cold-welds. Welding 14-gauge steel to 20-gauge steel will likely end with lots of burn-through on the 20-gauge because it is much thinner than the 14-gauge. This means that you need to purchase a quality reproduction panel because it is made of material similar to the factory floor.

Another potential headache with floorpans is that they are available in many forms, from small sections to entire floors. Buying a single-sheet floor is nice, but actually fitting it into the car is difficult, especially for post or 4-door B-Bodies.

Buy the sections you need. Measure the area that is damaged and replace only what it necessary. Make sure you know which models use the pan; sometimes variances require modification in order to fit the panel.

Tools

To properly install a set of floorpans you need several tools.

MIG welder: You really don't want to do this type of work with a stick welder; using a MIG torch is much easier and the results are significantly better. Flux-core wire works, but a solid wire with separate shielding gas is the best option for welding sheet metal. For the wire, .030-inch is okay, but .025-inch is optimum for thin-gauge sheet metal.

Cut-off wheel and die grinder: Either air or electric; you need a way to cleanly cut the rusty metal out of the car. A thin cut-off wheel works best. Air-powered die grinders are more maneuverable, but electric

I worked on one side at a time; this keeps the rigidity of the chassis secure during the repair process. You can see the various subframe and support structures that are critical to keeping the B-Body together. Note the seat belt location; this is not marked on the new panels. Take lots of measurements before you cut!

Upon first glance, these floorpans are not horrible, with just a few small holes. A closer look reveals much more. The surface rust has gone on much too long; this metal is paper-thin. It is surprising that it actually supported a person in the seats.

The finished repairs look like factory and these new panels are coated with electro-deposit paint (EDP) to resist rust.

90-degree grinders with a thin cut-off wheel slice through rusty steel as if it were butter.

90-degree grinder with flap wheel: This is for cleaning up the welds after the install. A flap wheel removes excess weld without leaving rough edges as does a standard grinding wheel.

Sheet-metal hole punch and 3/8-inch drill bit: Floorpans are spot welded in many places, including floor braces, brackets, and along the rocker panel. You need a drill bit or spot-weld cutter to remove these welds and a hole punch or drill bit to drill matching holes in the new floorpan. You can't eliminate these spot welds; they are critical for the structural integrity of the uni-body vehicle.

Skill Level

One saving grace for the novice welder is that floorpans are always hidden from view. If you are not an experienced welder, that is okay; the best place to learn is by welding in a floorpan. The biggest problem here is that B-Body Mopars are uni-body chassis, so the floor is structural to rest of the vehicle. Take care with this project and start small; don't cut out the entire floor first.

Floorpans and Uni-Body Tips

Welding floorpans is a large task, but it is a great way to become familiar with sheet-metal repairs. Take your time and be patient; you will be rewarded with excellent results.

Proper Fitment

Don't just hack the car apart without careful measuring and fitting. The last part you cut is the car itself. Always fit the replacement panels to the vehicle *before* you cut out the old rusty stuff. If an area of rust extends beyond the patch panel, now is the time to figure out how to handle it.

Support the Chassis

You don't want to chop the whole floor out of the car without supporting the weight and dimensional areas (door openings, etc.) first. For post cars, you have less to be worried about, but convertibles and hardtops can move around when the floor is removed. The best bet is to support the vehicle at several points, taking the weight off the suspension. This spreads the weight around and ensures that areas such as the front subframe, which holds the torsion bars, don't move when not supported by the floor.

Weld Small, Warp Small

The biggest mistake most builders make when welding sheet metal is to weld too much too fast. Stitch welding is the process of welding short (about an inch at a time) beads all around the panel, slowly connecting the stitches to form a solid weld bead. Spread the stitches 6 to 8 inches apart. You can use an air gun to blow cool air over the fresh welds to help cool them as well. Don't forget the spot-welds, they are crucial. Try to reproduce the welds in both location and number.

Prep Coatings

Fresh welds are immediately susceptible to rust. Paint the edges and hidden areas that are welded with a high-zinc weld-through primer. This primer reacts when heated by the weld and the zinc settles onto the cooling steel, providing a protective layer against rust. The last thing you want is for the rust to come back five years down the road. ∎

Roof Skin Replacement

By Restorations by Rick

Not many 1966–1970 B-Bodies need to have their roof replaced, but many of them came with a vinyl-top option. Because vinyl-top cars had only primer coats and topcoat color only around the perimeter, it's common to find serious rust issues under the vinyl. On cars with a severely rusted roof panel, it can be much easier and result in a better quality job to simply replace the roof skin. Although this project features a third-gen Charger, the procedures are universal.

The first thing you must do is dig out all the seam sealer in the drip-rail trough. You can use a small chisel or screwdriver; sometimes you have to tap the chisel with a hammer to get it all out. Be careful not to damage the drip-rail lip.

Thankfully, the roof skin is relatively easy to replace. Spot welds found around the entire perimeter must be drilled out. A specialized spot-weld drill with an adjustable-depth setting is the easiest, but a spot-weld cutter bit in a drill works fine; it's just a little slower. You can also use a die grinder with a cut-off wheel and carefully grind off the weld. No matter which method you choose be sure to wear eye protection and gloves.

Work from the center out on all four sides. Also, take advantage of the replacement top being accessible from both sides before installing and work out any dings or dents at this time.

A "rough cut" around the top is recommended first. This way the top is easier to manage in pieces. A rough cut allows you to pry up what is left after the spot welds are drilled. Do not forget that the sub structure is right under the top layer; do not cut so deep that you cut into the framework under the roof skin.

Installing the replacement top is simply a matter of aligning and clamping it in place, then welding the spot welds back together. Remember: Always work from the center out on all four corners. Be sure to strip off all of the black coating the panel may have on it from the factory.

You can use either a TIG or MIG welder to weld the new spot welds in the roof skin with similar results.

Roof Skin Replacement

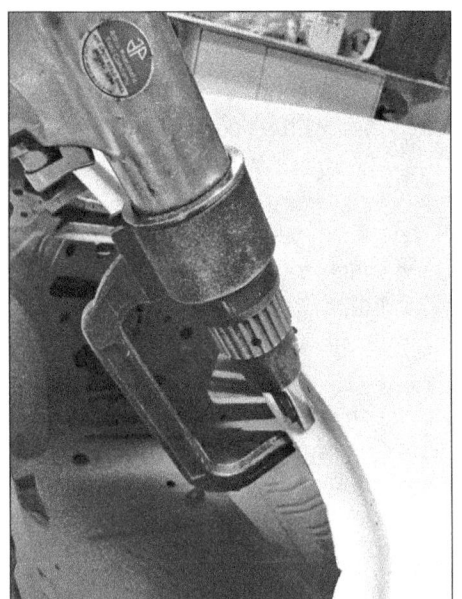

1 After digging out all the seam sealer from the drip-rail trough, grind or drill out all the spot welds around the perimeter of the old roof. Also grind out the original lead used to fill the roof to the quarter seam. Remove all of the old roof skin.

2 Grind all the spot welds that are rough after removing the roof skin. Clean up all rusted areas and treat them with a rust killer or converter. Shoot everything with weld-through primer. Although not a B-Body, this E-Body serves the purpose for these steps.

3 Now is the perfect time to clean and prime all the substructure and inspect for any other areas that may need special attention. If any of the sub-structure has been dented or pushed in, straighten them back into the original shape.

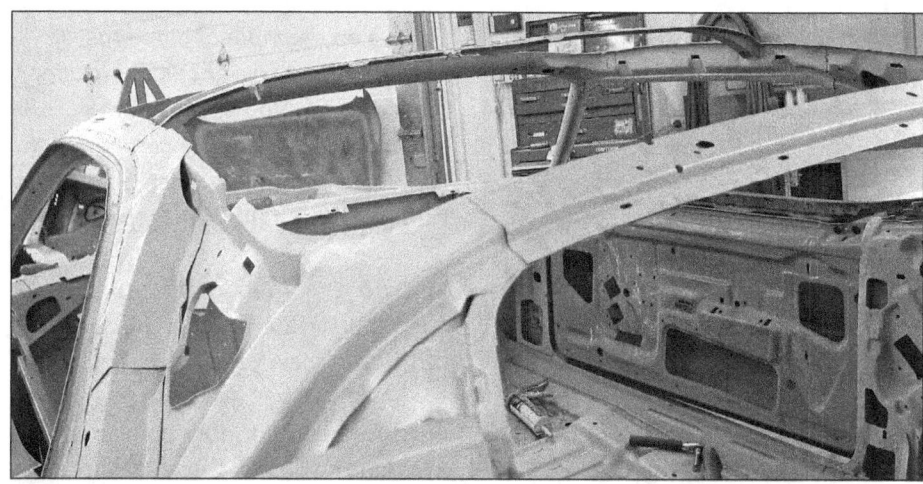

4 *If you are leaving the original quarter in place be sure to grind out all the lead and prepare the seam for welding. If you are replacing the quarter with full new sheet metal remove all the black factory paint and shoot with weldable primer.*

5 *On this example the drip-rail lip is in good shape, but it must be straightened where it was moved during the removal of the old roof skin. Carefully inspect all metal for any rust damage. Repair or replace any metal that is not in good condition and make sure you are ready to install the new roof skin over these areas.*

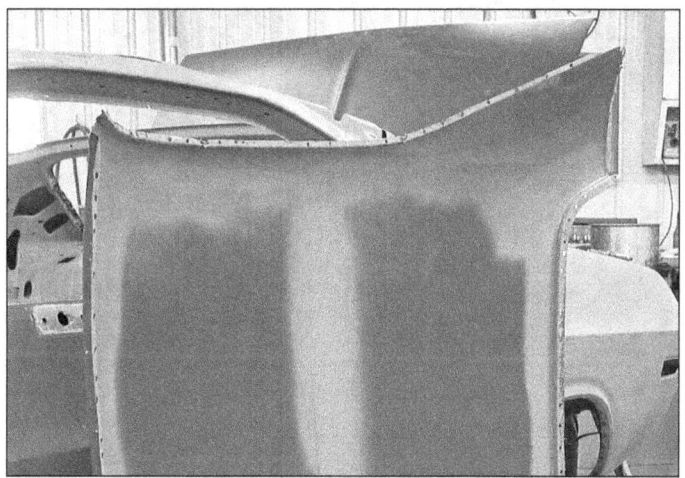

6 *Pre-drill all the holes where you are going to weld the replacement roof skin onto the car. Cover with weld-through primer and alternate weld locations working from the inside outward.*

7 *Grind all the spot-welds flush and re-lead the seam. Refinish and prime the roof skin. Whether you use original metal (shown) or replacement metal the process is the same.*

Quarter Panel Replacement

By Restorations by Rick

How do you decide whether or not to replace a quarter panel? As a general rule, if you have rust at the front and back of the wheelwell and a significant area above it, the car likely needs a full panel. I've heard of special cases where a car still had presentable factory paint and the owner wanted to preserve as much of it as possible.

In this example, the restoration shop purchased a half skin and used it to fit replacement pieces. This can be an excellent way to make quick, accurate patches if you elect to repair only rusted-through areas. Meticulous butt-fitted patches that are TIG welded are the best way to go, but it does require a high level of skill. If a new replacement panel isn't available for your particular model you have no choice but to repair what you have or find a used panel in good condition; this is seldom an easy proposition.

If the panel in question has massive accident damage that can't be repaired easily it may also push you toward the decision to replace. It's also possible to remove the panel

Here is an example of some rust-through on a survivor car. The owner does not want the entire quarter replaced. After carefully cutting out the rust, I discovered that it can be repaired without using a full quarter panel.

and do the metalwork off the car, then reinstall it. A great deal of work, but it may be worth the effort.

If you have rusted-through areas and you're in doubt, trim a couple of inches around them. Inspect the backside of the trimmed-off metal and keep trimming back until you see solid, clean steel. Also inspect the areas exposed behind the panel for corrosion. If you're seeing a great deal of rust it may be better to replace the whole panel. The areas behind the panel can be cleaned up and preserved better with full access.

Trunk floor extensions, wheelhouse replacement or repair, etc., are all much easier to do without the outer skin in place as well.

Patch Panel Installation

1 *Using a half skin, cut the new metal carefully to the exact shape of the fender that was removed.*

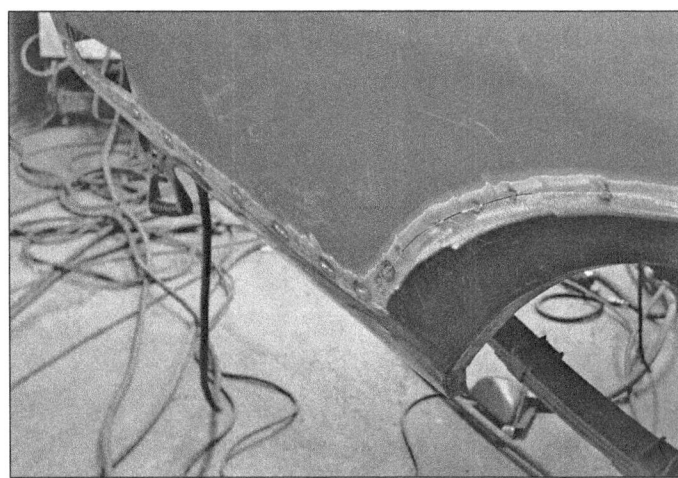

2 *After making sure everything is aligned for a good fit tack weld the patch panel in place.*

3 *Stitch weld alternating from front to middle to back, so you don't get any one place of the metal too hot and warp it.*

4 *Grind the welded seam flat and be careful not to go through any part of the seam or patch panel. Dress the seam with filler, and mask and prime until you are ready to apply topcoat.*

5 *Stay below the bodyline so that you do not need to paint the entire quarter. Pre-fit the wheel trim molding. Mask and shoot the topcoat right up to the bottom of the bodyline. Blend in the new paint with the old just under the edge of the line so it is not visible. Also, if your B-Body has wheelwell molding, now is the time to pre-drill the holes.*

6 *Color sand and buff the new paint to match the texture of the original paint. Apply the stripes and you still have most of the original quarter and paint saved.*

Quarter Panel Installation

Panel alignment begins at the quarter panels and is limited by the welded-on cowl position. First, align the deck lid, doors, fenders, and hood with the car sitting on its suspension. Door position is set relative to the quarter panel at the doors' back edge and to the rocker panel at the bottom. It's common for the rocker panel–to-door gap to be wider because the car was assembled originally. It's usually possible to install the new quarter panels slightly lower to allow the doors to fit closer to the rocker panel.

Doors without glass and a window regulator should be adjusted slightly higher at the rear edge to compensate for the weight difference. If any glass is in the car when welding or grinding, be very careful to protect it from sparks. You'll hate yourself if you ruin good glass!

Fenders align to the doors first then to the hood between the fenders. If the hood side gaps are too tight, the fenders must be moved outboard

and the doors tipped outward at the top. In some cases, it can be beneficial to push the quarter panel tops outboard slightly with a porta-power. Also note that B-Body doors can twist fairly easily. The vent window assembly helps stabilize this.

Because of the fixed cowl position on B-Bodies, the back of the hood–to-cowl gap can sometimes be too wide; the width of the door-to–quarter panel front edge gap is ideal. To make the hood back gap an acceptable size, the front edge of the quarter panel can be moved back.

To do this, cut a slit approximately 3/16-inch behind the front edge and tap it back, followed by tack welds. Do a 3-inch section at a time to prevent the panel from losing its shape. After tacking the whole edge in its new position, finish weld. You can follow these general procedures for quarter panel installation:

Support the car before the original quarters are removed. The front and rear frame rails are supported with two jack stands, one on each end. Verify that the doors align to

the quarter panels after supporting the car. This procedure ensures that the body doesn't sag or move when the quarter panel(s) is removed.

If you're installing reproduction quarter panels, compare the edge widths to the car's originals. Trim the edges to match the original. Incorrect widths on these edges are a dead giveaway to panel replacement and look awful. This is the ideal time to trim them.

Study the placement of spot welds and bracketry carefully. A digital camera is your friend! Take close-up pictures of all welds, brackets, edges, seam sealer placements, and so on. A rough trim staying a couple of inches from the panel perimeter using a plasma cutter or other cutting tool saves time. Inspect the cut lines closely to avoid accidentally cutting support structure behind the panel.

After the rough trim, drill spot welds using a Rota-broach bit. Use cutting oil on the bit to maximize its life. If the original panel is being scrapped, the spot welds can be ground thin with a cut-off wheel and popped easily. With the rough-cut method, you're left with strips of metal that are easier to pop loose, rather than fighting the whole panel.

Strip the paint using an abrasive stripping wheel or wire wheel in the spot-weld areas to make them easier to find.

Melt out the lead joints at the roof and rocker panel seams. A basic propane torch does the job, but be sure to wear a respirator.

Inspect your replacement panel closely to be sure you're not trimming too much of the original panel. An example of this is at the lower lead seam where many replacement panels don't extend all the way to the front.

If replacing the full panel, the roof seam area of the panel can be butt fit just below the overlap. This technique makes fitting the new panel much easier and removal of the original much less invasive.

Some restorers prefer to leave the factory spot welds and front edge flange in place and seam the front edge of the quarter panel just behind the door. If the replacement panel has a well-formed flange and crisp edge you can use it, as it allows more alignment options and reduces extra welding and finish work.

When a quality full panel is available it generally gives the best overall finished job. Partial panel replacement with a full-length weld seam requires much more welding, grinding, and finish work. Special care must be given to prevent weld "telegraphing." If a thick weld is left after finishing, the weld moves in the sun, showing a slight puffing outline. Grinding the weld flush on both sides of the panel prevents this.

Convertibles require seaming at the top edge around the deck. Leave the factory step in place and butt fit a seam approximately 3/16 inch from the edge. For the perfectionist, tack fit this seam and then drill out the spot welds on the step and remove the whole panel to finish the weld off the car. This way the seam can be perfected on the top and backside. An alternate method is to form a step flange; however, it's difficult to make it exact for a perfect fit of the stainless trim that attaches here.

Address any issues behind the panel. Now is the time to clean up any rust and treat accordingly. Wheelhouse rust repairs are especially critical because this panel sets the curve of the quarter panel as viewed from above. Unless the repairs are minimal, it's usually better to replace the wheelhouse. Trunk floor extensions should also be closely inspected and often require rust repair or replacement. The trunk floor is much easier to access for replacement at this time as well.

It's time to flop that new panel on and see how it fits! Clamp it in place and check the gaps. When the gaps are established, mark areas for trimming, such as the top gap or lower rocker joint. Mark the placement of spot welds and be sure they're positioned correctly.

Pull the panel back and drill or punch 1/4-inch holes for plug welds if you're MIG welding. A spot welder is another option and preferred by the most particular restorers; however, it requires a high-quality machine for proper strength.

If you're minimally experienced with MIG welding, it's a good idea to spend time practicing on some scrap metal. Use the same-gauge metal as the panels. To get the flattest plug weld, set your welder on the "hot side" and do a fast circular pass. With practice you wind up with a nice, flat-to-slightly dimpled finished weld that minimizes finish-grinding time. The factory spot-weld appearance can be accomplished many ways, such as re-melting the dressed plug weld with a TIG welder, pressing with a fabricated dimpling tool, pressing a pencil eraser in wet primer or filler, etc.

Now is the time to work out any dings or flaws. It's much easier with the panel off and you can do a much better job when you have access to both sides of the panel.

Sand the back of the panel and apply epoxy primer. Apply sound deadener/undercoating using your original panel for reference. Cardboard can be used as a mask template for the front edge, the side-marker opening area, etc. A cardboard square held above the deadener spray area works well to create the fan pattern stop build-ups often seen on factory applications.

Allow the sound deadener to dry overnight to prevent damaging it and/or igniting it with weld sparks while installing the panel.

Hang the panel on the car. Once again, clamp it in place.

It's best to start with the critical alignments first because they have to stay where they belong. First, weld the front-edge spot welds, being mindful of aligning to the door curvature and maintaining an even gap. Keep the gaps reasonable; 3/16-inch is a good target. Primer and paint thickness reduces it slightly.

Next weld the edge next to the deck lid, again being careful to monitor the alignment gap and rear-edge matchup. Test fit the quarter panel rear extension to be sure it matches the deck lid. Verify the fit of the deck filler panel and weld it at the end underneath where it meets the quarter panel and at the trunk trough jamb corner. At each end of the deck filler–to–quarter panel gap, weld approximately 3/16 inch and grind judiciously to slightly below the desired finish-seam sealer level. This helps prevent this sealer from cracking in the future.

Move to the wheelhouse next. It's important not to "trap a warp" in the area above the wheelwell; avoid this by starting in the middle and working outward. Be sure to alternate between front and rear.

Weld the front of the wheelwell at the rocker panel. The vertical seam to the rocker panel is welded solid to prevent moisture creeping under the lead work.

Next weld the rear edge where it attaches to the tail panel. Test fit the quarter panel extension to verify alignment. Now the area behind the bumper and the lower edge behind the wheel opening can be welded.

Last, weld the top roof seam. Just like the lower vertical rocker seam, you want to weld this solid to prevent moisture from creeping under the lead work. To prevent telegraphing of this weld, I highly recommend leading this seam as well as the lower rocker joint. Then grind off the excess lead and finish the seam with filler and primer.

Quarter Panel Replacement

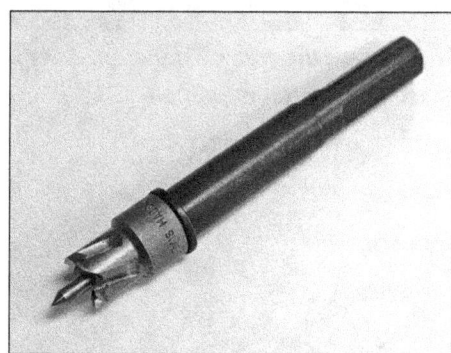

1 Use a good spot-weld cutter and a drill to remove the original spot welds. You may have to sand or grind off the original paint so you can see where the spot welds are.

3 After you remove the quarter, inspect, remove, and repair any rusted inner structure or supports and then finish in a good epoxy primer.

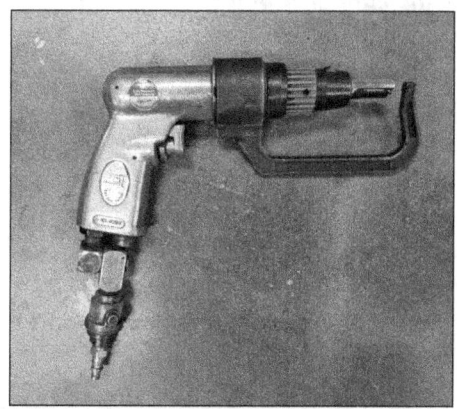

2 If you are planning on doing more of this kind of work in the future it is a good idea to invest in some heavy-duty equipment so the work goes faster. This drill for removing spot welds is great!

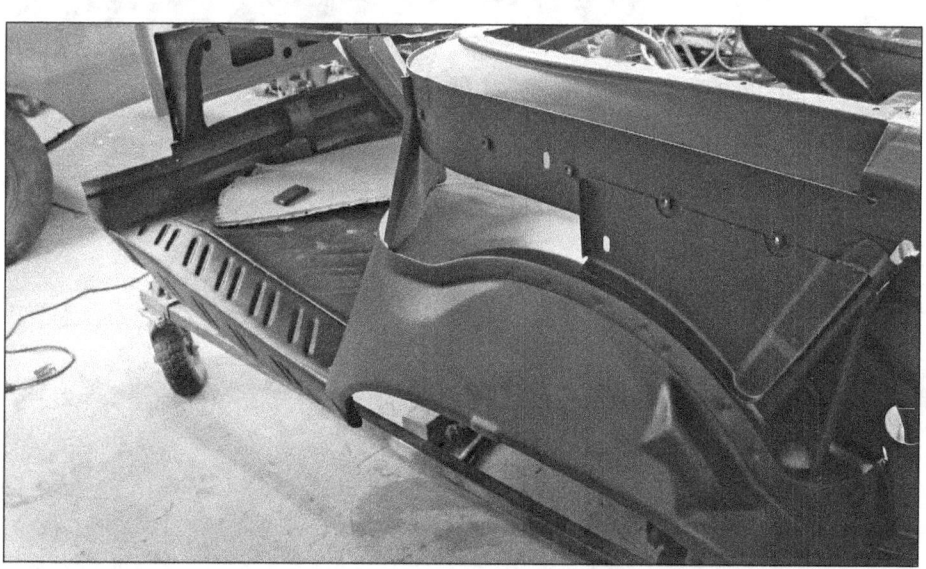

4 Notice the unique wheelwell housing on this convertible B-Body. If your convertible is rusted you must fabricate the replacement from a full hardtop wheelwell to create the flat top of the housing.

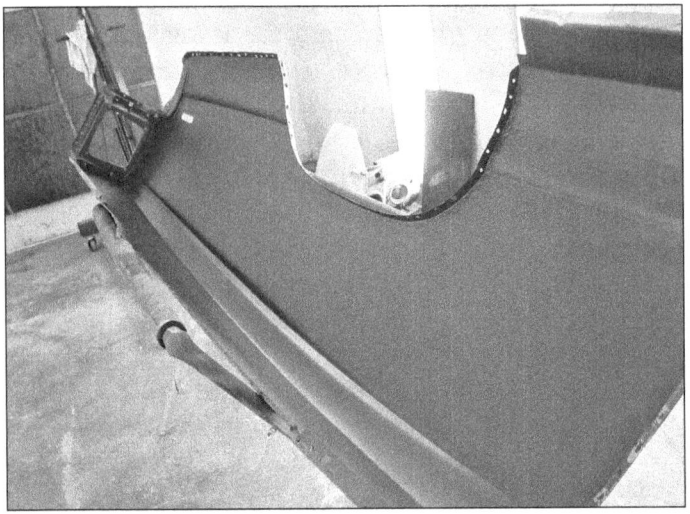

5 *Before installation grind down the wheelwell lip and rear lower edge to match the width of the original. Drill the spot welds and perform any bodywork to ensure the panel is straight when attached. Paint it in epoxy primer.*

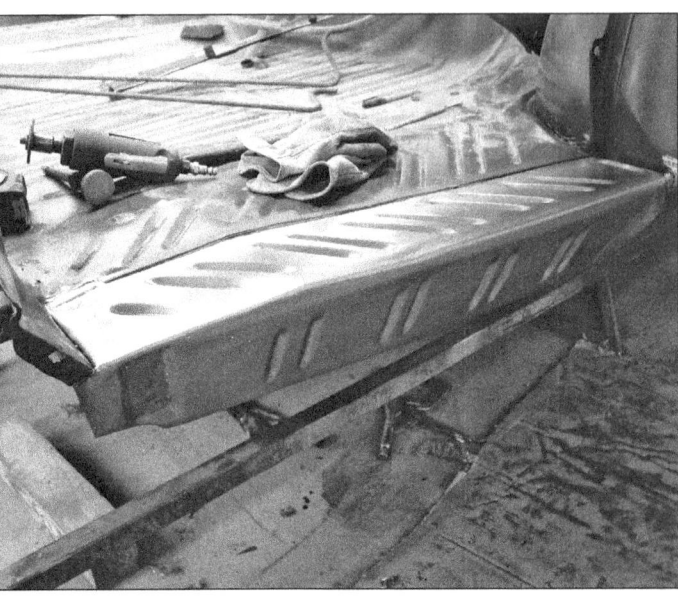

6 *You may need to replace the trunk extension. After all the correct welding, paint it in primer.*

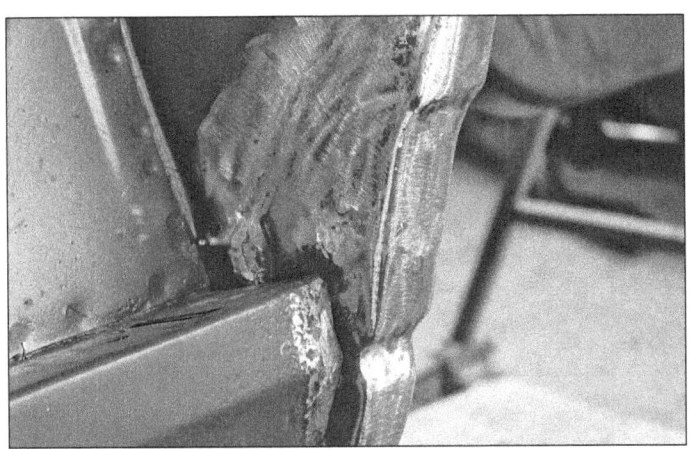

7 *If you have damage at the edge of the wheelwell opening you need to patch, weld, and finish it.*

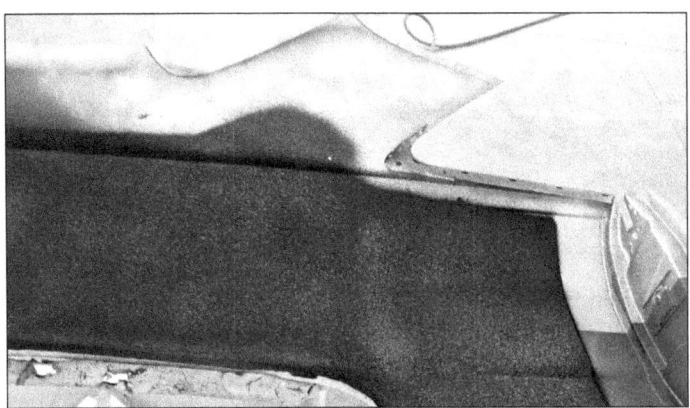

8 *After you apply the light gray primer, spray the sound deadener on the inside of the quarter before installation.*

9 *On a convertible body the original panel may need to be cut off about 3/16 inch from the top edge because the step for the trim is nearly impossible to duplicate. You then cut a new quarter to match and tack weld it into place.*

10 As you can see, the important door and quarter seam is perfect in height and in width. Tack it in so it does not move from this desired placement.

11 Stitch weld the entire seam alternating locations so that you do not warp the metal.

12 Grind down the welds and finish with filler.

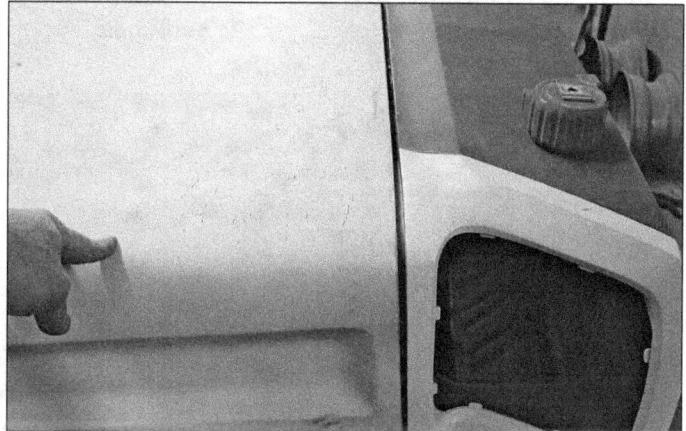

13 Having pre-fit the quarter with the correct trunk seam and with the rear taillight housing you can be assured of the correct gaps and final fit.

14 After finishing and applying epoxy primer the quarter is ready for sanding primer and final blocking before it is ready for its topcoat.

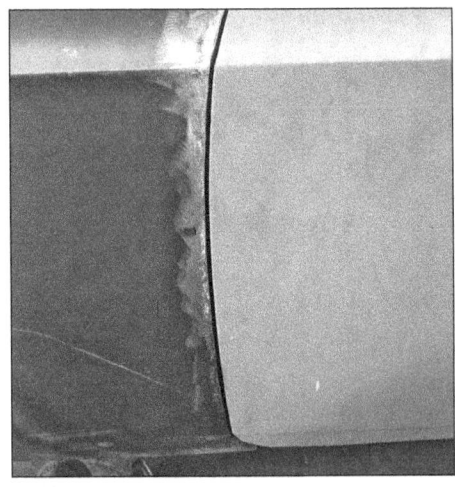

15 *You can save the original doorjamb along with all the factory spot welds and features by seaming the new quarter before the jamb corner.*

16 *Even though this is an E-Body it is a fine example of a horizontal seam replacement on this quarter. By leaving the top of the quarter and only replacing the side of the quarter panel on the original, you can save important bodylines.*

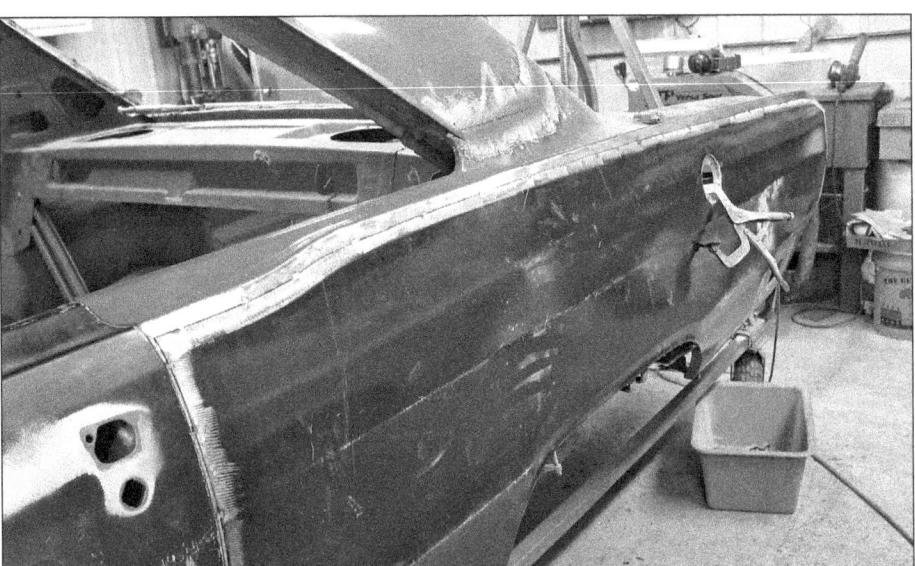

17 *As you can see here, only the metal was replaced on the quarter panel and C-pillar. Many go overboard and replace more metal than is needed. Don't do that.*

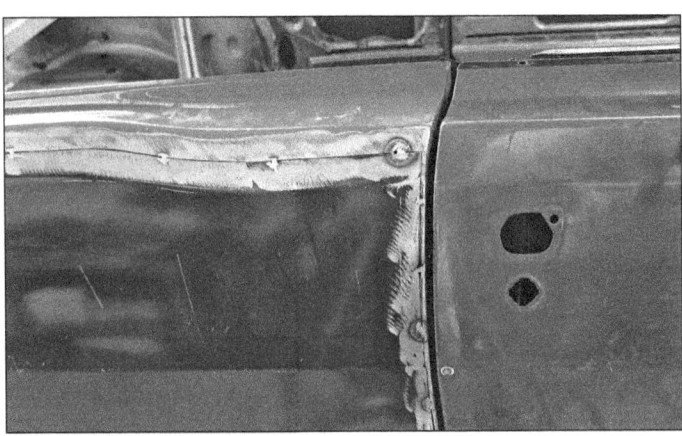

18 *Even though this is a roofline of an A-Body the seam is of the same design as on the B-Bodies. You weld the seam from the middle out and grind down the welds until they are smooth.*

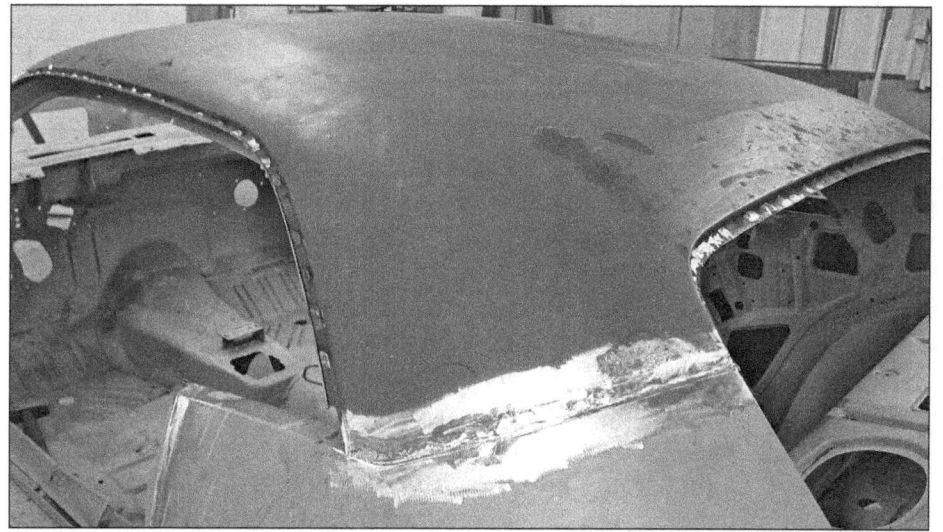

19 *On this E-Body, lead was applied to the seam just as the factory did it. Eastwood Company has all the instructions, tools, and supplies if you are not familiar with how to accomplish this skill. Be sure to use a respirator.*

Door Hinge Rebuild

Many times the doors sag after years of use and do not close or fit correctly. The culprit is usually worn-out door hinges. It is important to rebuild these now rather than after you've painted and aligned all of the panels. If you don't feel comfortable restoring your original hinges, replacement aftermarket hinge kits are available through outlets such as YearOne and Classic Industries.

You can use the following procedure to disassemble and restore your door hinges.

1 The upper hinges have pressed-in bronze bushings; each side has two. Catch the top edge of the bushing from the inside. With a relatively soft blow, drive the bushing out. Strike the bushing from various spots to drive it out evenly.

2 Inspect lower hinge bodies for cracks. Weld any cracks found being sure not to leave any weld buildup that would interfere with hinge movement.

3 Remove the lower S-springs. This is easily accomplished using a bench vise and an adjustable wrench. Clamp the round end of the S-spring in the vise. Now use the adjustable wrench and pull toward you; at the same time, tap on the hinge body to drive the spring past its stop. Release the wrench.

4 Ream the pin holes in the lower hinge bodies oversize to 11/32 inch (.3437). The reamer bit cuts without pre-drilling. Use oil for best cutting. De-burr the holes. The upper hinges don't need to be reamed; new bushings are supplied in the kit.

5 Inspect the detent rollers. Use penetrating oil and rotate the wheels with a vise grips. Be sure to

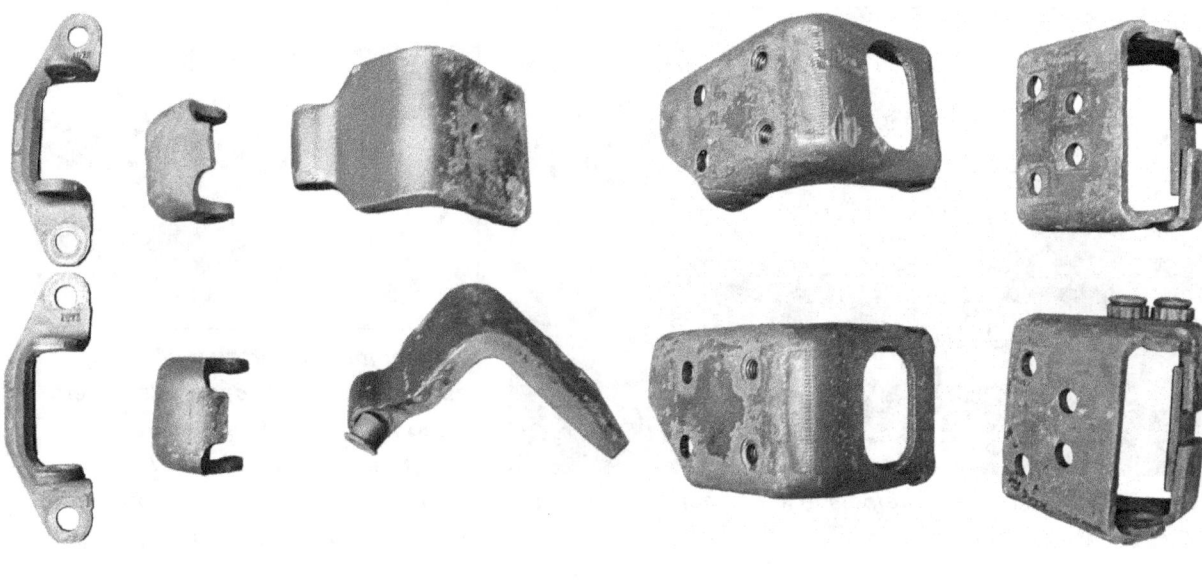

Take photos of the hinges from several angles for reference when reassembling.

have new pins and wavy washers available to replace them if the detent rollers rotate too far out of round (requires welding). These are not included in the standard door-hinge rebuild kit.

6 Purchase your new pins and wavy washers from Resto Rick or another supplier. Hardened star washers don't wear out and are re-used. Sandblast the body before installing the new pins; you don't want to fill them with grit. Liberally coat the parts with grease.

7 Clamp the washers in place with a copper bar. Blow cool air with an air gun after each weld to prevent overheating the wavy washer.

8 Grind the weld to approximately 3/32-inch thickness to avoid interference with hinge parts.

9 Clamp the upper hinge in a bench vise and tap in the bushings evenly. Soft taps are best.

10 Assemble the upper hinges (grease pins and bushings) first, and then tap in the pins. Be sure to orient the parts correctly; it's possible to put them together upside down. Install the pins from opposite sides. When installed on the car, the pins should be oriented with the heads on the top.

11 If the fit of the door swing bracket is too loose, you can tighten it with a slight squeeze in the bench vise. It should have a little play.

12 For the lower hinge assembly, grease the pins and slide them through while holding them together. Also grease and rotate the detent rollers a few times. Tap the pin all the way down to seat the knurling while aligning the parts.

13 Be sure to orient the pins from the opposite sides.

14 Finally, test the function of the detent rollers. Congratulations! Your door hinges are ready for paint and installation.

Wheel-Opening Molding Installation

By Restorations by Rick

It's always a good idea to pre-fit all of your trim before painting. Screwing on those pieces of automotive jewelry can become a huge disappointment if you don't take time to install them before paint and adjust them while you can. Even the factory original trim on original panels can often be improved.

Wheel-opening moldings are one of the more commonly missed items. An excellent way to begin installing wheel-opening moldings is with a few spring clamps. They allow you to position the trim correctly and determine what adjustments might be needed. Weld closed any old molding screw holes; they seldom line up to the re-fit molding.

Getting the fit just right might mean simply bending an edge or perhaps using a shrinker-stretcher tool on the molding. Sometimes the body panel needs some reworking to correct a contour.

When the fit is perfect, clamp the molding in place with a few spring clamps. Start at the center drilling a 1/8-inch pilot hole and install a screw. Use a temporary screw of the same size as your finished ones; that way you're not deforming the screw head while cutting the initial thread. Drill one hole at a time working from the center out, alternating front and rear. Be sure to verify that the trim is fitting snug as you drill each hole.

Installing trim on your beautiful paint job will now be simple!

Spring-loaded clamps such as these are great tools to keep your panel in place until it can be carefully spot welded into place.

Whether merely patching or wholly replacing a quarter panel, it's imperative to align key contact points. Align the former spot-weld hole (which should've been drilled out) with the pilot holes drilled in the new panel.

PAINT PREP AND PAINTING

The very first thing everyone does when they walk up to a car for the first time is to look at the paint. It requires your very best effort and the most attention to detail that you can give it.

For those who want to do *everything*, who don't want to hand off their car to a restoration shop, this portion of the build can be the most demanding, or the most thrilling. It all depends on how you view paint preparation, painting, sanding, and polishing.

Certain people look at an engine and reel in terror whereas others find

it to be the most exciting part of a car build; so it is with paint. This chapter is aimed directly at those who can't wait to jump into the challenge of aesthetically restoring their Mopar to as-new condition.

Though far more detailed than a beginner-level discussion, this chapter does not go into the same level of detail as books and videos dedicated to teaching you how to paint your own car. We strongly suggest you use them to learn the basics of painting a car.

This is a "how to" book on 1966–1970 Plymouth and Dodge B-Bodies.

It is a great tool for learning the differences among these cars. We cover specific painting techniques and tips along with how to reproduce the factory painting process.

Pulling Out Dents

Sometimes the fender or door may be free of rust but has a large dent or crease. When you can save original body panels you should take the extra effort to do so. You really need a good hammer and dolly set to work on these types of repairs. Companies such as Eastwood sell these quality tools at reasonable prices and they are a good investment if you plan on restoring or repairing more than one car.

You can use the old-fashioned dent puller that uses a metal screw that is drilled into the lowest part of the dent and then by sliding the moveable weight out you can pull the dent back to its original position. This still works but it puts holes into good metal that are not necessary with today's technology.

A stud welding system, which is available through Eastwood among others, is a great way to pull out dents and creases. Instead of drilling holes

It takes a great deal to get your project car from the way you found it to a finished paint job. In this chapter you find all the steps necessary to prepare your car for paint, and learn how to replicate the exact process that Chrysler used at the factory.

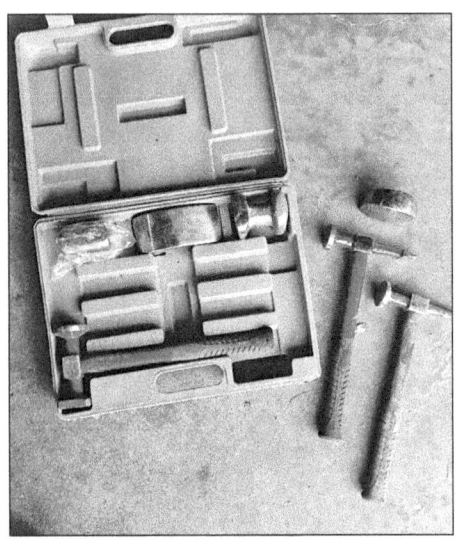

A good hammer and dolly set are a good investment for anyone who does paint and bodywork.

you weld a stud onto the metal and pull the dent out starting from the deepest part of the dent and working gradually outward until the dent is removed. After you get the metal back to its original shape all you have to do is cut off the stud and grind the weld smooth. You always have to use a dolly and hammer to get it really close and then dress the repair with body filler.

Body Filler Basics

Body filler (or Bondo) has received a bad rap for years. It is true that misuse of this important tool in preparing a car for paint can be found on many of these older cars. It should never be used on exceptionally thick patches or as a substitute for missing metal. It is used to fill in minor irregularities in the metal's surface and to dress repairs.

It can be applied directly to bare metal, but we prefer to spray the car with epoxy primer first and then use the body filler. We prefer to use as little as possible, whereas others coat the entire panel and then level it with the correct grade of sandpaper.

Regardless of the method you choose, do not buy the cheap stuff. Use the best grade of body filler available and you never have to worry about it failing and replacing it after the car has been painted. You can purchase your body filler from the local PPG distributor. Several different brands are available to suit your specific application.

The most common beginner mistake is to sand off too much of the filler. The next most common mistake is to use too fine a grit when shaping the repair. When the body filler has been sanded you skim coat it with a body glaze. Mix a small amount of body filler in with your final glaze filler so that it sands easier.

Always use the longest sanding board possible on a repair for a more level finish.

Primed and Ready

After you have performed all the metal work, body filler work, and finish sanding, it is time to use a sanding primer. We have already mentioned using epoxy primer on the bare metal before making body filler repairs. Epoxy primer is very difficult to sand and should not be used after the body filler is finished.

For this next step use a high-build sanding primer. Shoot two to three good coats on the entire body and all panels. Then sand with 100-grit paper and again use the longest blocks you can for the area you are working.

Apply a good "guide coat" in a contrasting color, usually black. As you sand the primer, the black helps to highlight any low spots that need further attention.

Shoot two to three more good coats and sand with 400-grit paper, again using a guide coat.

Finally, shoot everything with a primer sealer and you are ready to apply the top coats.

Paint Types

Single-stage or base coat/clear coat: Which should you use? When these cars were originally painted, the factory used single-stage enamel paint. They had a lot of "orange peel" and you could actually see repairs under the paint. If you are trying to re-create this original factory look use single-stage enamel paint. If not, use base coat/clear coat. It looks better and lasts much longer if you use modern paint technology.

When you use the base coat/clear coat process, it is much easier to produce better results. You shoot two or three coats of the base color over all parts of the body and panels. Be sure to observe the proper flash times between coats. Then you shoot three coats of clear over the base. The end result is a deep shine. This look cannot be re-created with single-stage enamel. If your car is covered in a metallic color it is very difficult to get good results without using base coat/clear coat.

Many top-level companies have good products. Now is not the time to try to save money. Buy the best paint and supplies you can because you really do not want to have to go through this again. We strongly recommend using PPG paint. They have all the original formulas for all the Plymouth and Dodge colors and their top-of-the-line clear produces a fabulous, deep shine.

Now the moment of truth has arrived. Can you paint your car

yourself and be happy with the final result? Only you can honestly answer this question. We covered selecting the right paint shop in Chapter 1. You may need to use that advice if you feel you cannot apply the topcoat and be satisfied with the result.

Even if you have never gone this far on a restoration before, the information in this chapter will guide you through the process to successfully paint your car and be proud of the final results.

Paint Booth

You can successfully accomplish many of the previous restoration work in a regular home garage or even in your driveway. However, applying color and clear requires having access to, or building, some kind of paint booth that helps you apply the paint with minimal dirt, dust, and even bugs getting in the paint.

The best thing to do is to contact several independent paint shops and inquire if they rent their booth over a weekend. This way you can be sure to have all the necessary equipment, lights, ventilation, compressor capacity, water, concrete floor, and space to put a quality paint job on your car. The better the environment you have to paint in, the better the results, and the less time you have to spend sanding and buffing out the flaws.

The next best thing is to build a temporary paint booth or convert part of your garage into a place where you can shoot paint and not fill your neighborhood with paint spray from your garage. We have seen many great paint jobs come from a home booth.

If you decide to build a temporary booth, several plans on the Internet provide step-by-step instruc-

---

Paint Booth Must-Haves

You must take into consideration several "must have" aspects to be able to lay down a good paint job.

- Containment: The area must keep out foreign particles and filter out the overspray from the paint gun before returning the air to the outside environment.
- Ventilation: Airflow must bring in fresh filtered air and return filtered overspray to the outside environment.
- Concrete floor: Your floor must be concrete and you must have a water supply and somewhere for the water to go after use.
- Dry compressed air supply: You need enough air capacity to shoot your gun through an entire pass around the car at a level of at least 60 psi.
- Lighting: You need as much light as possible! You cannot apply the paint evenly if you can't see what you are doing.
- Protection: Modern paints have toxins and you must take precautions to protect your health, including a respirator mask, gloves, and eyewear.
- Cleanliness: Every surface must be as clean as possible, including all nooks and crannies of the car and all of its surfaces.

---

tions on how to build one. Choose the plan that fits your specific needs and ability, and build it.

Vehicle Preparation

The factory painted these cars completely assembled. If you are going to return your car to its original factory condition you can either paint your car completely together or paint it in pieces but have a final result that "appears" as if it was painted fully assembled. If your car is non-metallic color it is much easier to paint it in pieces than if your car is metallic. Be sure to paint all exterior panels at the same time when shooting metallic; otherwise the paint does not match from panel to panel.

Disassembly

Because the undercarriage and interior received only an overspray of color, we recommend assembling the entire car and all joints. Also, ensure that gaps are correct before

painting the interior and undercarriage. It is best to apply as much seam sealer and sound deadener as possible. Also, before you paint, make sure that you have assembled those parts that show an oozing of this filler.

Don't forget to use grease when you mount the trunk sliders in the car. Yes, they do get painted (grease and all), because that is the way the factory did it.

After lining up everything and straightening all of the gaps, drill a small pilot-positioning hole in several areas. This way, you can reassemble all of the parts after you have painted; you won't damage the paint by having to reposition these parts.

Drill one hole on each side in the middle of the trunk hinges where they attach to the trunk. Then drill one hole on each side in the middle of the upper and lower door hinges where they attach to the body. Drill all the way through and use the drill bit to reposition these hinges after paint.

With your hood properly aligned, use a small drill bit to make a guide hole through both the hinge and the hood itself.

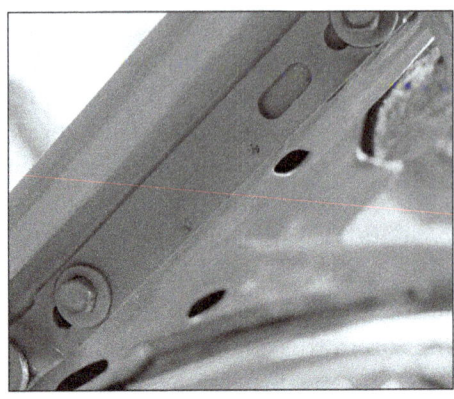

When your hood and hinges are painted, you can use the pilot holes to realign the hood to the hinge. When aligned and tightened, simply fill in the tiny hole with some silicone and paint it over so it is not visible.

Remove the doors, hood, and trunk and hang them vertically for paint. Leave the fenders on the car and the hinges on the doors. (You do this because of the factory seam sealer and the fact that the car was fully assembled before it was painted.)

Hang the hood, trunk, and doors in the room so you can shoot them in the same order as you removed them from the car. This way the color is consistent from panel to panel.

Mount all the loose attaching bolts into cardboard with the heads sticking up. Shoot them with color and clear at the same time you shoot the car and panels.

Cleaning

Clean the car well before putting it in the paint booth. After it is in the booth clean it again. Blow it off with air and wipe it down again. Wet the floor and blow the car off again. Use a tack rag on all areas to be painted.

Always wear a disposable paint suit and cover your hair and face. Wear gloves and a respirator. Wipe off the air hose. Do anything you can to keep everything as clean as possible.

Assembly

Carefully assemble the doors, hood, and truck using the pre-drilled pilot holes. Any paint that chips off the attaching bolts can be touched up with a brush. After assembly fill the pilot holes with silicone and with a fine detail brush paint it with color.

Within one week begin the cut-and-buff process discussed at the end of this chapter. The longer you

Tools and Materials

Before painting, be sure to gather all the materials listed below for this very detailed process. We recommend PPG paints.

- Paint
    - 1 gallon of epoxy primer, reducer, and activator
    - 1 gallon of sanding primer
    - 1 gallon of plastic filler, plus hardener
    - 2 gallons of base
    - 2 gallons of reducer
    - 2 gallons of clear, plus hardener
- 6 to 10 tack cloths
- 2 empty gallon cans
- Stir sticks, filters
- Masks

- Tooth picks, tweezers
- Lacquer thinner for clean up
- 20 sheets of 2000-grit sandpaper
- Sanding film for palm sander: 1500- and 2000-grit
- Masking tape and paper
- Measuring stick
- 3 paint guns: two down-draft HVLP and one touch-up
- 2 water inline filters
- Pads: cotton buffer, white foam, and black pad
- Rubbing compound (such as 3M Perfect-It 3 Compound)
- Finishing glaze
- Fine-line masking tape for stripe
- 1-quart Organisol, plus reducer (if your car has stripes)
- Masking wrap (plastic)
- Measuring cup ∎

PAINT PREP AND PAINTING

wait the harder the paint is and the harder it is to color sand and buff.

Make a Spray Plan

Plan out where you will start shooting color and the order of where you will go next so that you never have a dry edge while spraying.

We start in the trunk and work around the car counterclockwise, until we arrive back at the trunk. Have plenty of paint pre-mixed according to the instructions because one trip around the car can use as much as 1/2 gallon or more of reduced paint.

Allow the recommended flash times between coats. Shoot two or three coats of base on solid colors and three or four coats on metallic. On lighter colors you may need as many as four to six coats to achieve good coverage.

Keep the floor wet, and complete the process by shooting three coats of clear. Let all parts dry for at least 24 hours.

How the Factory Did It

Just how did the factory paint your car in the first place? One source takes you step-by-step through the factory process: Winged Warriors National B-Body Owners Association. Their website (wwnboa.org) is dedicated to the Winged cars and provides complete information about the unique assembly and painting processes used at the Lynch Road plant to build these amazing cars.

The following is a summary of everything we have learned over the past 30 years. This will help you understand what you find when you strip down one of these cars and how to duplicate it with your restoration.

Your car began in the metal shop, where everything that would receive paint was assembled and welded together. Each area of the mated surfaces of the panels was treated with a gray weld-through zinc primer before welding. When you take the doors off you see a green primer between the door hinge and the body. This was brushed on in several areas to prevent rust. Seam sealer was applied between the front fenders, taillight extensions, etc., and on many seams on the cars' bodies when they were assembled.

The trunk sound deadener was applied to the inside of the quarters before they were welded together.

The fender tag at most plants was attached to the body with one front screw and the tag was bent upward so that paint and inspectors' stamps could be applied along the way. At the Lynch Road plant the tag was hung inside the car with a paper clip. Upon leaving the "Body in White" metal shop, all parts of the car that would receive paint were completely assembled.

As your car entered the paint shop it went through several rinses, and then was treated with metal etching primer. After that it was dipped into a water-based dark primer vat, about halfway up the body. Then the exterior was hosed off before the dip primer dried. This dip line can easily be seen inside the doors, inside the backseat side panels, and on the inside of the cowl under the dash.

You can also see where this primer puddled in the ribs of the trunk and interior floors. The primer dripped out through the holes found in the floorboards and trunk, and left drip marks on the undercarriage around these holes and along the ribs.

Next, a black seam sealer was applied to the interior joints and a white hard drying sealer was applied in the trunk. A dark gray primer was applied to all doorjambs, trunk, under-hood areas, etc., and a final automated coat was applied to the exterior.

Immediately after, the interior color was sprayed and the car went into the oven to cure. After curing, the outside of the body was sanded, wiped off, and the interior color was masked off by hand. The body color was then applied and it again went into the oven to cure. Only an overspray of color partially covered the interior and undercarriage of the car.

All vinyl roofs were then attached (note that no body color was applied on the roof if it was a vinyl-top car).

Understanding the factory process helps you document your car when it is disassembled and stripped of its old paint. Then, as you restore it, you can duplicate your car's unique fingerprint and have a car that is finished to its very own factory original condition.

Painting Your Car Body

The decisions you make and the actions you take at this important step of restoring your car have impacts on the quality and value of the car for the rest of its existence. We cannot emphasize enough how important it is to take the time, effort, and expense to get this right! Frequently, an owner is so excited to get their car done that corners are cut or important steps are missed that come back to haunt later.

If you can finish restoring your car and not say, "I wish I had done this differently," you are in the minority. We hope this section can help you get to the finish line and say, "I am glad I did it the right way."

Body and Paint Preparation

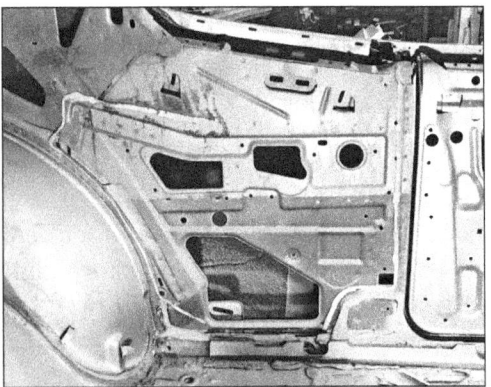

1 Here is a great example of the factory's "dip primer" line left after the entire body was dipped into the primer bath. You find this line on the doors and also on the firewall under the dash. Also notice the "sound deadener" inside the panel proving that it was applied before the car was welded together.

An E-Body is featured in this sequence, though the procedures are the same as for a B-Body.

2 Removal of all the undercoating from the undercarriage can be daunting. This is a factory-undercoated car, and as you can see they did not skimp on coverage for this car. It really does help to have a rotisserie rather than having to lie on your back to remove the undercoating.

3 A good MIG welder and cart are a great investment even if you do not plan to restore another car. If you have a large amount of metal replacement on your car it pays for itself the first week.

4 Using the pick side of the body hammer you can tap down any high spots and also create a better surface to improve the adhesion of the body filler.

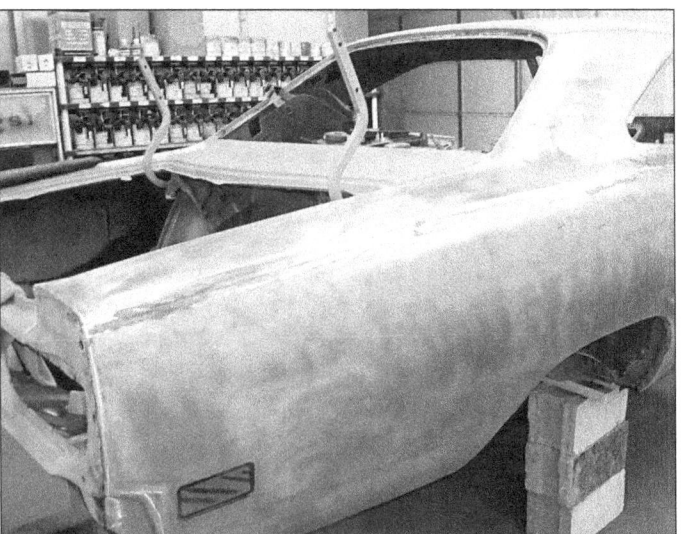

5 After stitch welding the seams (left), grind down the weld to make a smooth, even surface (right). Always remove the "black" protective coating on replacement panels. (Photos Courtesy J&J Repair and Restoration, Hazen, North Dakota)

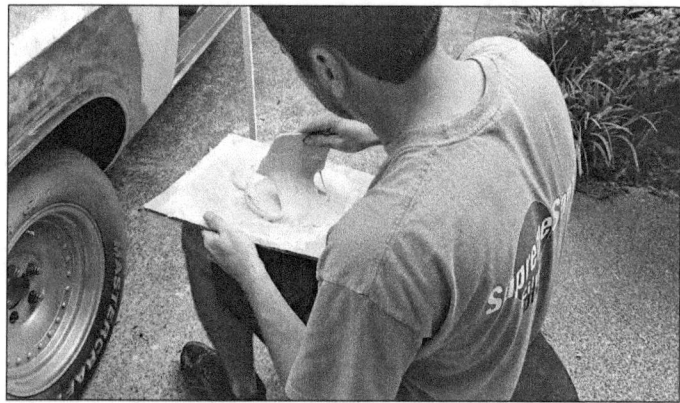

6 After replacing and completing all the metal work it is time for the body filler application. Be sure to buy a good-quality filler. It sands better and never has to be replaced after painting. You can use a good square of heavy cardboard to mix the filler and hardener.

7 Coat all surfaces with a filler. This is the best way to make sure the entire surface is completely straight.

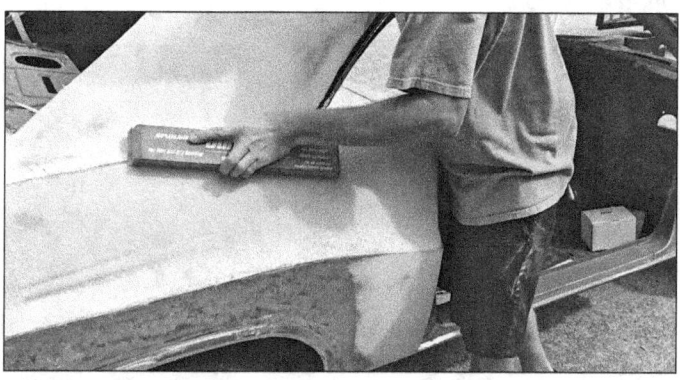

8 As soon as the filler gets tacky and before it dries completely, take a long board with 60 grit and rough form the filler. Use a wire brush to clean the paper off the filler to use it again.

9 As you can see, filler quickly fills the low spots, and the high spots also show up. Always sand away from the edges and bodylines.

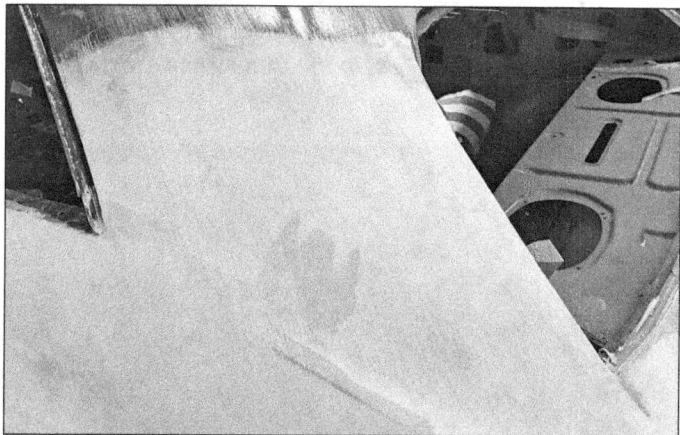

10 Even after using what may seem like a lot of filler you may still have good-sized low spots. If the car has a lot of replacement panels this process works well in getting the aftermarket panels even and smooth.

11 This car not only had new quarters, but the roof was replaced also. Using the filler created a seamless, even surface. Use additional filler and smoother-grit sandpaper until the filler is ready for sanding primer.

12 *This car only needed some minor repair to straighten the body. It was stripped to bare metal and covered with two coats of epoxy primer. After spraying a guide coat and sanding with a long block and 100-grit paper the low spots showed up.*

13 *Rather than coating the entire quarter and C-pillar with filler, just use enough filler to fix the areas that need attention.*

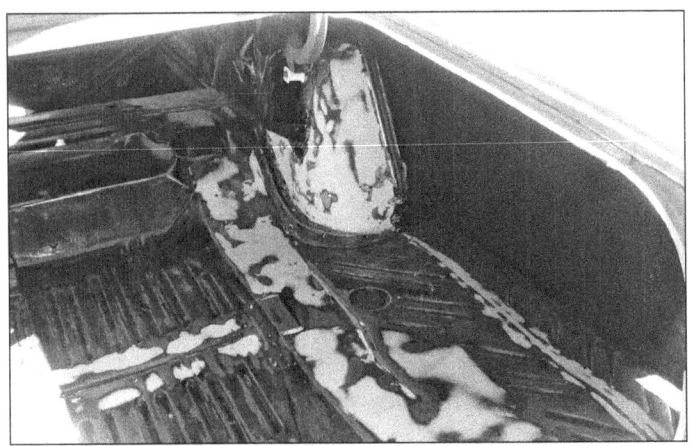

14 *The trunk can have many small imperfections and you must use a lot of patience in making sure every flaw is finished. The wheelwells should always be perfect because they are seen first in the trunk when the pad is installed.*

15 *Here you can see the taillight extensions attached with seam sealer. It oozes out when tightened. To achieve the correct factory appearance, wipe the seam with your finger. Contrary to what some suppliers tell you, there wasn't a foam gasket between the body and the taillight extension from the factory.*

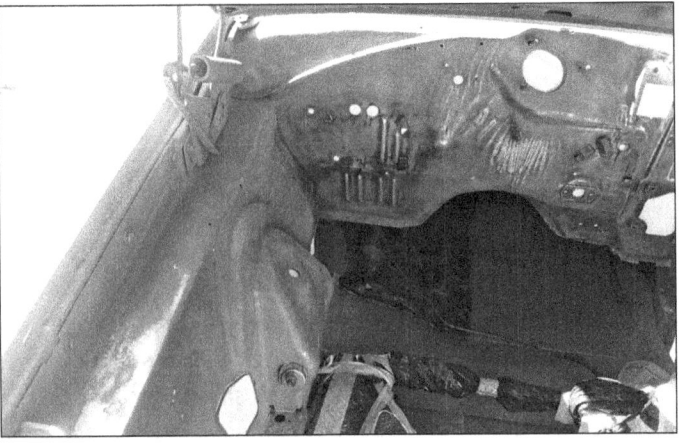

16 *There isn't any seal sealer between the fender and the inner fender panels yet on this car. You apply it before the final coats of primer are sprayed. Also be sure to weld up any extra holes in the firewall and fenderwells.*

17 A new AMD hood was used on this car because the original was unusable. You remove the black protective coating with 100-grit discs and a DA sander, then epoxy prime it.

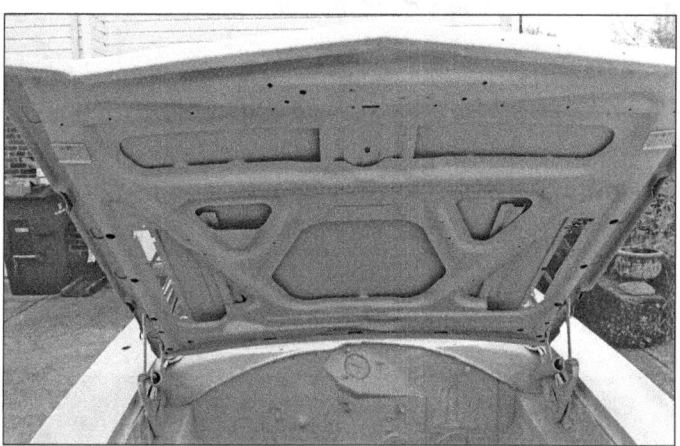

18 It takes hours to hand sand the underside of the new hood, but it must be done. The hinges, hood, and fenders have been pre-fitted and primed. Now it just needs to be scuffed with 400 to be ready for topcoat.

19 The trunk is now perfect. Wait until after paint to drill out the drip holes with a hole-bit to the correct size for the body plug.

20 After the car has been sealed and scuffed with 600-grit and a block you can take it to the paint booth that you rented for the weekend.

Painting

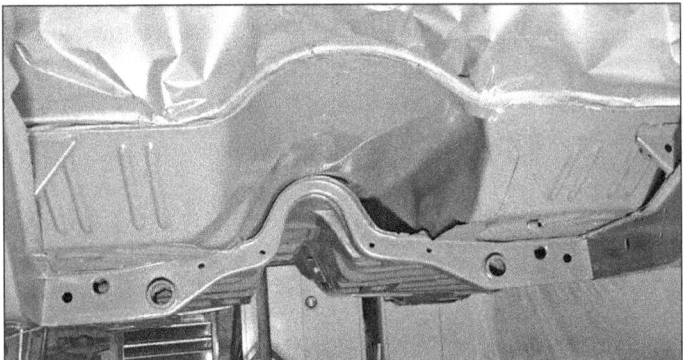

1 No need to waste the paint by spraying it where it does not show. We recommend masking off the whole car while priming. If you have already sprayed the entire car with epoxy primer there is no reason to apply more material.

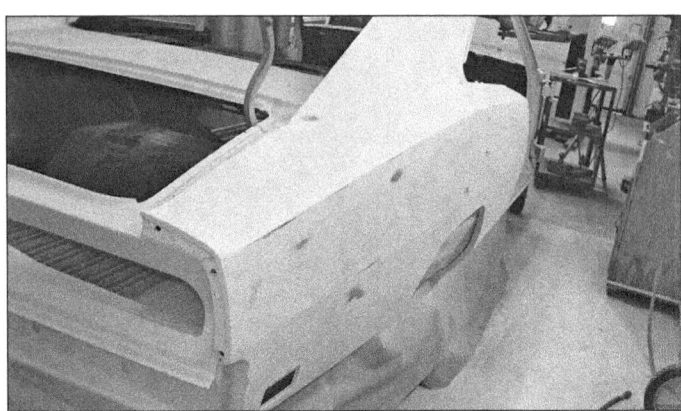

2 When the car is in the booth remove and hang the doors, trunk, and hood. Blow off any dust and thoroughly wipe down the car with a tack cloth. Tape and section off the underside of the car.

3 Be sure you have everything you need before you begin the painting process. Always have extra paint cans so you can mix the two gallons and have the same color. The objective of the base coat is to achieve really good coverage of color on all areas of the car. It does not have a shine so do not make the mistake of applying too much paint at one time.

4 You do not need to paint the top with color or clear if you are installing a vinyl roof.

5 We recommend that you hang the hood and the trunk when possible. If the trunk vertical panel is difficult to fully cover with paint when hung you can put it on a stand (shown). After the paint dries completely mask it off and paint the underside.

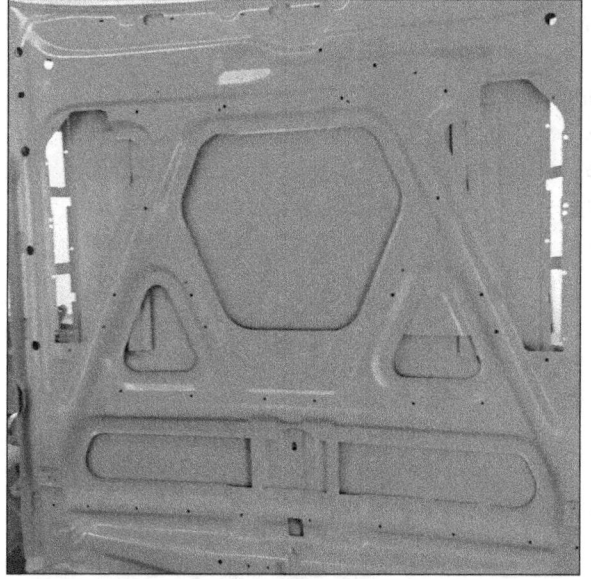

6 With the hood hung it is easier to spray the front and backside at the same time. The backside of the hood has many curves and irregular surfaces. Take your time to avoid dry areas and runs.

7 Usually two good coats of a solid color and three or four coats of a metallic give the paint job a good color base for shooting the clear. Always allow the correct amount of flash time between coats. If you need more coats to cover you should have enough paint because you started with two full gallons of unreduced color. We usually end up with 1/2 to 1/3 of a gallon left just in case a panel ever needs repair. Follow the instructions for the recommended flash time for your brand of paint. The average flash time is 15 minutes.

8 Start in the trunk with the clear coat. Before shooting, lightly go over the car with a tack cloth to remove any overspray or dust nibs. Work your way around the car making sure you do not have any dry lines. Complete each panel with the spraying motion before moving to the next area.

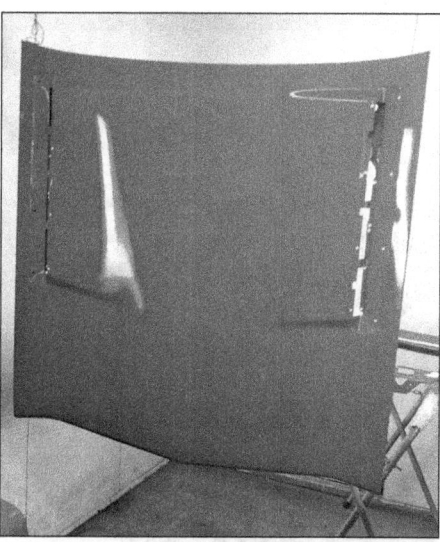

9 The first coat goes on wet, but remember that you have three more coats to apply so do not apply so much clear that you cause a run.

10 The engine compartment is the most difficult to shoot. Carefully climb into the engine bay and have a helper hold the air hose up so it does not touch the car. Move very carefully and deliberately. Plan each movement.

11 *Shoot any extra panels off the car unless they have sealer between the joints. You have less overspray with it apart.*

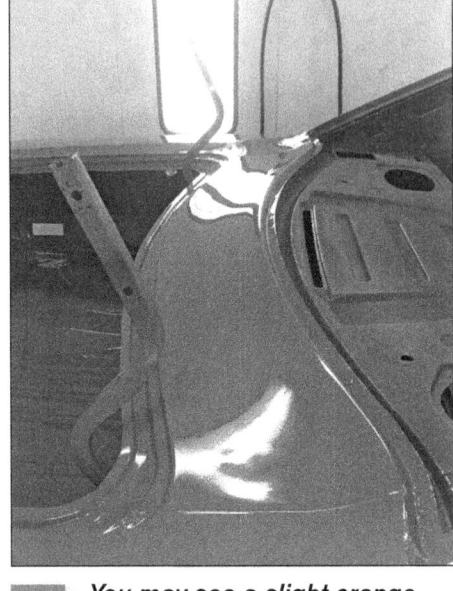

12 *You may see a slight orange-peel finish in the clear. This means you are shooting everything the right way. This all sands and buffs out later.*

13 *When you have applied all the base and clear coats walk away and let the paint flow out. You will be amazed at how the paint changes appearance and improves as it dries.*

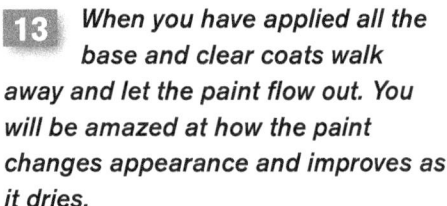

14 *Secure the doors, trunk, and hood so they are stable while transporting the car back to your garage or shop from the paint booth.*

Interior Color

Your car may have an interior door color that is different from your exterior color. A prime example is a red car with a black interior. You have to mask off the car and shoot this color. There isn't really any better way to do this.

Your tapeline should follow the holes in the door where the door rubber seals snap in. Scuff the paint and shoot with single-stage enamel. Use the color designated on the fender tag. After it dries remove the masking.

If you have a post car, remember that the interior part of the post also receives interior color.

While you have the car masked off it is a good idea to shoot the hood stripes and the blackout behind the grille.

Grille Blackout

Ma Mopar did not like to see body color shining out from behind the grille on these cars. Many say that the darker cars, such as black and dark green, did not receive the blackout. We have seen blackouts on an original black car so be sure to document your car if you have an exception to the rule.

There is also much discussion about where and how much blackout was applied to these cars. If you are fortunate enough to have this area original on your car, undisturbed, just take pictures and reproduce what you have. It will be messy and sparse in places, and masking was not used to prevent areas of overspray.

Basically, the semi-flat black paint was originally shot from the front of the car in a slightly upward direction. The area included is behind the headlight buckets to the lower part of the radiator support all the way up to the bottom of the upper radiator support, not extending over the lip, except with small irregular areas of overspray. The grille supports

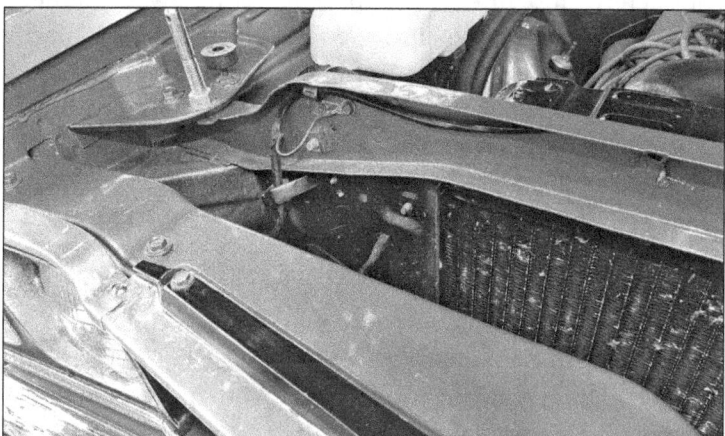

Although Chrysler B-Bodies are iconic for their body-color engine compartments, Chrysler never intended for the body color to shine through the grille. That is why the forward-facing core support and headlight bezels were blacked out.

You can see the black-out spray pattern on this original 33,000-mile Road Runner. Some of it has worn off over the years, but you can tell that it was not done with very much care and did not evenly cover the color of the radiator support.

This blackout area behind the grille was done to today's standards. The factory would have applied less paint and it would have never been this even.

were painted, but not the back edges because of the direction of the spray.

Most people cannot bring themselves to do this the same way the factory did. They mask off the area and completely, and uniformly, cover it with an even coat of paint. We recommend using a spray can of black paint that is not flat and that has no more sheen than a semi-gloss color.

Body Stripes

After sanding, buffing, masking off, and painting the interior door panels it is time to add stripes. Most of the original painted stripes used Organisol. This is a flat-black, slightly textured lacquer paint. You can purchase the lacquer-based Organisol from several restoration sources. Most PPG paint suppliers have the formula but do not sell anything but enamel.

The factory bulletin outlined how they shot these stripes originally with the lacquer-based Organisol. The original formula is difficult to paint with a tendency toward too much texture and a rough finish. Most restored cars have way too much texture in their Organisol. You can achieve better results with the enamel formula. Use about a 25-percent reduction in the shine of the color by adding a flattening agent.

Unfortunately, it's not as simple as this makes it sound. Hood stripes, and entire hoods, as is the case for the 1969½ lift-off hood Road Runner and Super Bee, are very difficult to paint correctly. Whether you use Organisol DDL 9355 (lacquer) or DCC9355 (urethane) is up to you. The process for laying out, scuffing, and masking is the same. The differences are in shooting the paint because each has its own application technique.

Different B-Body models have different stripes. You can find specific details on your stripes dimensions on the Internet. Different panels and other areas also were painted with Organisol on some models. Be sure to research your specific application before painting.

Stripe Layout

The following discusses the layout for the hood stripe on a 1969 Plymouth GTX and Road Runner. This can serve as an example of the basics of how to paint these stripes.

You need a roll of fine-line masking tape as well as a good-quality 1/2-inch masking tape. Never use the cheap masking tape you can buy at a school supply store. Only use a high-quality tape designed for automotive applications.

The stripe starts at the corner of the A-pillar, even with the edge of the cowl. It runs straight down the length of the fender and wraps over the rounded edge of the fender. The center gap measures 11¼ inches and is positioned evenly, with 5⅝ inch on each side of the centerline of the hood. Lay these lines out with the fine-line tape and rub down all the edges well with your finger.

After laying out these lines carefully scuff the paint right up to the edge of the tape using a red Scotch-Brite pad. Wipe with a clean cloth and tack rag before shooting the paint.

Mask off the center gap and the outside of the fenders, cowl, and windshield. Do not worry about trying to mask below the cowl vents

Allow the color coat to dry for about a week before applying the Performance Hood Paint. Mask off the car for the hood stripes, door interior panels, and grille blackout.

because, first, the factory didn't and, second, there is no access to do so.

The stripe goes all the way to the windshield trim. Do not mask off the gap between the fender and the hood because the factory didn't. The overspray pattern that is created when you just shoot the stripe is random and matches the factory technique. Some prefer to mask off this gap so that no overspray is present inside the hood area.

Emblems and Decals

Many emblems and body stripes were used as decals on these cars. The earlier 1966–1967 cars had few of these decals. But by 1970 almost every car had some kind of decal or stripe. Application of emblems and decals can begin in as little as two weeks after the car is painted, sanded, and buffed.

All these decals are reproduced and can be purchased from many sup-pliers. All are applied in the same fashion and turn out great when applied correctly. Purchase the better-quality decals so that they are more correct in color and size and last longer.

The most difficult part is installing the decals in the correct location and making sure they align with the body correctly. If you are in doubt about the decal location on your specific car, turn to one of the many factory documents detailing where

Don't forget to also spray the hood louvers for the Air Grabber if so equipped.

Shoot the interior door panels and the grille black-out first. After they dry re-mask those areas and shoot the hood stripes. Don't mask the hood-to-fender gaps if you want it to look like the factory did the stripes. Just let the overspray happen naturally.

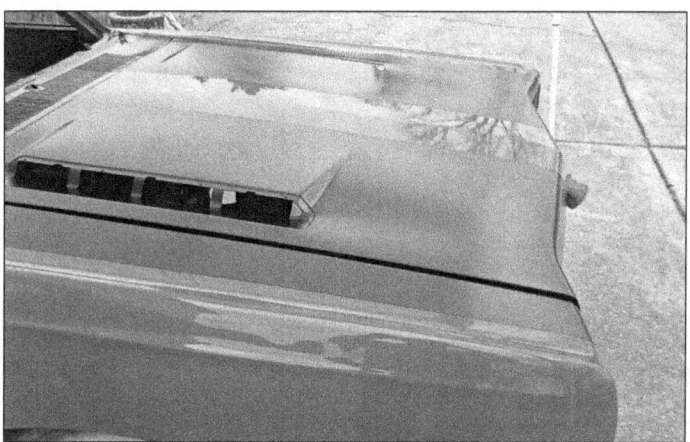

After the stripes have dried past the point of being tacky, carefully remove the masking. The fine-line tape creates the edge; pull it off with a slight direction toward the painted area. This leaves a crisp line. Never remove it from the freshly painted area.

This freshly painted, detailed, correct, beautiful paint job will last for years and bring pride when someone asks, "Who painted your car?" and you can say, "I did!"

DDL 9355 Lacquer

If you're using the original formula of Organisol on the hood, follow these guidelines. Shoot one good coat of black epoxy primer over the stripes. This gives a good color base and protects the existing body-color paint from reacting to the lacquer paint. The Organisol paint must be sprayed on wet. If shot dry, the texture creates too rough of a surface and cannot be wiped with a rag.

Using a gun with a tip of 1.6 mm or larger, shoot four wet coats of Organisol thinned with the slowest thinner you can find. Allow each coat to dry for 30 to 45 minutes. Check for good coverage and apply additional coats if needed.

Always use alternate patterns of spray, first lengthwise then crossways, so the coats are even, without any tiger striping.

For a single-stage urethane we use the following formula to mix the paint:

- 4 parts DCC9355
- 3 parts DT reducer
- 1 part DCX61 hardener
- 1 part DX685 flattening additive
- 1/4 ounce (per pint of mixed paint) DX1999 texture additive

Shoot one good coat of DP90 epoxy primer. Then shoot two medium wet coats of the urethane. By using this formula you can clean the stripe with a mild cleaner and a rag without any problems. With both paints you should never apply wax or polish on these stripes: It does not come off. ∎

---

these are positioned on the car. These documents are easily found on the Internet. If you cannot find one of the factory documents, catalogs such as the one from YearOne has many good color pictures to help you, or you could attend a national car show and look at top-level restored examples of your car.

Installation Tips

Follow the installation instructions provided with your emblems and decals. The following basic guidelines and tips will help you get them correct:

Measure as close as possible to where they go and put several pieces of masking tape about a half-inch wider than where your decal needs to go. This gives you a good guide for positioning it.

Apply smaller emblems and decals dry. There is always paper on the side of the decal that sticks to the body and a semi-transparent paper on the outside of the decal. Trim the top edge of the paper of the decal very close to the actual shape that you want on the car.

Then with another piece of masking tape, position the decal in the exact place you want it to be, and put the tape over the top of the paper of the decal and the body. This way you can lift the decal and put it back down in the same exact position because of the "tape hinge" you have made.

Lift the decal and remove the paper from the sticky side. While you work from the top down, press the decal in place (be precise because you cannot adjust the position). Rub

it to eliminate any bubbles and make sure you have good adhesion to the body. Remove the masking tape and slowly remove the semi transparent cover paper while making sure the decal stays in place.

Apply larger decals wet. You can position them by using the "tape hinge" method. Just use water with a drop or two of soap in it on a cool surface. This allows you to slide the decal and adjust its position.

Carefully squeegee out any air bubbles toward the outside edge working from the middle, and let dry.

Vinyl Tops

Many Mopars from this era had vinyl tops. They were a popular add on that often made the car look better. Sometimes the vinyl roof was added to cover up poor bodywork, as in the Wing car line. Because cars in general were left out in the elements, those with vinyl roofs did not fair well. They allowed moisture to get next to the metal and then the moisture became trapped under the vinyl. The result was a direct and

---

Overspray Removal

After shooting the interior color, the grille blackout, and any hood stripes, remove all the masking and inspect the car for overspray. You can wipe off the overspray using a rag that is only damp with alcohol or reducer because the paint is fresh.

Wipe again with a dry, clean rag. Never use lacquer thinner; it removes the paint. If you see a lot of overspray you may have to remove it using a buffer.

long-lasting association between a vinyl roof and a rusted car.

Today, vinyl roofs are much better and last much longer, mainly because these cars are usually not daily drivers and are garage kept. Some restoration books claim that vinyl tops are removed completely during the restoration of all cars. This could not be further from the truth for the 1966–1970 Plymouth and Dodge B-Body cars.

If your car came with a vinyl top you need to restore it with a vinyl top. Your local upholstery shop can install it and guarantee it is installed correctly. They prefer that you bring the car in before you install any glass. However, you can install a top with great success if you take your time, use the correct supplies, and follow some basic guidelines and tips.

Many videos show how to install a vinyl roof. We suggest you watch some of them, because seeing the process will help you install your top correctly. In the end, all you are really doing is gluing a large piece of vinyl onto your metal roof and trimming off the excess.

The following basic guidelines and tips will help you successfully install a vinyl top:

Tools and Materials

Here is a list of what you need to install a vinyl top:

- 3 or 4 cans of adhesive
- Single-edge razor blades
- Scissors
- Screwdrivers
- Measuring tape
- Felt-tip marker
- Straight edge
- Chalk line

1 Enlist the help of a friend to get the top to lay out without bubbles or lumps.

2 Purchase a high-quality, correct grain and color top from a source such as Legendary Interiors. They can help you make sure you get the correct top for your specific application.

3 Use a high-quality glue in a spray can such as 3M Super Trim Adhesive.

4 Lay out the vinyl top in a warm environment for at least a week so that most of the folds and wrinkles smooth out (you may need a buddy to help).

5 The unpainted roof should be free of glue or residue. Thoroughly clean the top area where the vinyl top will be applied. The roof of the car should have a good coat of epoxy paint on it.

6 Tape off and mask the hood, trunk, doors, and quarters so that the spray glue does not get on your fresh paint.

7 Place the top on your car and check for proper fit.

8 Fold the top, seam-to-seam, finished side to finished side, and mark the center at the front and the rear with the marker on the unfinished side of the top. Pop a chalk line on those two marks. You now have the centerline of your top marked.

9 Take three measurements of the car's roof, front, center, and back, and mark the center of those measurements on the roof. Pop a chalk line on those marks and the centerline of the car's roof is marked.

10 With the top folded in half align the centerline of the top and the centerline of the car.

11 Apply a generous amount of adhesive evenly to the top and to the car's roof from the centerline all the way out to the seam on the vinyl top from front to back. Let the glue become almost dry but not completely.

12 Line up the centerline marks, and with your hands and a plastic filler spreader, press the top into the glue from the center and work out to the edges. This is where a helper can hold the vinyl top off the glue until you press the top onto the car's roof. Be careful, because when the two-glued surfaces touch they cannot be adjusted.

13 When you have one half of the top applied from the centerline to the seam, fold over the other unglued side and repeat the process. You should now have the top completely smooth and applied to the roof, seam-to-seam and front to rear.

14 Spray glue and attach the top from the seam outward to the edge following the same gluing procedure as on both sides of the roof.

15 Spray glue and attach the pillar posts, using the same method as above.

16 Trim any excess vinyl leaving the material well glued and pressed down in the channels around the back glass and windshield.

17 Mark the location of the trim clips holes with a small piece of masking tape on the roof.

18 Overlap the drip-rail edge so that when the molding is installed it locks over the vinyl-covered lip. There is a difference between original drip-rail molding used on non-vinyl and that used on vinyl-top trim. They do not interchange. New reproduction stainless is designed to be large enough for use with a vinyl top.

19 Trim along the holes for the molding that separates the vinyl top from the quarter panel.

20 Clean up any excess glue on your top or on the car with adhesive remover.

21 Attach the stainless molding clips following your tape marks.

22 Attach the trim after you have polished and buffed it.

Inner Fender Masking

The undercoat patterns on the inner fender are similar but seldom identical from one car to the next. Using pictures of your original undercoating or a similar car gives you a good guideline.

The edge of your layout has a special foam rope material that has an adhesive strip. It leaves a nice, tapered, slightly spattered edge, much like what you see on original applications.

After the rope is pressed down firmly, mask off the rest of the area you want to protect from overspray. If your paint is older than about a week, you should scuff sand it to ensure good adhesion for the undercoating.

Inner Fender Masking

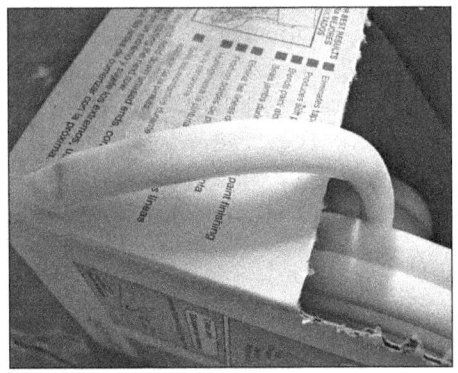

1 Purchase a box of self-adhesive rope foam tape. It can be cut to any length and pressed to stick in any form.

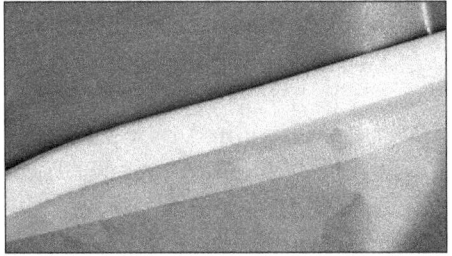

2 By using reference pictures from your car or from another car, place the rope tape where you want the edge to appear. Then with regular masking tape and paper cover the surrounding areas to keep excess overspray off the car.

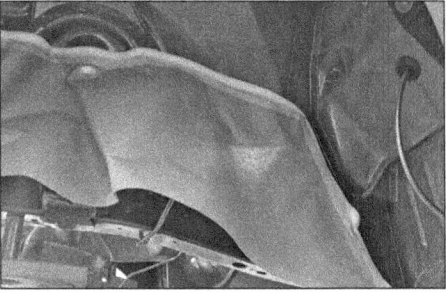

3 Notice that the emergency brake cable, grommet, and inner splash shield are all restored, but they are coated with undercoating. Take "before" pictures for reference that these parts were restored.

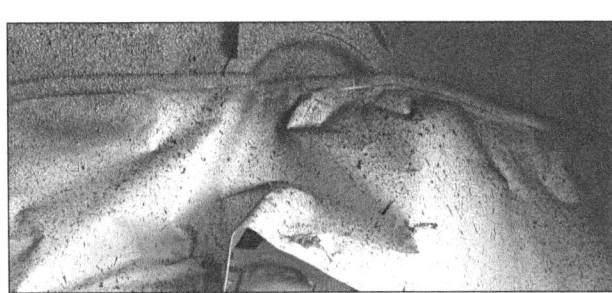

4 Spray the undercoating following the product instructions and guidelines. With the masking in place the other areas do not get the spatter from shooting the undercoating. The factory gun had a more controlled pattern than today's Shutz gun.

5 Remove the masking and rope tape after shooting several coats that are allowed to dry between applications, and when you are happy with the final results.

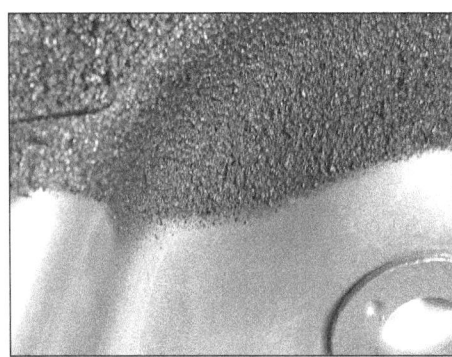

6 Even up close the results are flawless.

Polyurethane Underbody Painting

By Restorations by Rick

The best mixture ratio is four parts primer color to one part activator to one part PPG DT-series urethane reducer appropriate for the temperature (4:1:1). Apply it in two or three medium wet coats allowing 5 to 7 minutes between coats. (The pot life of the mixture is 48 hours.) After preparing the substrate as desired, apply one or two coats of epoxy primer prior to the underbody paint.

Undercoating Application

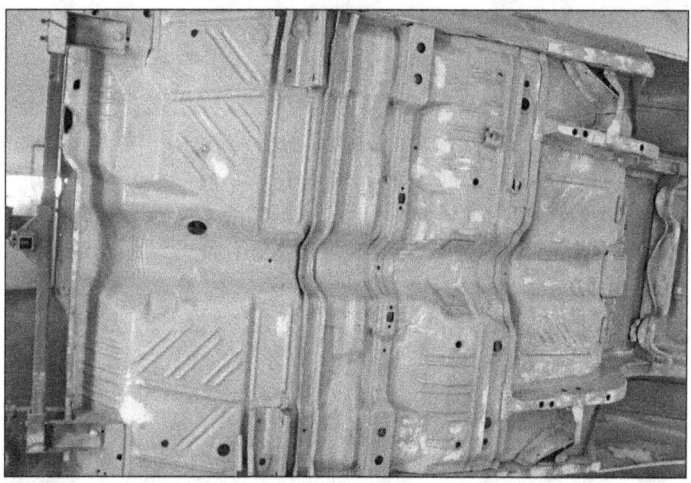

1 *Apply one coat of epoxy primer. This gives you time to perfect things without having rust form. An excellent epoxy primer is made by Southern Polyurethanes Inc. It has etching properties and dries to a tough coating. Another big advantage is that after curing it sands without gumming up the sandpaper as most epoxy primers do. That's a huge time saver on a large, complex area such as an underbody.*

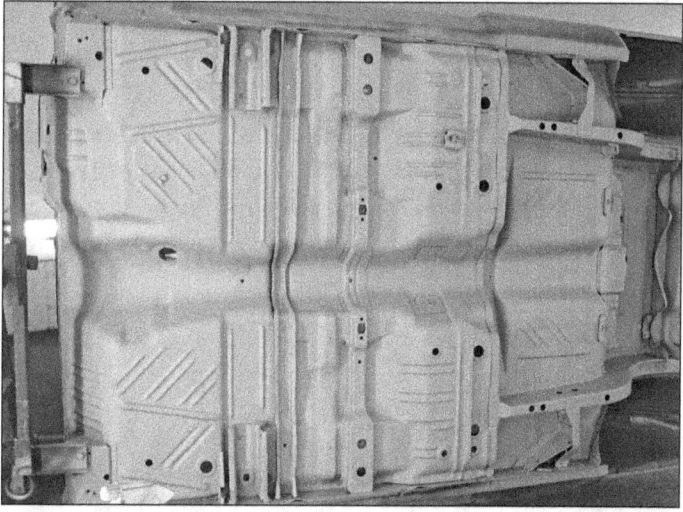

2 *Smooth out flaws such as pitting, scrapes, and dings with body filler. Sand epoxy primer in repair areas with 80-grit sandpaper before applying the filler. Finish sand the filler with 180-grit sandpaper. Also, scuff sand unworked epoxy primer areas with 320-grit before the next step.*

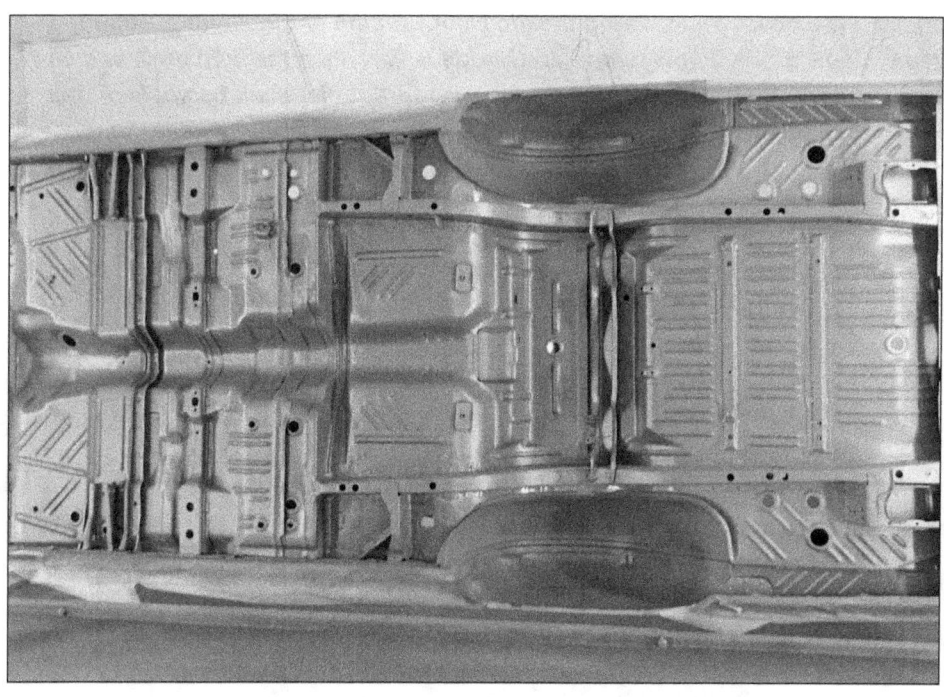

3 *Apply two coats of epoxy primer followed by three or four coats of primer-surfacer. Allow one day of dry time after epoxy primer application before primer-surfacer application. (This can be done sooner but I prefer to allow the extra cure time.) Allow drying time according to manufacturer's directions before sanding.*

Keep in mind that you should use only as much primer as necessary to do the job. Excessive primer thickness makes the finished coating more susceptible to chipping and edge puckering around fasteners and other irregular surfaces. It's a good practice to sand down the edges around screw holes to a minimum thickness.

4 Start sanding with 180-grit paper, followed by 320-grit, and finish with 500-grit. You'll likely have missed flaws to touch up after the 180-grit step. Reapply primer to these areas.

5 Blow, vacuum clean, and wipe with wax and grease remover. Apply the wax and grease remover using a spray bottle and wipe it off with a clean, disposable towel. You use a lot less product this way and eliminate potential contamination of the can.

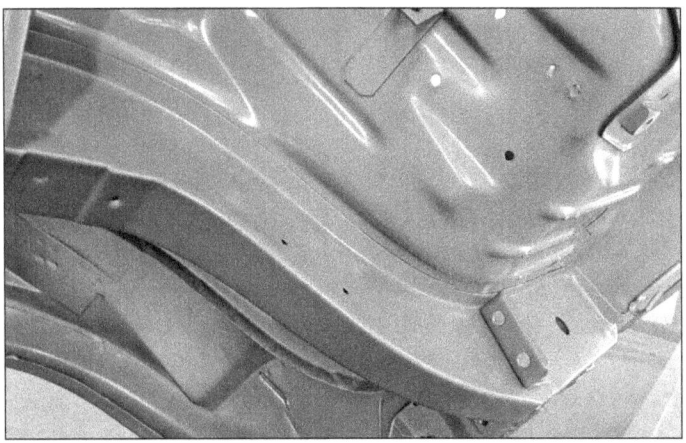

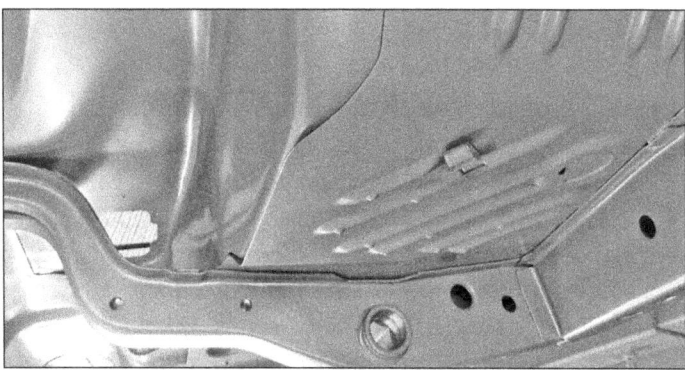

6 Apply one or two coats of epoxy primer. (Two coats if you have multiple bare-metal areas.) Allow a minimum of one hour to dry (one day is even better) before applying RestoRick Polyurethane Underbody Paint. Flatten and tack wipe any dust nibs.

7 Apply underbody paint in three coats. I like to focus on the hard-to-reach pocket areas first. If you're following the dip color with the original primer color oversprays, red oxide is first, then the light gray, and last is the topcoat color. Overspray colors can be applied after the dip-primer color dries for 15 to 20 minutes. For best adhesion, apply it within 48 hours.

Cowl Painting

By Restorations by Rick

Here are two good questions: What's the best way to paint inside the cowl (under the grating)? And what is the best way to sand between the slots on the cowl? Let me answer them with a real-life example.

I worked on a Road Runner a few years ago where I replaced the cowl; it was great because I was able to paint that area before installing the replacement cowl top. I just stuffed a damp towel over the paint while welding; then masked it off while doing exterior paintwork.

For routine refinishing work, this area can be pre-painted somewhat by using a touchup gun and placing the nozzle close to the openings while blasting paint.

The gun can be rotated slightly as well. You can also get a pressure pot

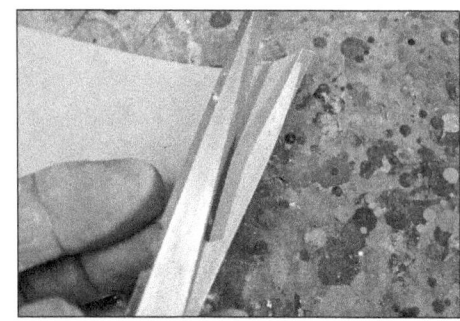

This is a great way to sand tight areas. This technique can be used on various small detail tasks.

fed gun up through the cowl fresh-air openings on the interior underside.

Sanding the slot openings is a pain!

I usually use a small piece of sandpaper folded over a couple of times so it is rigid. This is used to sand in line with the slot opening. I then finish with a single thickness and my

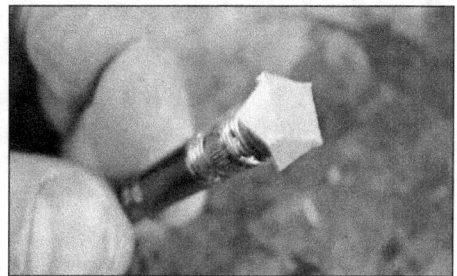

The sandpaper used is an adhesive-backed type and is simply cut into squares before adhering to a pencil eraser.

Undercoating Tips

By Restorations by Rick

Preparation

- Lay down plastic sheeting to protect the floor. Set up an area with cardboard or newspapers to fill the gun. Wear rubber or disposable gloves.
- Prepare areas to be undercoated by first cleaning with wax and a grease remover. On paint older than a couple of days, scuff the area to be coated with a Scotch-Brite scuff pad to ensure the best adhesion. Scuff up to the edges of the intended coating area, but not into the blend edges.
- To duplicate the masked-out area around the rear side marker lamp hole, use thin cardboard taped to the quarter panel loosely from behind the opening.
- A scrap of cardboard held in front of the spray pattern can be used to re-create the vertical fan pattern buildups often seen on areas such as the inside of the quarter panels.

The Mixture

- The undercoating produced with the 4:1:1 ratio is a rubberized product with texture additives that provides an exceptional re-creation of the original undercoating texture and thickness. It can also be used for coating the inside areas of quarter panels and be painted over.
- Mix thoroughly! A paint shaker is ideal but not mandatory. If the product has been sitting for an extended period, cut off the top of the can for better access to incorporate the settled texture additives. Pour the product through a piece of common metal window screen to strain any possible chunks; this becomes more critical as dry clumps form around the spout.

The Gun

- Undercoating can be sprayed with a conventional 3M Shutz–style undercoating gun. No tube modifications are necessary. Wear proper breathing and eye protection! A respirator rated for painting use is mandatory.
- It is very important to work with a clean gun! Due to the thickness of this product, the gun must be perfectly clean and kept that way. If clogging develops, first verify that the bleeder hole in the top of the cup lid is open. If it's open, hold a rag over the output nozzle and press

This close-up of a piece of cardboard shows how well it creates the spray line when taped to the area you are trying to keep free of undercoating.

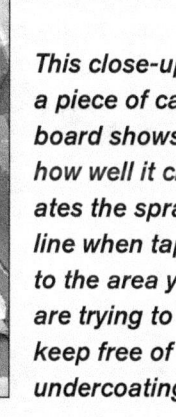

Tape a piece of cardboard in the desired shape to create the spray line on the front of the quarter.

Undercoating Tips CONTINUED

The brake, fuel lines, and clips were already in place when this undercoating was applied. Also notice the uncoated area behind the lip of the inner fender well. It is important to let these distinct areas of coverage and non-coverage remain just the way the factory did.

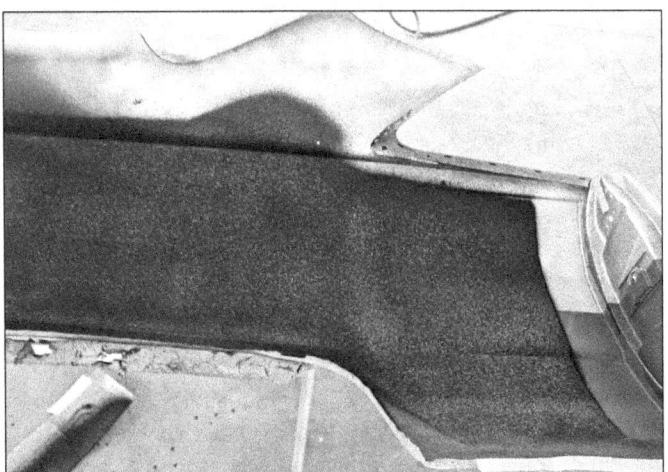

Sound deadener was applied before the quarter was welded in place at the factory. When replacing a full quarter be sure to follow this sequence. Take pictures for future reference of everything you do in your restoration.

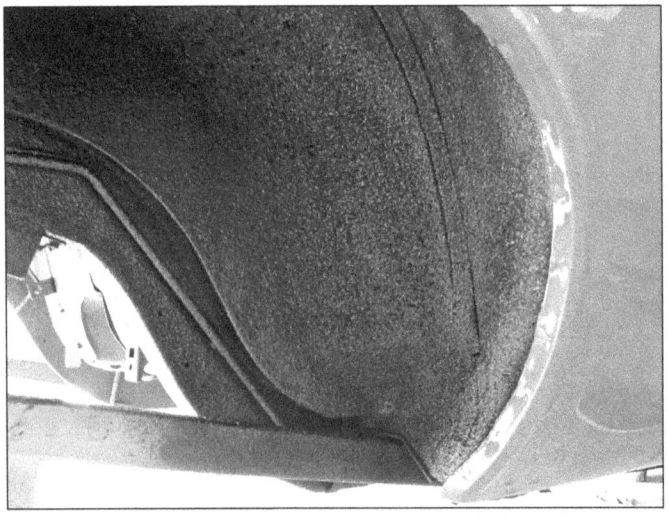

The rubber bumpstop for the rear end was bolted in place before the undercoating was applied. Remember that the bracket for this bumpstop was painted yellow even though it is partially coated with undercoating; some of the color still shows, replicating the factory process.

the trigger to backflush the gun. Important: Do this with the gun removed from the cup and aim the pickup tube away from yourself into a suitable catch container. Attempting this with the cup attached can result in a face or eyeful of undercoating. Finally, spray some thinner through the gun to clean.

- Air pressure to the gun is the maximum allowed. (This varies depending on the cup construction, but is generally 60 psi.)

Before You Spray

- Some items are put in place before you apply undercoating.

The Application

- Apply in medium coats, allowing at least 15 minutes between them. The longer you wait between coats the better. Maintain a gun distance of about 10 to 12 inches and use quick passes. Where a thicker appearance is desired, apply in multiple thin coats rather than a single heavy coat. Heavy applications flow out and create too smooth a texture.

Completely cover the inner wheelwell and outer frame well with undercoating, covering even the lines and clips. Notice that the area in the background is covered only in dip primer with no color overspray or undercoating.

- Lay down one coat, covering the desired areas first. Let that dry well and then slowly build the texture with quick dry coats; after this add the "accent" areas such as the vertical fan pattern stops usually seen on original cars. Again, let it dry well and follow with a couple of dry misting coats to get the best "peaky" textured look.
- For the best possible appearance allow an overnight dry before the final coats; this works better because the first layers of dried undercoat have a sponge effect on the solvents and the coating stays more textured.
- Undercoating can be painted over after 30 minutes, but it's best to wait overnight. It can be directly painted, but I prefer to epoxy prime it first.
- Although this product can be thinned with lacquer thinner, it is not recommended as it applies too smooth and tends to flow out. If not mixed thoroughly and the product is too thick as you get to the bottom of the can, small amounts of lacquer thinner may be added. ■

You can see the directional spray pattern. It is important to re-create it because a line worker would never stop to eliminate these patterns. You can also see that the body plug was already in place when the undercoating was applied.

You can create a very clean line; however, it must be noted that for high-level OEM competitions these areas are way over-restored compared to the sloppy applications of this deadener from the factory. It is up to you to decide how neat or sloppy you choose to be. (This example is not from a B-Body quarter; it from an E-Body quarter. However, the process is the same for all models.)

Here is a great picture of the dip primer line with undercoating applied after primer was applied, followed by the application of the undercoating with a factory stopped spray line. This original look can be achieved with careful attention to the details.

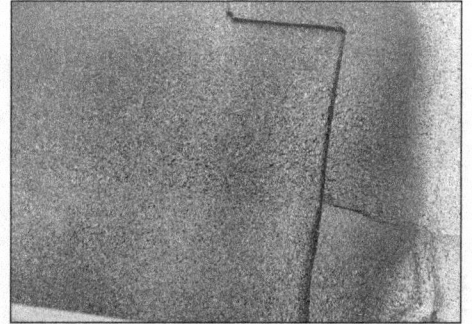

This survivor 1969 B-Body shows the exact factory undercoating. It is very difficult to reproduce the thickness of the original undercoating. In this specific case we would not strip the original off but would instead clean, scuff, and paint over it.

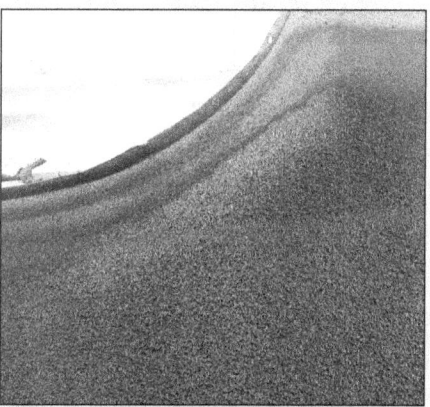

The undercoating goes all the way to the edge of the fender lip. You can see that it is easy for overspray to get onto the edge of the painted fender or rocker.

finger for rounding and blending the edges and ends.

I also use a paint stir stick with Stikit sandpaper occasionally.

To align the slots just right I block sand perpendicularly over them to reveal the high and low spots. Then I use a pull rod tool to adjust them. You may obtain slight correction from the primer block sanding effect too.

Wet Sanding

Many people are so focused on getting paint on their car that they neglect the final two critical steps that really make the difference between a "driver" paint job and a "show car" paint job: wet sanding or color sanding. During these processes you take a freshly painted car and sand out all the imperfections to create a perfectly smooth surface.

You follow the wet sanding with a buffing and polishing process that removes any super-fine scratches left in the paint after color sanding. This process can take from 30 to 60 hours, depending on the quality of the initial paint job.

The following list identifies the products, techniques, and tips for shine so deep you think that it is wet, and so clear you can read the newspaper in the reflection.

Materials

Wet sanding and buffing create a very big mess. It is always best to do all of your sanding and buffing before assembly. It is also good to do this on a concrete floor in a well-ventilated area.

Always remove any residue and especially any compound that is left over from the buffing and polishing

session. If you do end up having to do a buff after the car is assembled, tape off and protect areas from the compound and sanding residue, including all glass, the vinyl top, the interior, all trim (especially chrome), and even the tires.

The basic materials needed for wet sanding a fresh paint job include the right grit of wet/dry sandpaper, a bucket of soapy water, sanding blocks, paint sticks, a squeegee, and wiping rags.

Always start with the least aggressive grit of paper appropriate for your application. If the paint is really nice with minimal orange peel and few dust nibs you can start with 2000-grit. If this doesn't do it, go to 1500, and finally, if you have any runs, you may have to use 1000.

Be very careful using aggressive grits. Stay away from the edges so you don't sand through the clear and into the base. The only fix is to re-shoot.

Hand Sanding

Soak the paper in a bucket of water with a few drops of dish soap. The soap makes the paper slide freely

and keeps the paper clean of buildup of paint.

Use a sanding block on flat areas and wrap a paint stick with the wet sandpaper to get a super flat surface in tight or angled areas. Use the squeegee to wipe off the water and clear coat residue, and then wipe the area with a dry soft rag. You are then able to see if the surface is uniform and flat, or any shiny low spots need more attention.

If there are at least three coats of clear on the car you can spend a lot of time massaging the paint without going through the clear. If there are only two coats be careful because there is less material between your sandpaper and the base coat.

For all the rounded edges and curves, wet sand by hand using 2000-grit paper.

Palm Sander

Most enthusiasts used to wet sand the entire car by hand until they discovered a palm sander and sanding film. Through the use of a soft-throw-air palm sander, you can reduce sanding time dramatically with fantastic results.

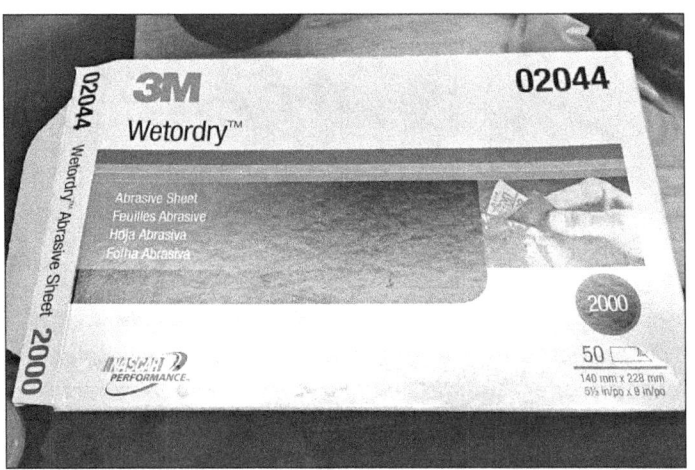

Soak your fine-grit sandpaper in water with a few drops of liquid dishwashing liquid to help the paper cut and reduce clear-coat build up. Also fully soaking the paper for a while softens the edges so they do not leave scratches as you sand. Fold the paper in overlapping thirds. 3M makes a great 2000-grit wet or dry paper already cut to the correct size. If you use a full sheet of paper just tear it in half and then fold it in overlapping thirds.

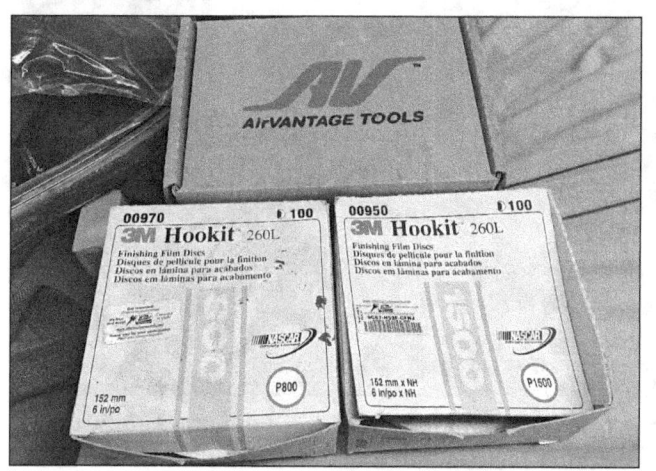

Finishing film sanding discs with a short-throw palm sander help to cut sanding time, and when used correctly produce a smooth, even finish. AirVANTAGE tools are great; I have used this one for years of maintenance-free service.

Start with a 1500-grit sanding disc. Use it on all the flat panels, staying away from the edges and bodylines. Try to keep the palm sander flat and move it uniformly over the surface to prevent waves or deep scratches.

Change the discs and the paper often so you don't create scratches from the buildup of material on the paper. Always wipe all the clear coat/water residue off the car because if it is left to dry it can stain the paint and be very difficult to remove.

Wet Sanding

1 Start with about a 2 x 2–foot area. You want to get right up to the edge but not hit the edge with the sander. Even with 2000-grit wet hand sanding, avoid the edges or you might sand through the clear.

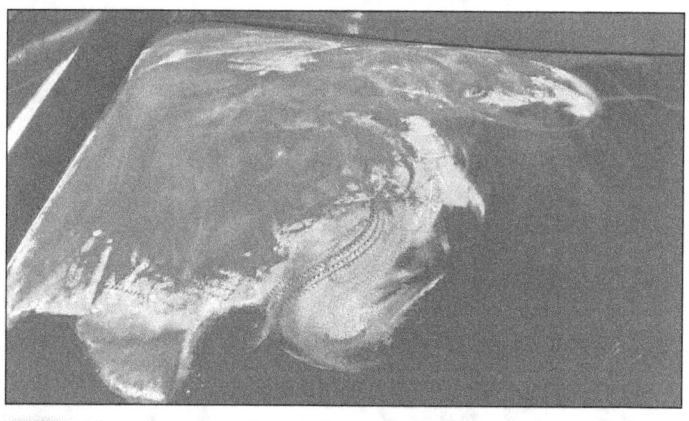

2 You can already see how much clear is removed with the fine white residue left behind. When "pig tails" start to appear, stop and rub your hand over the disc to remove the buildup. If you don't these "pig tails" can be difficult to buff out.

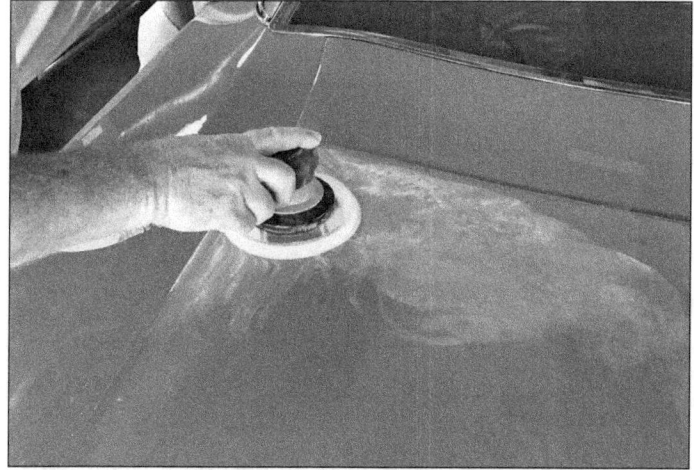

3 After wiping the residue off you can go back and work on the area until all the flaws are smooth.

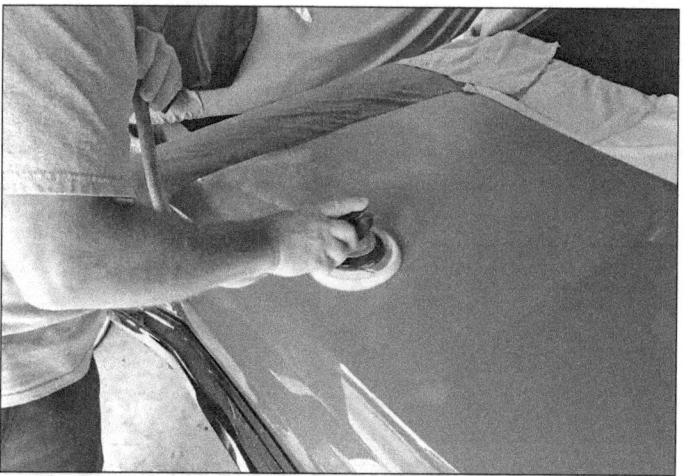

4 Continue sanding a section at a time until the designated area is flat and smooth.

5 *We covered the surrounding areas that were already finished with soft towels. You can also mask off these areas to protect them.*

6 *Use side lighting so that all of the flaws show up during the sanding process. A plain light bulb in a droplight shows everything. Here you can see small flaws that still need attention.*

7 *After completely working out all the flaws wipe clean with a microfiber towel.*

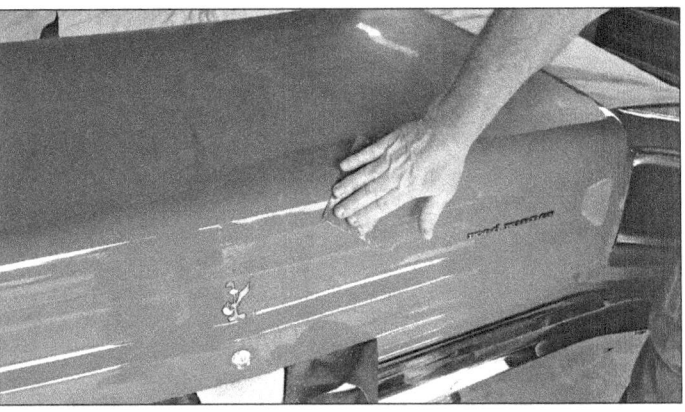

8 *Use wet sandpaper to work the rounded edge, removing any dust nibs and smoothing out the orange peel. We do not use a block or paint stick on these areas, but be sure to hold your fingers in a tight, even grip on the paper.*

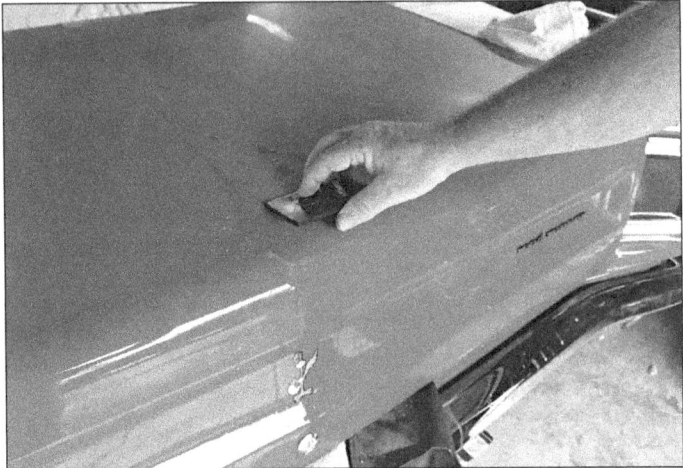

9 *Using a 3M rubber squeegee you can remove the water and sanding residue so you can see what you have done to the finish.*

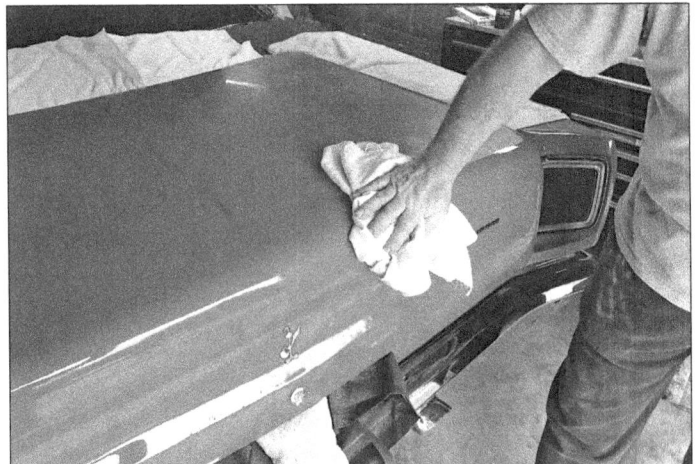

10 *With a dry, soft cloth wipe off the rest of the water. Asses whether you have removed enough of the orange peel to for a smooth, even surface.*

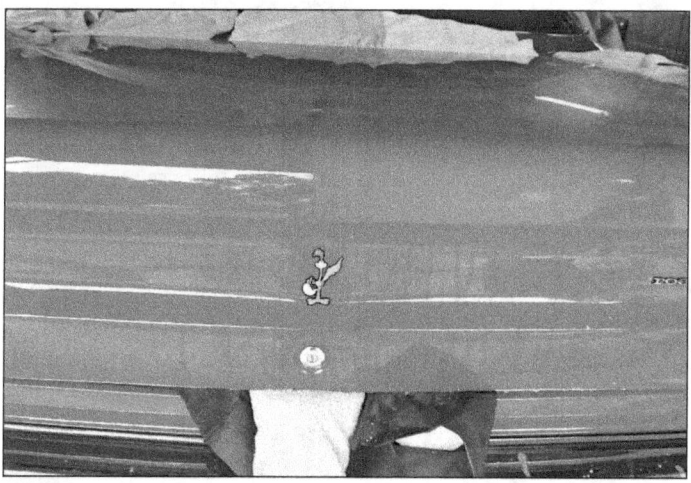

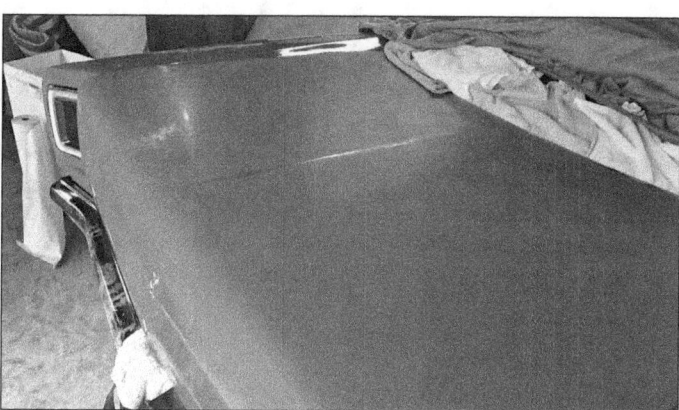

11 *Here the inner part of the sanded section is flat. Toward the outer edge of the sanded area you can still see orange peel.*

12 *All problems have been sanded and much care was given when sanding the lower trunk recessed panel. In fact we only sanded the small imperfections and not the entire panel, because this area is very difficult to buff without burning through the paint.*

Paint Buffing

The basic tool for correctly buffing out a color-sanded paint job is a variable speed right-angle polisher with a "hook it" backing plate to mount the wool buffing and foam polishing pads to the polisher. Orbital polishers are useless for this level of polishing out sanding scratches. For the beginner it is very scary thinking about buffing through the clear and having to re-shoot the panel with paint. However, more pressure

on the buffer is required to get the desired results than you would think.

Until you get the hang of just how much pressure is needed, work slowly and carefully examine the surface you just buffed. After several passes you are able to tell how much pressure is needed.

By carefully massaging the paint, a fabulous finish can be achieved. Even though it seems like a scary procedure, with patience, knowledge, and a little practice, even the most inexperienced novice can create a

professional looking finish. The following is an overview of the general process for buffing your paint.

Start with the wool pad and the number-1 rubbing compound. Apply small drops to the area you are going to buff. You don't really need much material. Spread the compound over a 2 x 2–foot section with the non-rotating pad. Bump the polisher a little at a time until the compound is spread evenly without slinging it everywhere. Start at the top of the area moving back and forth with

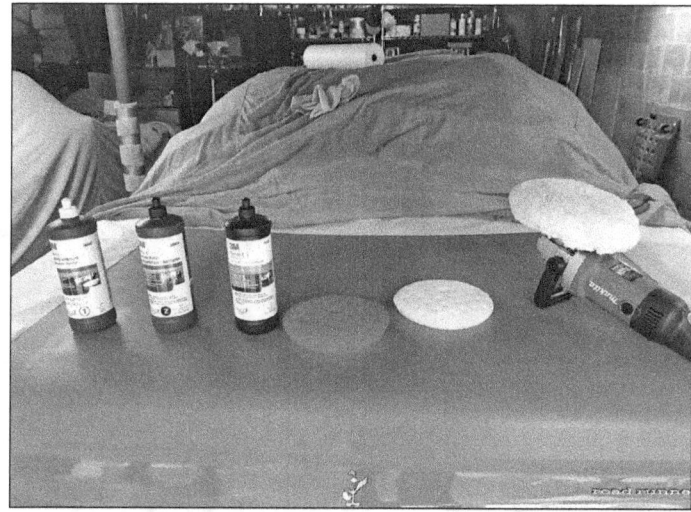

A variable-speed buffer, various buffing compounds, and foam pads buff out sanding scratches to a flawless shine.

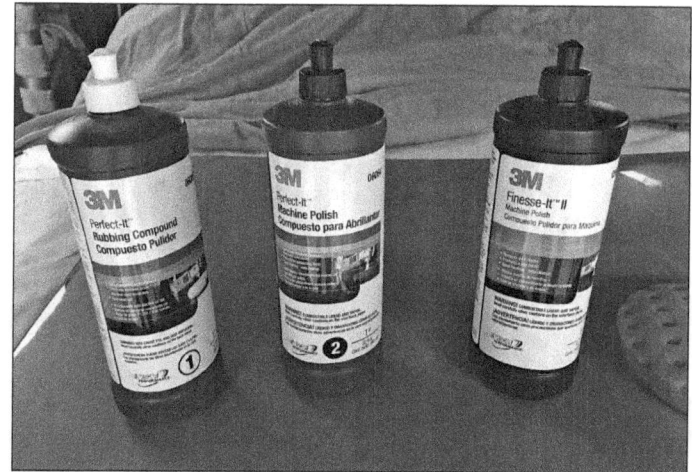

3M makes a great line of buffing compounds that are numbered so you know which one to use first. This makes it easier for the beginner.

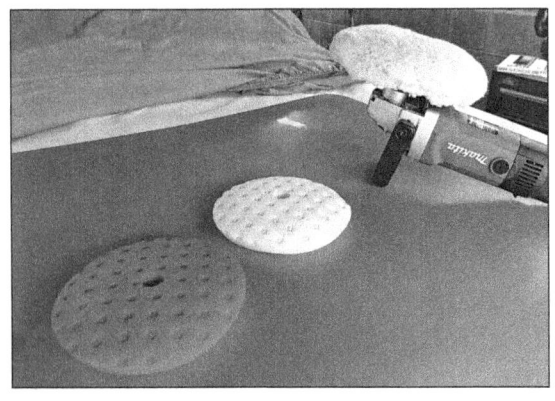

A wool pad (right) is the most aggressive pad and is the main tool for removing wet and dry sanding scratches. Foam pads (left and middle) polish the paint further, remove any buffing swirls, and intensify the shine.

even, slow passes using only one half of the surface of the pad at a time.

When moving from right to left, use the right half of the pad. When moving left to right, use the left half of the pad. Never try to keep the pad flat or it bumps up on you.

Work the compound into the area with firm pressure, gradually becoming lighter as the compound disappears. Always use the number-1 setting on the buffer.

When you approach the edge or a bodyline, make sure the buffer rotation is away from the edge. Catching an edge is the easiest way to buff through the paint.

Wipe off any residual compound with a clean cloth.

Repeat this process section by section until you see a non-hazy shine. If the area you just buffed has a hazy shine, buff it again with the same process until it has a good, clear shine. Do not worry about buffing swirls; they are removed with the next level of pads and compounds. Clean your wool pad with a "spur" to remove any built-up compound. Do this outside because it creates a lot of dust.

Next, use the red pad with the same number-1 buffing compound. Less pressure is needed with the foam pads and you should move the buffer a little faster across the panel than you did with the wool pad because you are actually polishing rather than removing scratches.

Cover the same area using the same technique. You should see more shine and fewer swirl marks.

Wipe off any excess compound with a soft cloth, but you cannot use a spur on the foam pads.

Next, use the yellow foam pad with the number-2 compound. Repeat the techniques you used with the red pad.

Last, use the black pad and the number-3 compound for the final polishing passes. Use a varying amount of pressure so you remove any remaining polishing swirls.

Always wash the pads after a buffing session. Spin them dry on the buffer, holding it close to the ground to avoid spraying the excess water everywhere.

For the novice, it's best to completely buff one area at a time so you can see how well the final results look. Mask off that finished area (such as a door, a quarter, or a fender) before proceeding to the next panel.

Experienced enthusiasts may buff the entire car with the first pad, then use each successive pad over the entire car. That takes a lot of practice!

Paint Buffing

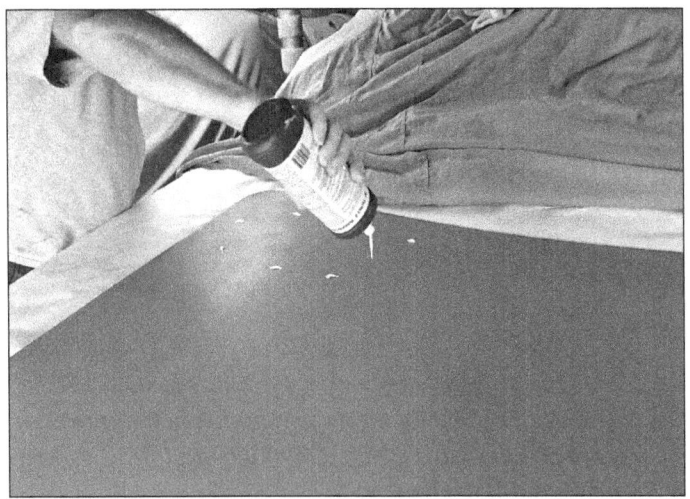

1 *Begin with compound number-1. Do not overuse the compounds. It only takes a few drops of the compound to accomplish the task.*

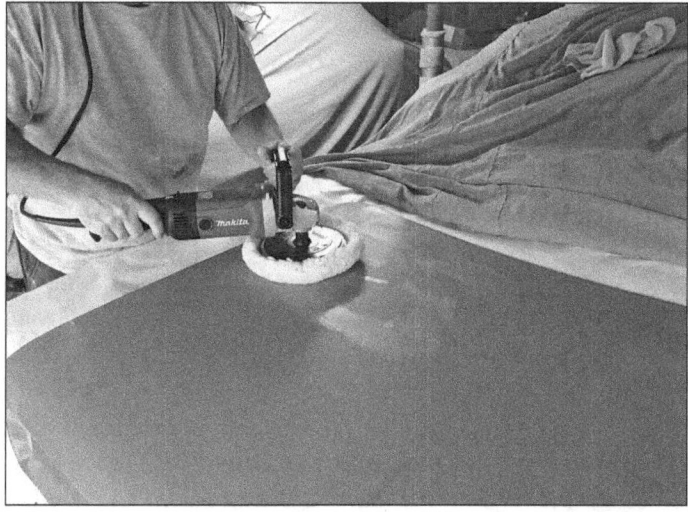

2 Spread the compound without the buffer running. Again, only work a 2 x 2–foot area at a time.

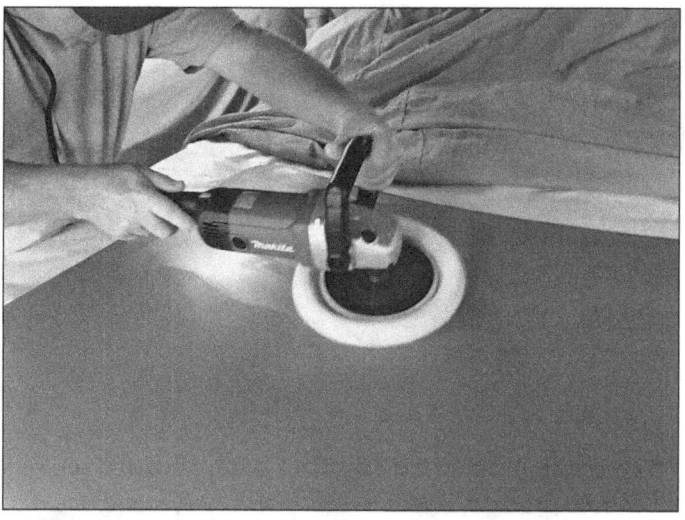

3 Bump the trigger a few times to completely spread the compound without slinging it everywhere.

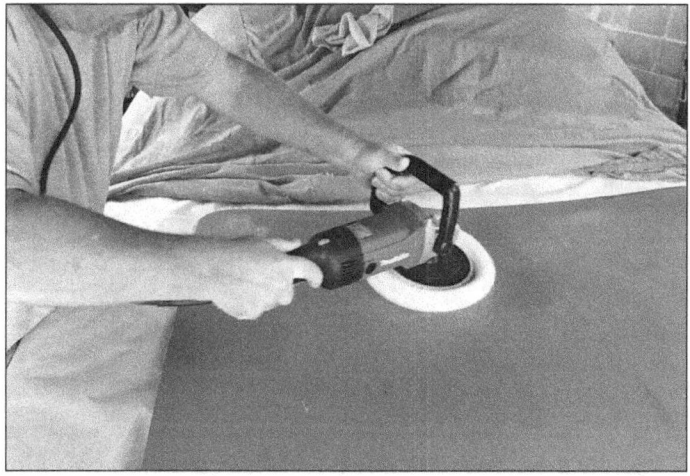

4 Run the buffer on the slowest setting, dragging the compound with the slow but firm strokes.

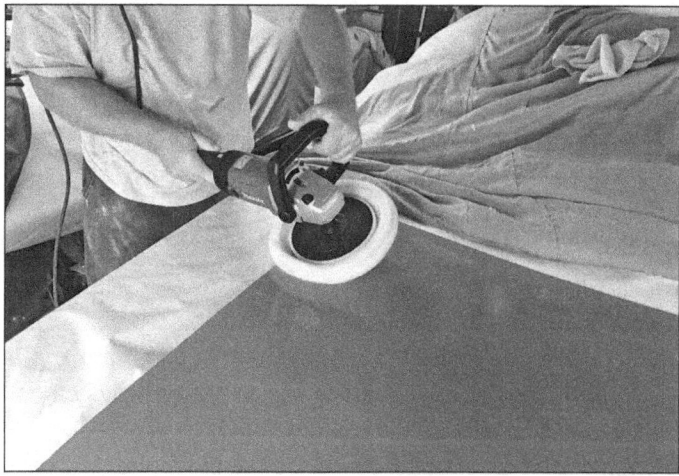

5 Always buff away from the edges with the rotation of the buffer.

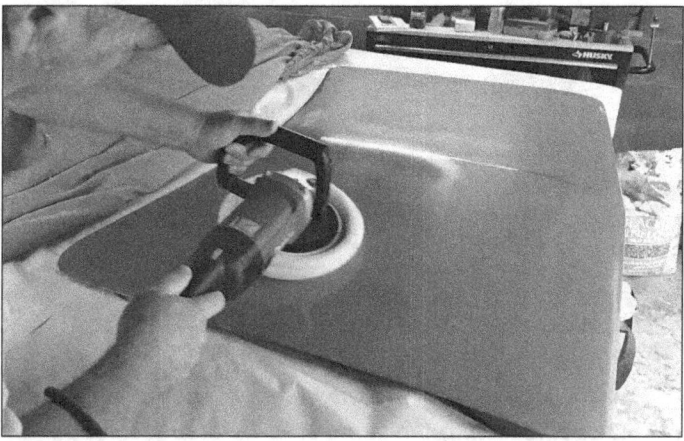

6 As the compound dries out it begins to disappear. As it does, apply less and less pressure on the painted surface.

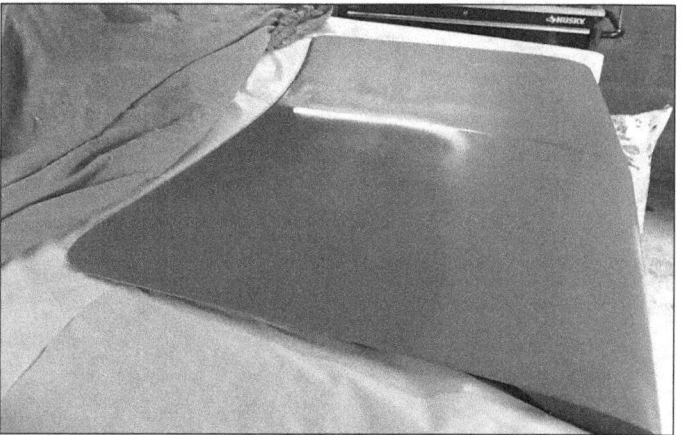

7 After the first pass and after wiping off the excess compound with a soft rag, you can still see a hazy shine. You still need to remove the scratches.

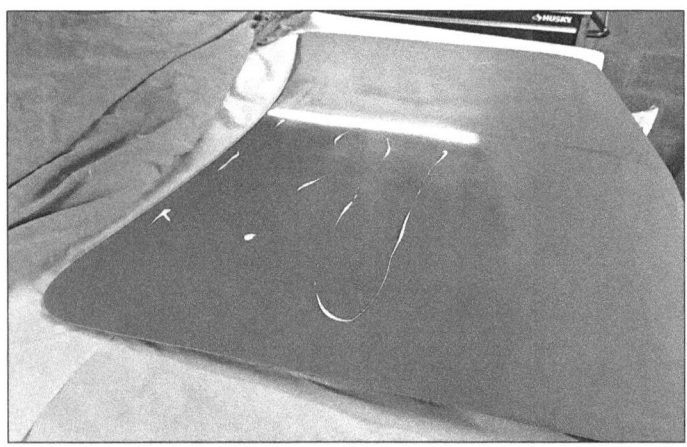

8 Reapply the same number-1 compound and repeat the process. Again use firm pressure, sometimes even hard pressure, while keeping the buffer moving. Never stay in one place or you burn the paint.

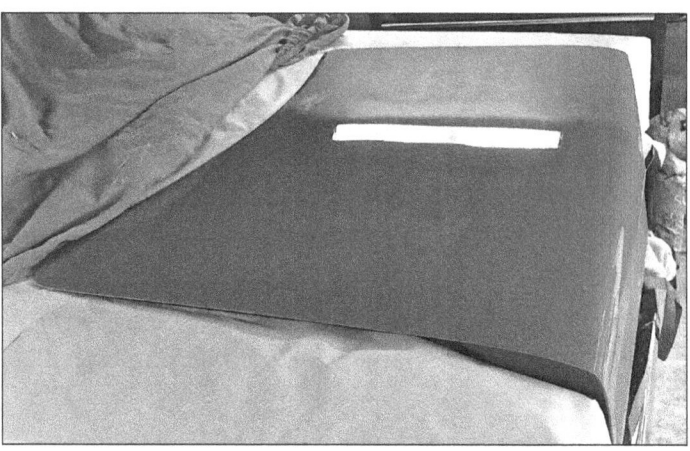

9 You know you have removed enough of the scratches with the number-1 compound and wool pad when you achieve a clear, deep shine. What a contrast to the dull-sanded area!

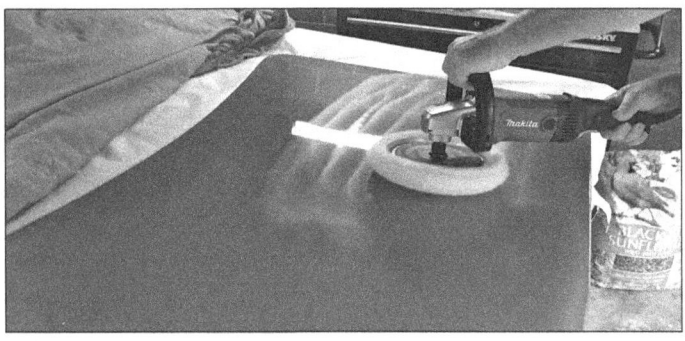

10 Continue to buff the rest of the area using the same process you have been using on the previous steps. This close-up shows the compound and how it is dragged along with the wool buffing pad. Notice the indirect light and how well it shows everything.

11 As the compound dries apply less and less pressure until you have a deep, clear shine.

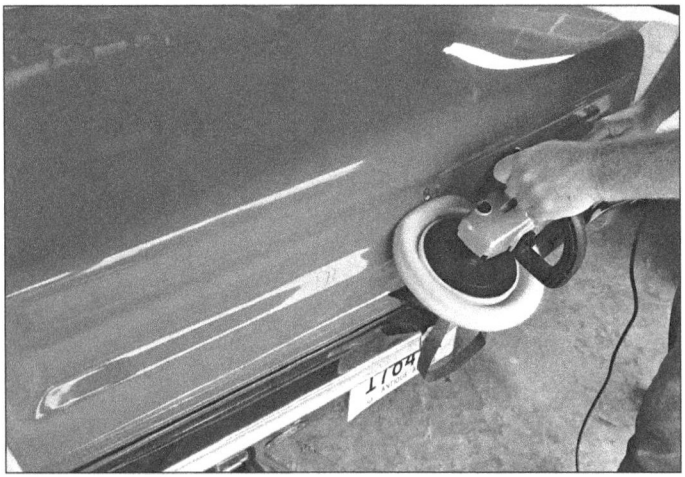

12 Hit the small detail areas with small amounts of compound and carefully use only as much of the pad as necessary to achieve the shine.

13 Now that you have a good clear shine with no haze, the area is ready for the number-2 compound and yellow pad, following the same step-by-step technique used previously. However, you don't use as much pressure as with a wool pad because you are now polishing and removing swirl marks rather than removing scratches.

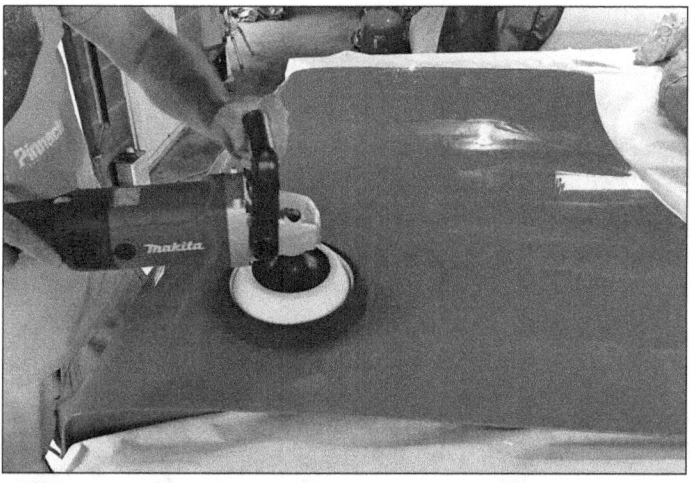

14 *After the yellow pad use the number-3 compound and the black pad. This is your final step and, accordingly, requires less and less pressure and more of a floating motion. You still only use the slowest speed setting on the buffer.*

15 *When you have used all the compounds and pads and have wiped up all the residue you are left with a deep, clear shine.*

Hand Glazing

When the entire car has been buffed with the black pad you can use a final hand glaze and micro-fiber towels to fill any almost-invisible swirls. Pull the car into the sun to inspect for any buffing swirls. Usually very dark colors show these swirls more than the lighter colors.

If you do see buffing swirls in the sunlight you can use the smooth black pad and 3M compound to remove them.

The final step is to use hand glaze for a "like glass" finish.

After hand glazing, the finish looks as if you could swim in the depth of the clear, and you can almost read the wattage on the light bulb in the reflection.

SUSPENSION OVERVIEW

The suspension systems of Chrysler vehicles, including those of 1966–1970 B-Bodies, were some of the most unique coming out of Detroit during the height of the muscle car era, particularly the independent front suspension. Using a unique torsion bar instead of the more conventional coil spring freed up room in the uni-body chassis vehicles and provided substantial weight savings.

The front torsion bar system, consisted of an upper A-arm, a single lower control arm with a forward-facing strut, hydraulic tube shock, sway bar (if so equipped), and a tempered torsion bar. It was lightweight, accessible in the wheelwell, and easily adjusted thanks to a threaded tension bolt below the lower control arm.

The upper A-arm mounted to perches on the upper frame rail while the lower control arms connected to the front crossmember (or K-member) through a pivot shaft. The entire front suspension (apart from the torsion bars) was assembled on the crossmember cradle prior to being attached to the vehicle during its initial assembly. And likewise, it's significantly easier to work on your front suspension with the crossmember out of the car.

Upon the vehicle being lowered over the powertrain and engine crossmember on the assembly line, the torsion bars were slid through their rearward perches on the mid-crossmember and fitted into the hexangular reliefs in the lower control arm pivot shafts. Then the upper control arms were attached to the body and eventually aligned.

The rear suspension was a far more common arrangement, with the live axle (be it a Chrysler 8¼, 8¾, or Dana 60 housing) attached to a pair of leaf spring packs hanging below the rearward frame rails. The leaf springs were attached to the body through a pair of shackles at the rear and large stamped steel perches in front. The forward frame rail perches differed in B-Bodies only if a vehicle was a convertible or equipped with the 426 Hemi, where a large reinforcement plate was attached over each perch.

The entire rear end (springs, shackles, emergency cables, brake lines, wheel hubs, and hangers) should be removed as one unit. This way you can disassemble each component and strip them to the bare metal, replace any worn parts, and refinish to the original condition. You reassemble all of the parts into the one unit and reinstall it in the car.

In this chapter, we discuss the proper steps to disassemble your 1966–1970 B-Body's suspension and return these components to stock OEM or similar-appearing status. Of course, many choose to replace original factory equipment with aftermarket components to improve drivability characteristics, and this is also a worthwhile endeavor. We strongly suggest "bolt-in" replacement parts over kits that require cutting, fabricating, or heavy modifications, as these kits often do not bear the desired results.

Aftermarket companies such as Hotchkis Sport Suspension and QA1 offer direct-replacement items that include upper and lower control arms, adjustable shocks, high-quality struts, torsion bars, and sway bars. They also offer leaf springs that have a long track record (quite literally) of significantly improving the road handling of Chrysler A-, B-, and E-Bodies, unlike a few coil over replacement kits that have garnered mixed results.

Even a stock car equipped with a 4-barrel 383 B block can easily break the 100-mph mark, and the last thing you want is a loose and questionable suspension. To someone who has never tackled the complete rebuild of the torsion bar front and leaf spring rear suspension, it can seem like something way above your pay grade. In reality, with some detailed guidelines, a good amount of mechanical experience, the help of a good machine shop, some designated garage time, and a reasonable amount of sweat, you can have a brand-new suspension that looks like it just came off the showroom floor.

Dropping the entire front suspension, which includes the crossmember with the engine and transmission, all together is actually recommended. The rear end assembly comes out significantly easier, and requires the use of two jack stands and a good floor jack. We recommend that you restore and install the rear suspension first. This provides you with a good support so you can elevate the car and slide in the entire front assembly at once.

Rebuilding a Front Suspension

The front suspension can be completely rebuilt without taking the entire front assembly and engine crossmember out of the car, but be prepared for a lot of time on your back or stooping low to the ground.

You can put the front end up on two jack stands and remove all the components. But it is a no-brainer to remove it all as one unit. Chapter 7 covers this removal process for a 383/440 big-block powertrain.

The main obstacle in the removal of the entire front suspension is the torsion bars. To overcome it purchase the specific torsion bar removal tool. You will use it many times.

The torsion bars were originally dipped in paint and have drip marks left by the thick paint. They also have identification marks made with light brown paint. The right bar has one stripe about 6½ inches from the front of the bar. The left bar has two stripes, one about 7½ inches and the other about 10 inches from the front of the bar.

Another tool to purchase (or rent) is a tie-rod puller. Many people use a fork when they replace the ball joint boots; however, anytime you need to separate the new suspension you cannot use the fork without tearing a boot or marring the new parts.

After complete disassembly, cleaning, and blasting, you have two options for replacement bushings: original rubber or polyurethane. You also have a choice in the type of replacement parts you use. Companies sell complete kits to rebuild your front suspension but they do not have the same appearance as the original MOOG parts. For a correct restoration use rubber and original MOOG replacement parts.

After building the front suspension and assembling it on a rolling frame, the entire engine assembly can be mounted in place followed by the transmission. Then the car can be lifted and the entire assembly can be moved into place and attached without any damage to the freshly painted car.

The mechanical restoration of your front and rear suspension is crucial to a fully functional car that can be driven and enjoyed. Just as important are the cosmetics of the components. They contribute to a restoration that can compete at high-level car shows.

Ideally, the car you start with has all of its original parts and markings so that as you remove the dirt and grime you can document each original part on your car. Beware, however, that this is seldom the case except for a few high-dollar, low-mileage survivor cars.

By researching other cars of your same model and year at high-level car shows you can find out what is accepted as "original." This chapter includes some basic guidelines for assessing the correct appearance of the many parts of the suspension. However, the only way to be certain something is correct for your car is to find it that way.

Suspension Rebuild

1 Remove the entire front suspension as one unit. Coat every bolt, nut, and moveable joint liberally with your favorite penetrating spray and allow it to do its work for several hours. Take inventory of any missing, damaged, and worn part that must be replaced and add them to your "parts needed" list. Document with pictures every castle nut, tie-rod end, and original part for later reference. Look for any factory inspection marks so that they can be documented and reproduced later.

2 If you find a rusted retaining pin in the end of the lower strut rod end, carefully remove it without breaking it off. Soak it in penetrating oil and push out with a punch and hammer. If it breaks you must drill it out so a new one can be installed. This is a fine detail that many people miss. You can see the clear cad finish on the washer.

3 Three castle nuts with cotter pins are used in all of the steering ends. You can see the way the pin was bent by the factory and the style of the original boots.

4 These are the original end link, sway bar, and tab locations for a 1970 B-Body. Earlier lower control arms have the tab mounted farther out on the control arm and use a different style sway bar. Note the bolt inserted from the bottom up.

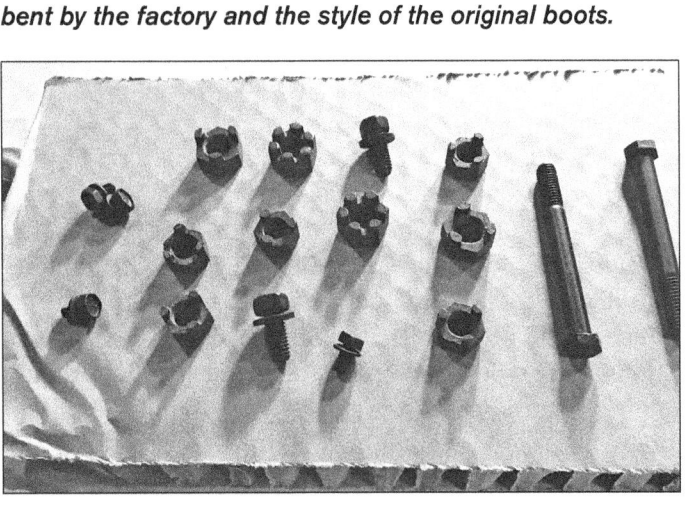

5 All the nuts and bolts are black phosphate. You can have them plated or do it yourself. Either clean them with a wire wheel on a bench grinder or blast them until they are completely clean.

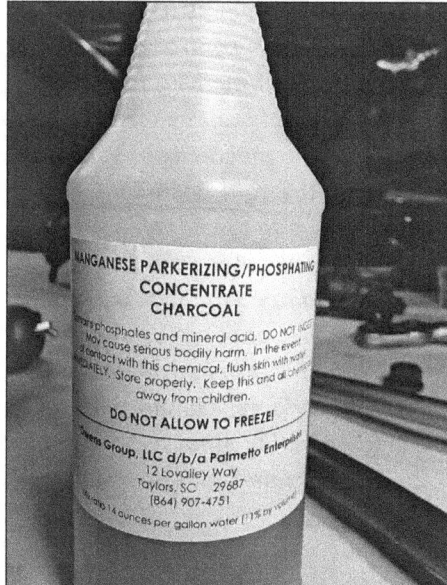

7 Clean, refinish, replate, and replace all of the components of the entire front suspension. Label them for installation.

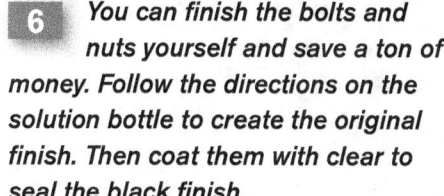

6 You can finish the bolts and nuts yourself and save a ton of money. Follow the directions on the solution bottle to create the original finish. Then coat them with clear to seal the black finish.

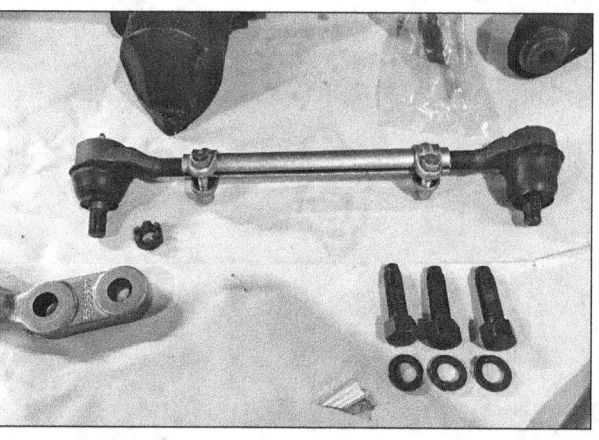

8 Restore tie-rod ends, tie-rods, and steering links in natural metal finish. Seymour's stainless steel paint is a great match. Tie-rod ends are Moog parts and are clear coated. These bolts and nuts on the tie-rod are incorrect. They are black phosphate, not natural metal.

9 Finish the lower ball joint, spindle, and attaching hardware. Protect the surface where the wheel bearings meet the spindle when painting.

10 These are the upper control arm bushings after removal with a cold chisel and a cut-off wheel. They must always be replaced.

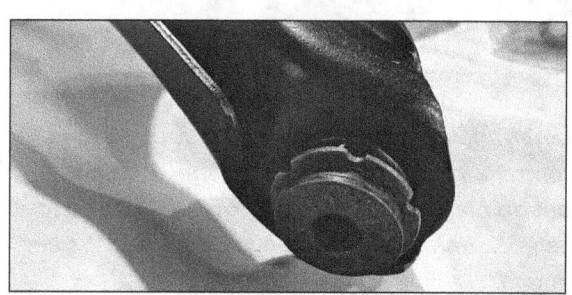

11 This is how the upper control arm bushing looks after being pressed in at the machine shop. Notice that on this car the upper arm is painted black. Original arms were natural metal and NOS arms (shown) were finished in semi-gloss black.

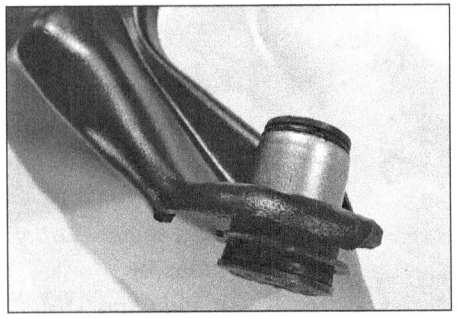

12 On late-1970 cars an additional sleeve can be found on the bushing. Earlier cars did not have this extra sleeve. With or without the sleeve the same bushing is pressed in the arm.

13 In 1970 a lower control arm with a lower bushing replaced a pivot pen pressed in by the machine shop. Notice the gold Cosmoline finish up to the knuckle. Originally these arms were dipped in the waxy protective coating. You can paint this arm to appear as original without the waxy residue that remains when treated with Cosmoline.

14 Completely strip and paint the K-member. Then add all the components to complete the front suspension. You can powdercoat it or paint it with enamel. Just be sure to use semi-gloss to create the original finish.

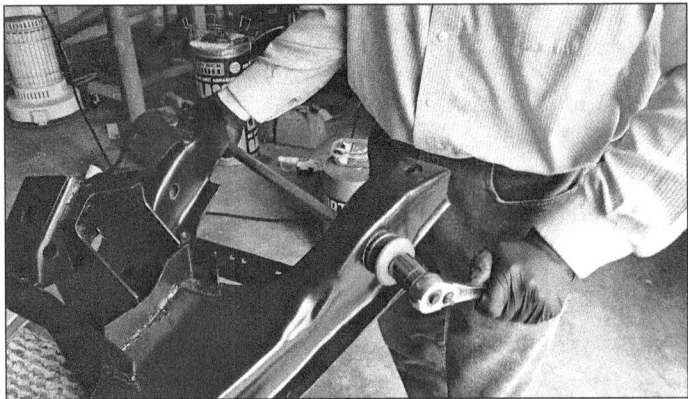

15 Install the lower strut rod and tighten the front nut. Notice the new rubber bushing, washer, and correct finish on each. I recommend original rubber rather than the harder and more prone to squeak polyurethane.

16 The self-locking nut is correct, as is the bushing and washer; missing is a retainer pin. Wait to install these until after everything is under load and tested just in case it must come apart. You do not want to install the pin twice or risk having to drill out a broken pin when it's in the car. Just do not forget to install it afterward.

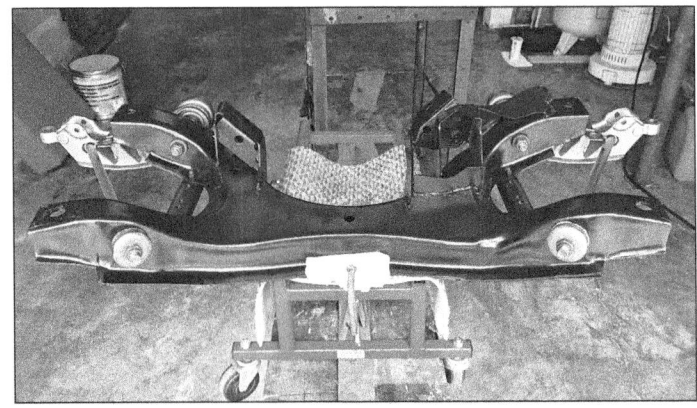

17 Slide on the complete, restored lower control arm assembly making sure to insert the strut rod and the lower control arm pivot at the same time. Attach the hardware but do not over-tighten or torque at this time. Make all the adjustments and torque to spec after the car is on the ground.

18 Hang the completed brake, ball joint, and spindle units on to the lower control arm and torque all bolts to spec.

19 These original appearing finishes stand up to use after the restoration is complete. Notice the castle nuts and cotter pin. It's important to note that the lower ball–to-spindle nut should not be a tri-castle nut. The upper ball joint–to-spindle should have the tri-castle nut and the lower multi-castle nut.

20 Make sure that the shoulder is correctly against the K-member and that the pivot has been correctly pressed far enough into the lower control arm. If it isn't, you will have problems when installing the torsion bars.

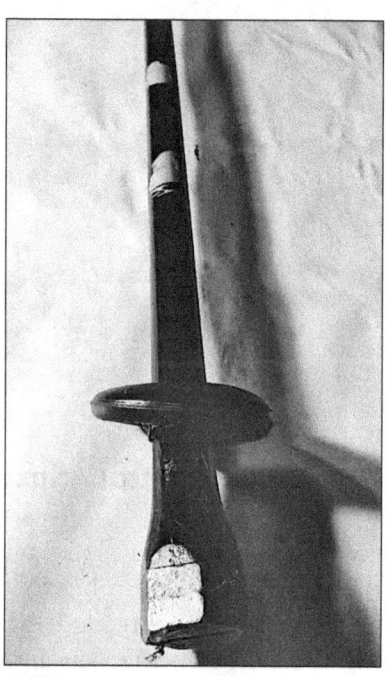

22 You can identify the right and left torsion bars by the casting found on the end of the bar. They are painted very heavy semi-gloss black so that the excess paint causes drip marks along the bar. You can find inspection marks on the bar about 6 inches from the front of the bar. The right bar has one stripe and the left bar has two. The marks are different colors depending on your model of car but most of the time they are light brown. Do not attach the torsion bars until the K-member is installed in the car.

21 Be sure to install the dust boot cover onto the torsion bar so that when the bar is inserted into the crossmember of the frame, the boot is toward the front of the car and seals out any dirt or water. It is very difficult to move the boot over the front knuckle of the bar. Use a liberal amount of grease and a major amount of effort.

23 *This lower control arm in a 1970 B-Body has the real Cosmoline on the arm. After it dries it can be shot with matte clear to make sure it is not sticky and does not easily rub off.*

24 *Many inspection marks can be found on these cars' front suspensions. This is a 1970 B-Body.*

25 *After you have restored the entire front suspension assembly, the engine and transmission can also be attached. Then you can install the entire unit from the bottom, just as the factory did, minus all the great assembly line machinery. When in place, install the torsion bars, adjust the height, torque all bolts to specification, and don't forget the retaining clips.*

Upper Control Arms

The removal and replacement of the upper control arm bushings can be a challenge. We recommend taking the unit and the new bushings to a machine shop and having them press the old ones out and then press the new ones in.

If you do take them to the shop you might as well have them also remove and replace the upper ball joint. You can buy a kit that includes tools to remove the bushings and a special socket to remove and install the ball joint if you plan to perform this process more times in the future.

An extra sleeve is on the backside of some OEM bushings. This is not present on most pre-1970 control arms.

Removal of the ball joint requires a special socket; again, unless you plan on restoring several cars, just have the machine shop remove and install the new ball joint. One unique detail is the use of tri-castle nuts on the front suspension. The tri-castle nut goes on the upper ball joint and the six-count castle nut goes on the lower.

Prior to installing your new bushings, take the time to have them media blasted. It makes your final result all the more satisfying.

The finish of the upper control arm is natural on most applications with some painted semi-gloss black. Most NOS or replacement upper control arms come painted black. The finish you choose is entirely up to you.

Lower Control Arms

The lower control arm is vital to the operation of the front suspension. The pivot shaft and the bushing are directly attached to the torsion bar, so every movement of the car actually goes through this shaft and bushing. It can appear daunting to remove the shaft and bushing, restore both parts, and then install them. But the process is not that difficult.

The first step is to press out the shaft from the lower control arm, leaving the rubber bushing in the arm. The rubber bushing can then be pried out. A novice may think it is time to put in the new bushing, but a closer look reveals that a metal sleeve is still in the control arm and another one is still on the pivot shaft.

If you are using polyurethane bushings, all you have to do is lubricate the bushing with the supplied lube (a must if you do not want squeaks) and push the shaft into the bushing. If you use the original rubber bushing, you must remove the sleeves.

Removing these two sleeves is by far the most difficult part of the front suspension build. You must use a cold chisel and a hammer to split the sleeve, cave it inward, and separate it from the control arm. Use care not to damage the arm. To remove the sleeve from the shaft, notch it lengthwise on all four sides and slip it off. Blast all of the parts except the pivot shaft.

To begin the rebuild process, press the shaft into the new bushing. Then press the bushing and shaft assembly into the arm. That's all there is to it.

Originally the lower control arm was dipped in Cosmoline up to the knuckle. This was a brownish-gold waxy preservative that kept the arm from rusting. The excess Cosmoline sometimes ran down the arm because it was hung from the knuckle. Some people like to find a spray paint that resembles this look and simply paint the arm.

If you want to truly re-create the finish, treat the bare-metal arm with Rust Preventative Magic or paint with Seymour's Stainless Steel

paint. While the arm hangs from the knuckle, spray on a heavy coat of Eastwood's Heavy Duty Anti Rust. Let it dry for several days and then spray with a matte-finish clear to seal the Cosmoline.

When complete, install the bumpstop, the torsion bar adjuster bolt, and the threaded metal block, which is designed to stay in place in the arm when it is under tension. Both the block and bolt are left in natural finish.

Now, take special note that all lower control arms for the 1966–1970 B-Body line of cars are the same, except for a welded sway bar mount tab. That tab is located near the ball joint stud hole on 1966–1969 B-Body cars. The tab is near the center of the arm on 1970 B-Body cars.

Other than the sway bar mount positions, all the control arms interchange. The reason for the different location of the tab is that in 1970 the sway bar configuration changed.

Front Components Finishes

The following is a short, general list of the finishes found on front and rear suspension parts.

Finish	Component
Semi-gloss black	Sway bar and brackets, K-frame, torsion bars, power steering box, brake drum backing plate, K-frame to radiator support bracket, access plates to adjust control arms, shocks
Natural	Tie-rod and tie-rod ends, steering link, idler arm, upper and lower ball joints, front strut rods, manual steering box, torsion bar adjusting bolts and block, access plates screws
Gold cadmium	Sway bar end links
Black zinc	All attaching nuts and bolts, tri-castle nuts
Clear zinc (silver)	Front strut rod washers, cotter pins

All brake drums for cars that have the sport wheels (including all chrome Magnum wheels, road wheels [black wheel with stainless spokes] and brushed trim rings in 1969 and polished trim rings in 1970, and Rallye wheels) were painted red on the outer edge by brush. This was not done carefully from the factory and runs from the red paint often appeared on the sides of the drums.

Brake System

The basic function and design of the brake system did not change much over the years, but the appearance changed substantially among models and through the years 1966–1970. Your specific factory service manual is a must and it shows detailed diagrams of your original equipment.

Manual Drum Brakes

Most 1966–1970 Plymouth and Dodge B-Bodies left the factory with manual drum brakes. That in itself could be one of the main reasons for the rarity of these cars. They were really fast, but often if you had to shut 'er down in a hurry the ditch was a quick option when the drums just couldn't stop the beast.

Under hard braking these drum brakes heat up rather quickly and experienced major brake fade. Brakes that didn't fade could lock up. On

Before disc brakes became standard equipment, manual and optional power drum brakes were common on Chrysler B-Bodies, even those equipped with B and RB-Engines! It's hard to imagine a Hemi car trying to come to a halt with a quartet of drums.

gravel, or on a wet, or even worse, icy road, locked-up brakes quickly caused many hard impacts. However, if they are in good working order, and you leave a little more room than you leave with your modern anti-lock power disc brakes, they will perform well.

One of the first things you learn growing up working on cars is how to do a drum brake job. Manual drum brakes are very simple and their repair is basic and relatively inexpensive. But if your car has been sitting a very long time in an uncovered state it is going to take more than 30 minutes and a set of new brake shoes to get your brakes in perfect operating condition and show-quality appearance. Be sure to examine your front and rear brakes to see if they are original in appearance and what needs to be replaced or rebuilt.

Because these parts are so important to you and your car's safety, the entire brake system should be replaced or rebuilt. That includes the master cylinder, brake lines and hoses, distribution block, wheel cylinders, bearings, brake drums, and shoes. If you plan to show the car, new brake lines are a must.

The actual components inside the brake drum are unique in color and appearance. As you disassemble your originals you will probably find that they have been replaced. You can refer to pictures that show how these components were finished and what colors were used from the factory. As always, different models, years, and factories used different part suppliers, so restore yours the way you find them or use a documented example of your car's specific application. On all drum brake cars with road or Rallye wheels, the outside edge was painted red with a brush, no matter the color of the car. Cars with steel wheels did not receive this paint.

Master Cylinder, Engine Compartment Lines and Distribution Block

The master cylinder is cast in appearance and carries part numbers and date codes. Make sure you have the correct master cylinder for your year and model of car. Early master cylinders can be a single-reservoir style; all later ones had dual reservoirs. When you have the master out of the car the pedal actuator rod may seem as if it will not come out. But it will and is just held in the cylinder with an O-ring.

One of the fastest ways to remove a stubborn rod is to put the master cylinder in a bench vise and run a steel rod through the hole in the end of the brake rod. Angle the bottom of the steel rod against the bench and use a hand sledge to hit the top of the steel rod away from the cylinder. It pops right out. You can buy a rebuild kit at most parts stores. Remove all the internal cup seals, plungers, and springs, making sure to pay attention to the order and orientation of the parts as they come out.

Check the bore for pitting and ridges. If the master is original you want to save it even if you have to send it away for sleeving. If the bore is in good shape, use a hone to smooth the bore so you have a surface that seals when you reassemble the unit.

The wheel cylinders also should be rebuilt or replaced. The process is the same with these individual units. The bleeder valve is usually stuck or rusted and is replaced with a new one. Save your originals if you can, but it is not the end of the world if you have to replace them because they are not visible. Their correct function is much more important than their appearance. They are also cast with black phosphate bolts holding them in place. A white foam gasket seals the unit to the backing plate.

The distribution block is usually usable and can be brought back to original appearance with a wire wheel because it is brass. It, too, is date coded and attached with a black phosphate bolt. Differences in this block depend on whether you have manual drums, power-assisted drums, or front disc brakes. They cannot be interchanged among brake systems.

Again, replace all brake lines. If you are going for a totally correct appearance know that the originals are not stainless. They can flash rust, so unless you are going to show in a high-level Original Equipment class the stainless replacements look good, keep a nice appearance, and last much longer. There is one drawback to using stainless: Because the tube is made out of much harder metal they can have problems with sealing.

Power Drum Brakes

Everything that needs to be done to a manual brake car's system must also be done to a power brake car with the addition of a power booster. These boosters can be model and year specific so make sure you have the correct one for your car. The master cylinder is also different and so is the distribution block. Most power brake booster and master cylinders are painted black and completely assembled. If you have a Hemi car you must have a Hemi assembly for it to fit.

Front Disc and Rear Drum Brakes

If your car was ordered with front disc brakes they are noted on your broadcast sheet. This option can also be coded on your fender tag. You need a different master cylinder and distribution block. These front disc brake units in complete original condition are hard to find and expensive to rebuild. The rotors and calipers are not reproduced in correct appearance. So if you have the originals be sure to save them. Turning of the rotors is a must and hopefully you have enough metal left to use your originals.

Drum Brake Rebuild

1 This is the heavy-duty 11-inch rear drum. If your drum does not have the extra-reinforced fins you probably have the smaller low-performance brakes. To upgrade to the 11-inch brakes requires replacement not only of the drum but of the entire brake assembly, including the backing plate. It is worth the effort and expense to upgrade.

2 Be sure that your rear drums have a minimum amount of metal so you can turn them before spending the time it takes to blast and paint them. Do not blast the drum surface where the brake shoes contact the drum. The best way to restore them is to use a micrometer to measure the drum and confirm that it can be turned. Then blast, have them turned, and paint with a darker cast metal paint.

3 If your car has any wheel except a solid steel wheel, it received a brushed-on coating of Ralleye Red paint. It was applied without any care given to how much paint was used and how messy the results were.

4 Here is what you can find when you open up the brake drum. Most of the natural metal is rusty and you can have paint that never came originally on the car. Correct finishes include orange upper springs.

5 The internal components of this unit are in really good shape and can be blasted and refinished correctly. Even though a lot of pad is left on these shoes they must be replaced with new pads.

6 Wheel cylinder, cross piece, spring, and wheel studs are all in good restorable condition.

7 Axles were pulled when the rear end was rebuilt. They were painted with Seymour's Stainless Steel paint. The backing plate was painted semi-gloss black. All of the components were replaced with new except the brake adjuster with the star wheel.

8 The spring in the adjuster cable and the lower brake shoe spring are green, and the brake shoe hold-down spring, rod, and caps are clear zinc or cadmium plated. Note the correct, original larger teeth on the adjuster.

9 The adjusters are unique to each side of the car. Make sure you have the right one by testing the direction they move when the adjuster cable is engaged. Notice that the adjuster has small teeth; because the original one was not usable it had to be replaced with a new one.

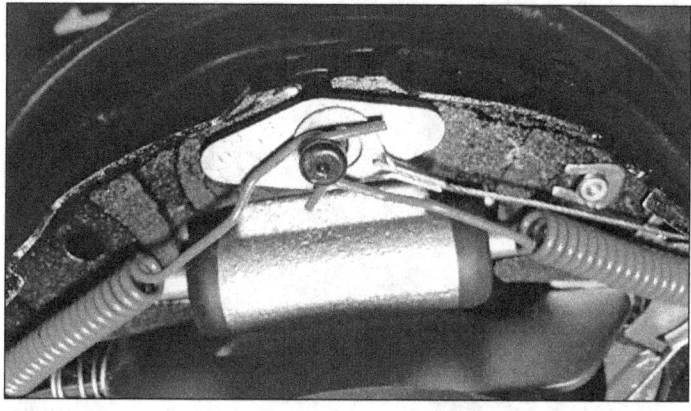

10 The wheel cylinder had to be replaced because the original had too many rust pits in its bore. Notice the lack of original part numbers on the cylinder. Orange springs and all-new hardware complete the assembly.

11 The emergency brake retainer was red on this low-mile 1970 Road Runner, so it was painted the same way it was found. When removing the cable be careful not to damage the retainer. The teeth must be compressed so that the cable can be removed from the backing plate.

This completed drum brake assembly has been finished the way it came from the factory. It now functions better than new. Even though it will be soon covered by the brake drum and wheel you have the pictures to prove you didn't cut any corners during the restoration.

Disc Brake Rebuild

1 This is an untouched original front disc brake assembly from a 1970 Plymouth. It has been steam pressure washed and care was taken to not remove the original orange, blue, and yellow inspection marks. Don't let the new nut and bolt that is from the stand fool you.

2 This galvanized dust shield and original brake hose have been painted black. Note how the factory bent the cotter pins and used a blue inspection mark on the driver-side assembly.

3 *The factory used a yellow inspection mark on the passenger-side assembly. Notice the three castle nuts on the tie-rod end and that the original cotter pin has been replaced. You can tell because it is way too long and not bent the way the originals were.*

4 *This close-up shows additional inspection marks. It also documents the clips on the caliper bolts that are almost always missing. The lower ball joint is held on by six castle nuts while the upper is held on by three castle nuts.*

5 *These disc brake assemblies are from a Dodge B-Body. They are identical to those on Plymouth B-Bodies.*

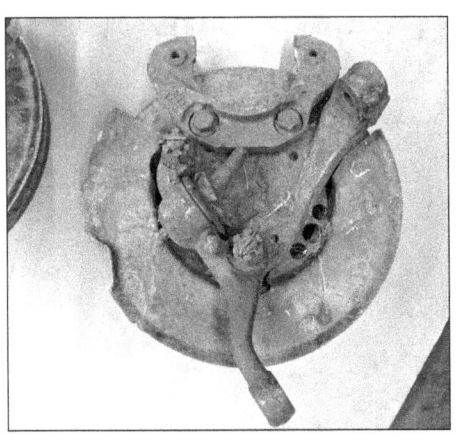

7 *Someone has done some previous incorrect work on this unit. At least it is clean and complete. The bearings and seals must be replaced. Always inspect the spindle and make sure it is smooth and in usable condition.*

6 *The back side of the assembly seems to be beyond saving. It isn't, and because it has all original parts, you should try to save it.*

8 Before spending any time on the original rotor measure it to be sure it has enough metal to be turned. Also do not overlook the condition of the wheel studs.

10 After carefully blasting the rotor without blasting the surface where the pads contact the rotor you can paint it with a dark cast color. Then have the rotor turned. Next using fine Emory cloth sand them with a circular motion. This makes a really good surface for seating the pads during the early miles of operation.

9 This pair of disc brake assemblies has one good dust shield and one that is completely unusable. New ones are available but are not the original finish. That is not a problem because they were painted black from the factory.

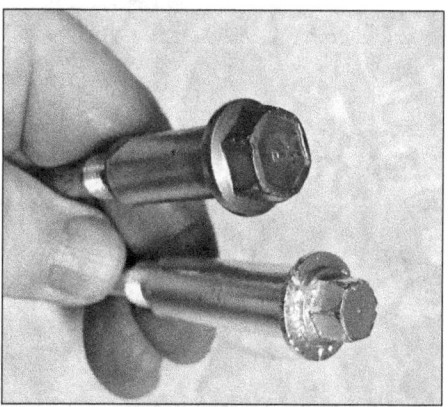

11 Even though the center of this hub has a slight chip in the surface the original rotor is worth using. Replacements are not identical to the original but can be used if yours are too far gone to save.

12 A brake rotor includes the notch, two-piece wheel stud plate, and balancing weights. By painting this rotor before it was turned it is ready to reassemble.

13 Here is a side-by-side comparison of an original caliper bolt (upper) and a replacement caliper bolt (lower). They differ in size and design of the head of the bolt. The original has been replated. You also can paint them with chrome paint, but the finish does not last as well as plating does.

14 All these pieces have been blasted and turned, and a new lower ball joint replaces the worn-out original. Moog parts are as close as you can get to original unless you find NOS examples.

15 The original spindles were in good enough condition to save. Do not blast or paint the surface of the spindle where the bearings and rotor ride. Original part numbers are on the spindle and the date codes are on both the spindle and the caliper-mounting bracket.

16 The first step in reassembly is the dust shield. It has been painted semi-gloss black and the attaching bolts are black phosphate.

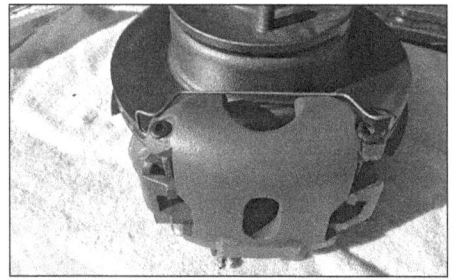

17 After having the original calipers rebuilt, the bolts should be replated. Next, clean and reinstall the rubber bushings that the caliper bolts go through. Also buy new brake pads. After that, the unit is ready for assembly.

18 Missing from this nearly complete assembly are the cotter pins and caliper bolt clips. The calipers were rebuilt. The paint is different from the paint on the other parts. The owner liked the contrast so they were not repainted. Originally they were not painted but in reality it is nearly impossible to keep the natural metal from flash rusting. So unless you are going to compete in a high-level Original Equipment class, just paint them. When you do, be sure to fog the last coat. That reduces the shine and makes it almost impossible to tell if the part is painted or not.

19 Here is a close-up of the anti-rattle spring. These almost never remain on the assembly and are not reproduced. If yours are missing be prepared to search long and hard to find them.

20 *Always use new parts if they are close to the appearance of the originals. These reproduction splash shields are not galvanized like the originals, but they are painted black and will look original when mounted on the car.*

Rubber Hoses and Brake Lines

All rubber hoses must be replaced. These are available new from any local parts store but do not have the finish or markings of originals. They are reproduced with a close appearance to the originals.

You can purchase a complete set of new brake lines from sources such as Fine Lines or The Right Stuff. They come packaged in a large box with a slight bend in the middle for shipping. This bend can easily be straightened for installation. They fit very well and are a must if you plan on showing your car.

A combination distribution block and axle vent is threaded into the rear axle. It is also brass and has a spring-loaded cap that vents the axle. Most of the time these are reusable.

Emergency Brake Cables

The routing of the emergency brake cables can be very different depending on the year and model of your vehicle, but a single cable always attaches to the emergency brake assembly. It has a grommet seal where it comes out of the interior to the underside of the car. On most B-Bodies this cable goes through the frame and a special clip holds the cable in place and does not allow it to move forward or backward during operation. This clip is hard to see, but it is there.

A guide attached/welded to the floorpan directs the cable to the inside of the rear frame rail. There the single cable goes into a double clip where the right and left emergency cables attach and then goes back to the brake assemblies. A threaded rod with a lock nut allows you to adjust the emergency brake so it properly engages. Two additional U-clips hold the right and left cable to the frame bracket.

These cables must be functional, and they are natural metal in appearance (uncoated). The rear two brake cables slide in a heavy-duty spiral reinforced case. These can be blasted and painted with Seymour's Stainless Steel paint for a correct appearance. Reproduced versions also have a great original appearance.

Leaf Springs

Unless your springs have very low mileage you should disassemble them, blast them, and replace all the inner zinc liners, the plastic spacer wear pads, and the front bushing. Also blast and then paint the front spring hangers (we use Seymour's Stainless Steel paint). Inspect the area on the front of the spring assembly that is protected by the spring hangers. You will know if your particular springs were natural or painted black by looking under the hangers. The factory used two swatches of color to identify which spring went on what car and on which side.

Taking several pictures to document what you find helps you restore your car to its factory-original condition.

If your springs are natural you can use Rust Preventive Magic and they never have to be painted. You can also paint them with Seymour's Stainless Steel paint. If they are black they can be painted before assembly. Some say they were dipped fully assembled but that hasn't been confirmed. Pictures of original cars do not show any paint on the exposed liners and we haven't found any heavy areas of paint that would indicate they were dipped and hung. The paint is black flattened at about 20 percent. Some say they were brush painted black after assembly.

After you disassemble the spring assemblies, blast all the leaves separately, and remove the large front rubber bushing. You can drill out the rubber in several places and then press out the bushing. After refinishing or painting the springs install a spring rebuild kit. Inexpensive kits contain liners made out of galvanized tin and clamps that are not very thick. We recommend that you purchase a kit from Frank Badalson. His kit includes zinc liners and heavy clamps. Lubricate the front eye bushing and press it in.

Lay out the springs in the proper order for reassembly. Get several C-clamps or welding clamps and a long shaft that fits the center bolt hole. Put duct tape on any surface that will touch the finished springs. You do not want to mar the newly finished surface. Lay out protective cloth where the springs touch your workbench.

Press in the wear pads until they snap in place and then assemble the leaves and liners. Make sure the leaves have an extra hole in the front and one in back. The clamps have a tang that goes into this hole.

When everything is laid out with the wear pads and zinc liners in place, run the shaft through so that all parts are lined up. Tighten the C-clamp and compress the entire assembly. Put the original black phosphate finished bolt/pin in place with the nut toward the bottom. The pinhead goes in the spring/shock mount. Wrap the nut and bolt with tape and tighten so as not to mar the finish.

When both assemblies are completed install the clamps. By using at least two C-clamps to hold the new "spring clamps" in place you can bend and secure the clamps with crisp corners and minimal dents in the surface of the clamps.

When you finish the assembly of these springs, if they are painted black, mask them off and paint them. You can do the same if they are painted stainless. Then you can set them aside until you are ready to bolt them onto the rear axle and install everything as one unit into the car.

Steering System

The steering box and linkage for all B-Bodies, no matter the year, is basically the same. Yes, there are differences and of course different date codes, but the design is basically the same. Removal and reassembly is not difficult. The steering column and dash can be removed and reassembled without a lot of trouble either.

Steering Box and Linkage

The steering boxes attach to the K-member. The steering column attaches to the steering box and is secured with a drive-through pin. The idler arm also attaches to the K-frame and the steering linkage, the inner tie-rod attaches to the center link, and the outer tie-rod attaches to the lower ball joint arm of the front brake and wheel assembly.

Your car has either power steering or manual steering. The appearance of these two steering boxes is different and so are the parts to rebuild them. If you have a manual steering box it is natural in appearance. The steering column is longer than the one that is used with the power steering unit. Usually the internal gears of the manual steering box are worn and the steering has a lot of play. Some of the play can be lessened, but you should have the unit completely rebuilt. Good shops can perform this rebuild; some are listed in the Source Guide at the back of this book.

If you have a power steering unit it is painted black and the steering column is shorter than the manual unit. It also requires the additional power steering pump and hoses to make this unit work. You should have this unit completely rebuilt by a good shop. When you have it rebuilt you can choose different levels of final performance.

The original power steering feel from the factory is slow and kind of soft in response. You can upgrade the feel and response to a quicker and tighter response. You can rebuild the power steering pump from a kit found at most local parts stores; NAPA carries great replacement parts. Two pump styles were used on these cars: Federal or Saginaw. The parts are different on each unit and their appearance makes these units easy to tell apart.

All of the steering linkage is natural in appearance. This can be achieved by blasting the parts; then either refinish with Rust Preventative Magic or paint with Seymour's Stainless Steel paint. All the castle nuts are three-prong versions from the factory except where the lower ball joint attaches to the wheel assembly.

Upon reassembly of the steering linkage you can get the alignment somewhere in the ballpark so that you can get it to a good shop where you should have the car completely aligned before driving.

Steering Column and Dash

Removal of the steering column is surprisingly easy. Remove the four bolts connecting the steering column flange to the firewall. Next, remove the pin from the rag joint connecting the column to the steering box. Finally, remove the four nuts connecting the column to the dash.

When removing the dash it works well if you have about a 3-foot piece of heavy wire to support the dash after you remove the five dash bolts. Loosen the two lower bolts but do not remove them. The dash pivots on the two lower bolts and you can tie the wire to the dash frame and body, so you can access all of the dash wire connections and heater control cables.

When you reinstall the dash use the same support wire you used on disassembly so you can access and hook up all the wires and cables before sliding it in place and re-bolting it.

POWERTRAIN

After you have documented your car (as outlined in Chapter 2), several decisions need to be made about how and to what extent you restore the drivetrain.

As you disassemble the engine, take pictures and take the time to bag and tag all parts. It is amazing how quickly you forget how that bracket goes back on. Many accessories go with the engine, but we focus on the long-block from disassembly to the completed unit with factory paint.

Type of Restoration

If your car has a numbers-matching engine and transmission and you want the car to have an original appearance, the best way to proceed is to build the car completely stock. Or at least any modifications should be bolt-on changes that can be easily changed. If the car has survived with its original driveline intact, and still in the car, it demands to be saved. If you really want to drive a modified car with major upgrades to the driveline, do not purchase an original numbers-matching car.

Some owners have restored their Mopar to original condition and shown it at many national venues. Then, after it has aged, they have removed the original engine, stored it, and then replaced it with a high-performance upgrade.

A popular and easy change is to drop a 440 into a 383 car. Many of the parts interchange and improved performance is soon experienced. Add a tri carb to a 440 and hold onto your hat. Another popular change is installing a crate Hemi. You have to make several necessary Hemi-specific changes if you choose this option, but the swap can be done with enough time and money.

If you do not have a numbers-matching driveline, you can really do anything you want in terms of engine, transmission, rear end,

It takes quite a bit of effort to transform an original, modified engine back to its factory-correct appearance. Fortunately, if you follow our tips your B-Body powerplant should look and perform back to factory specs.

etc. You can also restore the car to original condition without a numbers-matching driveline. Once the original driveline is gone, the date codes no longer matter. Some sellers advertise that they have replaced the block with a date-correct block. Although some view that as important, it really doesn't mean anything if the block is a 1966 or 1970. The block still appears original and fits and performs just as great.

Another popular trend is building a "tribute" or "clone" car. These terms are merely used to increase the value of a basic "hot rod." If the car came with a 318 and you replace it with a 426 Hemi it is still a 318 car. These cars will never be worth the same amount as a "real" car. However, if one of these cars is done right, it can bring much more money than the sum of the parts.

A number of books have already been published that help you build a high-performance upgrade to any of these cars. This chapter is dedicated to saving and completely rebuilding a numbers-matching car to original appearance that, when completed, can be enjoyed and even can win national-level awards.

The level to which you restore the driveline is completely contingent upon the correct date-coded parts used and the attention to detail while restoring those parts. The smallest detail is important and you should do everything possible to acquire and install correct original parts, if this is the final goal of your restoration.

383/440 Strategy

If the thought of actually disassembling, restoring, and installing the engine in your car terrifies you,

this section is just what you need. Unless you are lucky enough to find a car with a fresh engine rebuild, most cars' powerplant needs attention. The engine and transmission are why you always dreamed of owning a muscle car. No one wants to drive an unreliable, slow, smoking, and leaking muscle car. Restoring the engine to factory condition can be expensive, but if you do all the work yourself you can save a load of money and have the gratification of saying, "Yeah, I built that."

The 383, or "B" block, and the 440, or "RB" block, are very similar engines. Many parts from the 440 were used on many of the original 383 B-body cars we know and love. Using the free-breathing heads and exhaust manifolds from the 440 on the 383 provided an immediate and inexpensive gain in performance. Because so many similarities exist between the engines, you see many 440s transplanted into 383 cars.

If your car is not numbers matching, and you want more bang for your buck, rebuilding a 440 costs about the same as rebuilding a 383. Now is a great time to evaluate exactly what you want to do with your car when it is finished. That final goal helps you make good decisions during the build of your car.

Tools

The tools and equipment needed to perform a restoration are listed in the Chapter 1 sidebar "Tools." Before attempting to rebuild the engine yourself, make sure you have (or have access to) the following: a garage with room to keep the car in a non-running condition, an engine hoist, a four-leg engine stand

(a three-leg stand works but be careful that it doesn't tip), a torsion bar removal tool, a ring compressor, and a hammer handle.

Process Outline

On a full restoration, we prefer to remove the engine, K-member, transmission, and front suspension, from the bottom. If the car is already painted and needs only the driveline rebuilt, you may opt to take the engine and transmission out from the top. If you do remove the entire assembly from the bottom it is very helpful to fabricate two welded stands with castors that can attach to the car's frame so that it is still mobile.

Pull the torsion bars and then disconnect the upper A-arms, brake lines, fuel lines, linkage, drive-9shaft, speedometer cable, all electrical connections, and anything else that keeps the engine and transmission from coming out of the car.

Lift the car with the engine hoist, slide a roller frame under the K-member, and then lower the car so that it is resting on the roller frame. The car pivots on the back tires and axle.

Unbolt the upper control arms, remove the transmission crossmember, and unbolt the K-member. Lift the car high enough to clear the engine and roll the entire assembly free.

Separate the transmission from the engine. If your car is an automatic, also remove the torque converter and torque plate. If it is manual, remove the transmission, bellhousing, and flywheel. Examine the condition of each unit and repair or replace as necessary. We recommend taking the transmission to a reputable rebuild shop to perform the repairs.

Machine Shop Work

Because this is a restoration book we stick with factory appearance with optional performance upgrades. You can build a high-performance engine; just be sure to back up such an engine with high-performance driveline parts and brakes. Take the bare block, heads, rods, pistons, and crank to a trusted or highly recommended machine shop. They can check the specs and condition of your parts and recommend what needs machining and or replacing. The block might only need to be hot tanked and honed or it may need to be bored out depending on the wear in the cylinders.

The same is true for the crank. It can be either polished or turned based on the amount of wear. The shop's technicians can tell if you can reuse your original rods and pistons or if they need to be replaced.

For example, if the block is bored out, a new correct-size piston must be used. After you purchase the parts, have the machinist assemble the rods and pistons, which have been stamped with a specific order and orientation in the engine. If the crank is turned, use larger bearings. After a complete assessment of your engine and its needed parts specifications the machinist can recommend what to purchase, including rings bearings, and a gasket rebuild set.

Cam size, headwork, springs, valves, and lifters must be considered at the same time. If you select a stock cam it requires little change to original equipment. If you choose a performance-oriented cam you need different springs. (Many sources, including Comp Cams, can help you choose the best combination for your desired end result.) Have the machine shop install the new cam bearings in the block, as well as a new distributor driveshaft intermediate bushing. ∎

Engine Assembly

It is extremely helpful to lay out all the new parts, existing original parts, gaskets, sealers, oil, tools, etc. By having an organized workflow you can save valuable time and ensure that you don't miss anything during assembly.

At about this time, you may start to get cold feet when you think about assembling the engine. After all, it will turn up to 6,000 rpm and needs to stay together for years to come. If you do, just pay the shop to assemble, your short-block, lower reciprocating assembly, or even the long-block, complete with heads, intake and rockers, and make it ready to paint. It depends entirely on your budget and your desire to build it yourself. Either way, it is important to strip, clean, and replace all engine components as necessary.

Rods and Pistons

Each rod and piston assembly is marked by the machine shop for the required assembly order and position. The rods are stamped with their position, the pistons are marked with a notch that goes toward the front of the engine, and the rods are marked with a dot.

Correct rod bearing and crank bearings must be cleaned, installed, and completely covered in assembly lube. Be sure to install the crank bearing with the oiling hole toward the block or you will have engine failure! In addition, use the lube provided in your new ARP bolt kits.

It is vital that you use a high-quality assembly lube on all the internal moving parts of the engine. We also use a heavy racing oil to coat parts and to dip the piston and rings in prior to assemble.

Check the block to make sure that all of the oil channel plugs are in place. The machine shop usually installs these, but never assume anything when building an engine. Double-check everything. On this block, one of the main plugs was left off. Without it, the oil pressure (if you have any) is low. Use red high-temp RTV to seal the threads and then install.

We recommend replacing all rod bolts and crank bolts with new ARP bolts. We use original bolts externally on the engine for originality, but why not use new hardware inside on the moving parts?

We like to get all the piston assemblies in correct order and orientation in the piston box to help with proper assembly order. To seat the new ARP rod bolts, assemble the rods and caps and then coat with the ARP assembly lube.

Torque the bolts to the manufacturer's recommended spec, which is different than the torque spec in the factory service manual. If you are using the original bolts, follow the manual's specs. Always torque everything to the correct and appropriate specification.

Rings and Bearings

It is now time to assemble the rings into the pistons. If you are using the original pistons, be sure to use a ring groove cleaner to remove any deposits or burrs that can restrict the rings' movement in the piston's groove. Follow the directions provided with the rings for their order and position. The lower ring is actually made up of three rings. Always stagger the gaps in the rings to ensure proper sealing.

Clean the rods with spray cleaner. Install the rod bearing into the rod assemblies. The bearings have different edges. Make sure the beveled side goes toward the front of the engine on the number-1, -3, -5, and -7 rods and toward the rear of the engine on the number-2, -4, -6, and -8 rods. This allows the less beveled side to mate to the rod that shares the same crank journal.

Crankshaft and Main Caps

Once all of the rod/piston units are assembled and in order, you can install the crank and the main caps. Install half of the rear main seal (after dipping it in oil) and follow the included instructions to make sure it is installed facing the correct direction. Offset it so that about 1/2-inch of the seal is sticking up above the edge on one side of the block. This offset helps to prevent the seal from leaking.

The main caps are numbered 1 through 5. Lube the main cap bearings with assembly lube. The main caps are a tight fit. Make sure to position them level in the block and tap them into place with a hammer handle. Install lubricated ARP main bolts and torque to the ARP recommended torque specs.

Put the crankshaft bolt in place so you can easily rotate the crank. Give it a few turns to make sure it turns freely. Rotate the block up to about a 45-degree angle. Wipe the engine cylinder walls with cleaner and then with a clean rag soaked in oil. Begin with the number-1 rod assembly. Double-check the position

of the rings based on the factory service manual instructions. Apply assembly lube to the rod bearings. The number-1 cylinder is on the driver-side front of engine.

Turn the crank so that the number-1 crank journal is at the lowest point from the block. Dip the piston into a bowl of oil; make sure that all the rings are immersed. Using a ring compressor tighten the rings on the piston. Insert piston and guide the rod; do not scratch the cylinder wall.

Once in place, tap the top of the piston with medium force until it is fully in the cylinder hole. Then guide the rod onto the crank journal while continuing to tap the piston from the top. Put the rod cap on and tighten the rod nuts leaving them only snug.

Install the number-3, -5, and -7 rods and then flip the engine block so you can access the other side; install the number-2, -4, -6, and -8 rods following the same procedure. Turn the engine over and torque all the rod bolts to ARP specs.

While the engine is bottom-up, dip the rear main rubber seal unit in oil and install. Be sure to follow the instructions so that the seal is in the correct position. Offset it about 1/2 inch on the opposite side from where you installed the lower seal before putting in the crank.

Install two sticks on each side of the seal unit. Apply RTV liberally to the channels on each side then press the sticks into the RTV. Apply RTV to the block surface and carefully slide the unit into place; make sure that the sticks remain in place and do not slide out of position. This is a must if you do not want the seal to leak.

Put in the special headed bolts and finger-tighten. Apply more RTV to the outside edges of the unit where

it meets the block. Let the unit set for 5 minutes and then torque to specs.

Timing Chain

Turn the engine to the upright position. Install the new crank timing chain's lower sprocket; the timing marks must remain visible. Clean the new camshaft with spray cleaner. Lube all of the lobes thoroughly with the assembly lube. Carefully insert the cam making sure to support it all the way in; do not nick or scratch the bearings. Lube the upper and lower timing chain sprockets with assembly lube.

Position the upper sprocket so that the "0" is at 6:00 and the lower sprocket's "0" is at 12:00. Line up the cam's peg with the upper sprocket's hole. When the chain, upper sprocket, and lower sprocket are lined up and partially on, tap the upper sprocket onto the cam.

Install the cam bolt (or bolts) and torque. Use red Loctite on the threads.

Install the oil slinger onto the crank.

Oil Pump

Install the stock fuel pump with the pump rod in place. Notice the correct-headed bolts. Use new gaskets and RTV seal when you attach the oil pump. We suggest you replace the stock pump with a high-volume pump. It looks stock but provides more oil flow to the engine.

Do not torque until you have installed the distributor driveshaft. Position the crank so that the number-1 piston is at TDC (top dead center) and the two "Os" or dots line up on the upper and lower timing chain sprockets.

Distributor Driveshaft

Lube the distributor driveshaft; use a large screwdriver to install it

---

with the slot in the 10:00 position. You have to turn the shaft as it goes in to get the gears to mesh. You may have to try several times to get the slot at 11:00. This position ensures that the distributor, rotor, and cap are in the correct position for the number-1 plug wire.

Torque the oil pump bolts now that the shaft is in place.

Windage Tray and Oil Pan

Now that the timing chain cover is installed, rotate the engine to the bottom-up position and install the oil pickup tube. Be careful when starting it; it is easy to cross-thread the unit. Tighten it with a pipe wrench until you have about 1/16- to 1/4-inch clearance between the pickup and the pan. Also check for clearance and fit of the windage tray.

The windage tray and oil pan require two gaskets. This engine's original gaskets were cork. Use cork gaskets because they do show after installation.

Spread a light coat of red high-temp RTV on the engine block. Place one gasket in the engine and coat it with a thin layer of RTV. Place the windage tray next. Coat the oil pan's rim with a layer of RTV and place the gasket on the pan. Then apply another layer of RTV to the gasket.

Place the pan on the block. Install the pan bolts, note the correct head marking, and snug all of the bolts.

Let it set for five minutes and tighten each one until you see the gasket start to swell toward the outside of the pan. At that point, do not tighten any further or you split the cork gasket.

Cylinder Heads

Start with the completed short-block in the upright position.

It is a good idea to chase each head bolt hole in the block with a tap to make sure they install correctly. Spray-clean all areas to remove any dirt or shavings; then re-wipe all of the pistons and head surfaces with a clean, freshly oiled rag.

Place the head gaskets on the block. Don't use any sealer on these gaskets.

Spray-clean the heads and wipe dry before installation. Then position each head onto the block. You do not have a left or right head; they are identical. Again, chase the threads where the intake bolts go. If using stock original head bolts, dip the threads in oil and insert them in the head. If using ARP bolts, apply the provided assembly lube to the threads and washers and then install.

Snug all bolts in place on both sides of the engine. Refer to the factory shop manual for the head bolt tightening sequence and torque spec. Remember that ARP bolts use different torque specs than the stock bolts. Spray-clean the new lifters and liberally lube with assembly lube, then slide them in the bores. If using new pushrods (or even the originals) clean and lube each end and install them in the lifter through the head. Lube each valve contact point. Stock rocker assemblies are very basic and yet very reliable for street use. The individual rockers have a left and a right, but the assemblies do not. The rocker shaft must have the oil holes facing toward the block. The spacer and all attaching bolts and brackets install a certain way. Clean each component and reassemble with oil on all parts.

Position each assembly on the head perches. It helps to have two hands to keep all the pushrods and rockers in line. Slowly tighten and

make sure you are not binding the pushrod that is not in the lifter and rocker recess.

Repeat for both sides. When the shaft is seated, torque to spec. We recommend using the valley pan gasket that has the heat crossover blocked. Unless you live in a very cold area or you plan to drive the car daily, you do not need the heat crossover functional. Also, if you do not block it off your intake discolors and blisters after a few hours of operation of the engine.

Only use the metal gasket; you do not need to use the additional felt gaskets that come in some kits. Be sure that the rails and bolts are cleaned and ready to install. Put a dab of RTV sealer in each corner and lay the gasket in place. Install the intake manifold and torques to spec. The negative battery cable on all wedge big-blocks is mounted underneath the return carburetor spring bracket. The cable was attached when the engine was painted. Many restoration articles have said that only a small portion of the cable was painted.

If you are lucky enough to have the original cable you need to duplicate the amount of paint actually on your cable. For most, however, that is not the case. Our engine has the original cable to use as a guide and it was almost entirely painted all the way to the end.

As you install the intake, be sure to mount the cable and then torque it down. On engines before 1970, a negative ground wire was used on the rear passenger side of the engine that was also attached and painted. We had the correct original bracket, with serration, bolt, and cable for a 1970 440 or 383. Harmonic balancer, water pump, water pump housing, inlet tubes, throttle bracket, any spark plug wire brackets, valvecovers with the PCV rubber grommet and valve mounted on the cover, and exhaust manifolds were also attached at the factory when the engine was painted.

Yes, exhaust; and the paint burned off as soon as the car was driven. Each owner has to decide whether or not he or she will paint the exhaust. Most people choose not to paint them, but to be completely factory correct they were painted.

Use cork gaskets on the valvecovers because they show. Attach all of the additional parts to your long-block. Then, mask off all open holes and wipe the entire engine with lacquer thinner.

Rebuilding a 383 Engine

The following is a step-by-step guide to rebuilding an original 383 engine.

Before you even start, make sure you have everything laid out, restored, and ready to install.

The block should have already been sonic tested, cleaned, and bored or honed before it's ready to assemble. The mains must be bored and ready to accept the correct main bearings, which are numbered for easy installation. Chase all threaded holes with a tap so you don't have any problems during assembly.

Be sure to check all plugs; and install them with sealer. You won't have any oil pressure if you miss one.

Remove the mains and clean them very carefully.

Bearing, Piston and Rod Preparation

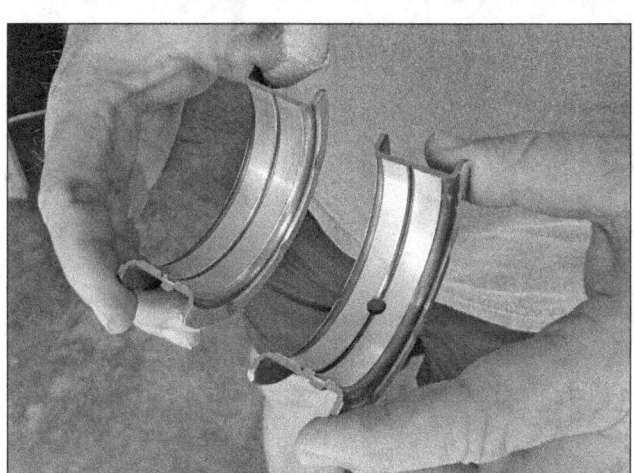

1 Open up the main bearings and identify the center main. The oiling holes must be inserted toward the top of the block.

2 Use assembly lube and insert the center main, followed by the other main bearings.

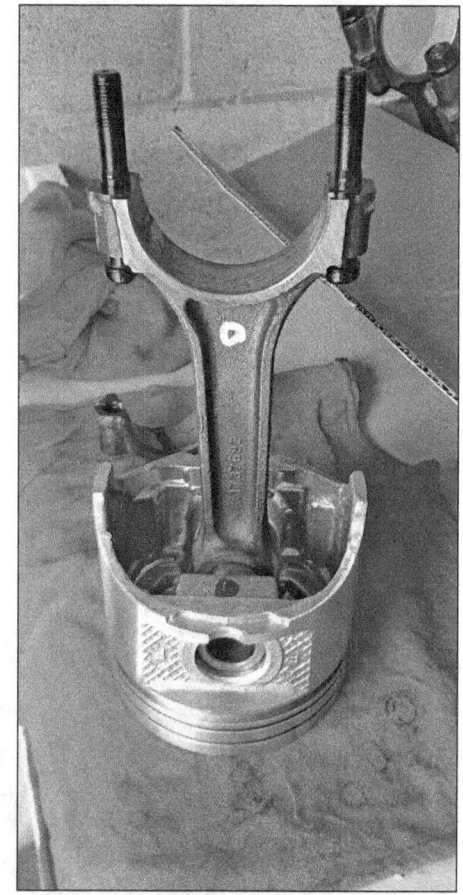

3 The machine shop returns the pistons and rods labeled correctly.

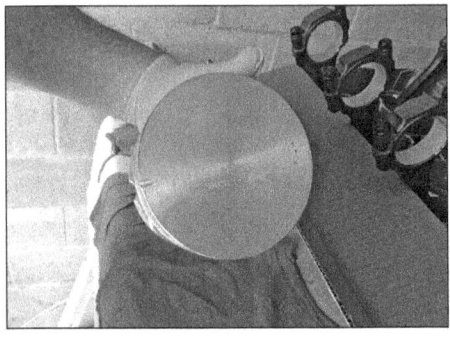

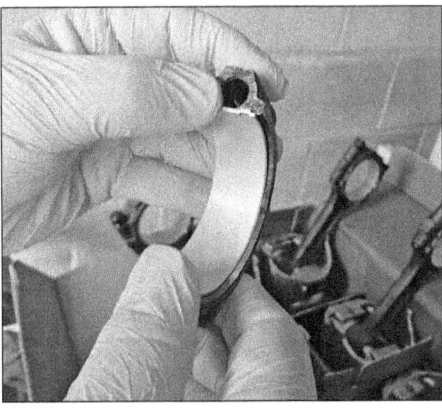

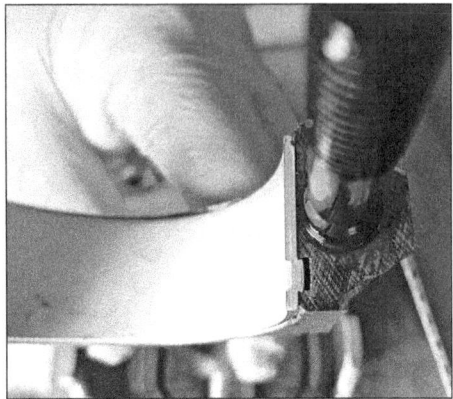

4 *The notch in the piston faces the front of the engine. The rods are always numbered and must match the rod and the cap with the same number.*

5 *Clean the bearing with spray cleaner, grease with assembly lube, and then install.*

6 *Notice the correct tang in the rod. The rod cap should always have a tang that matches.*

7 *Be sure to use the correct lube when seating the rod bolts and bearings. We recommend using new ARP rod bolts on an engine build. They are much better than original and almost never break.*

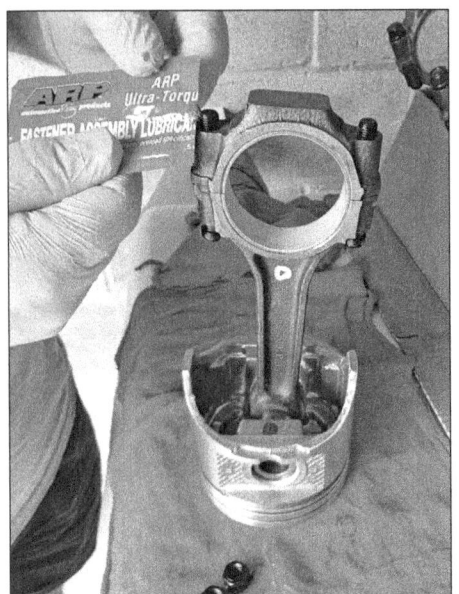

8 *Tighten the new rod bolts to specification in a vise before installation to seat them.*

9 *After all bearings are installed and all rod bolts are seated, place all of the pistons and rods in numerical order for installation into the block.*

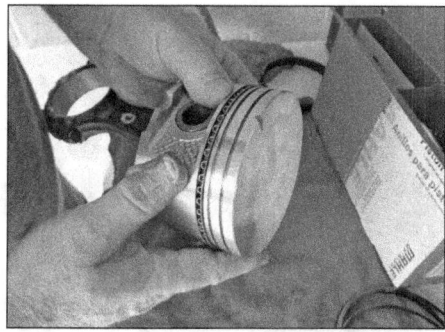

10 Following the instructions that came with the ring kit. Place the oil ring first. Next, place the upper and lower oil ring retainers; be sure to stagger the gaps according to the instructions.

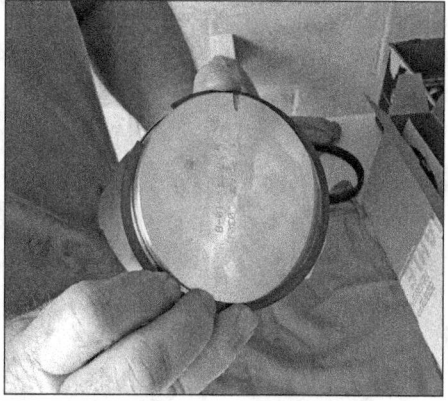

11 Install the compression rings next per the instructions. Be sure to insert the ring properly with the correct beveled edge upward.

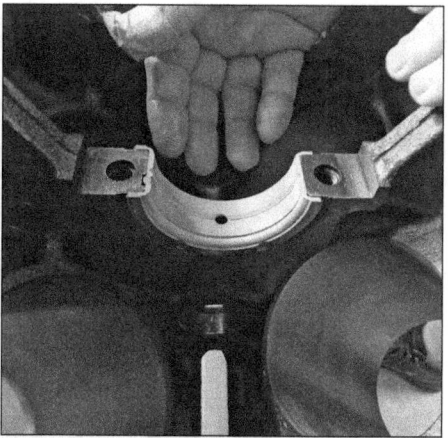

12 Double-check the main bearings and make sure the oiling holes are lined up.

13 The engine mounts are specific to each side and for what bolt and nut goes where. Take pictures or follow this example to install them correctly.

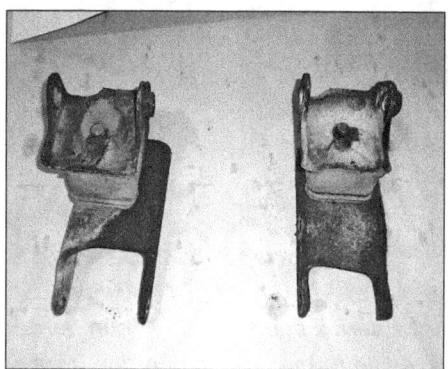

14 We always recommend purchasing new engine mounts when rebuilding an engine. Years and years of torque being applied weaken them over time.

15 Always use a certified assembly lube when building an engine. Under startup conditions it ensures that no damage occurs until the oil flow reaches the bearings.

16 Coat each bearing with moly lube and make sure the oiling hole is lined up properly. Be sure to install the upper rear main seal in the block. Follow the instructions provided with the seal.

Crank Installation

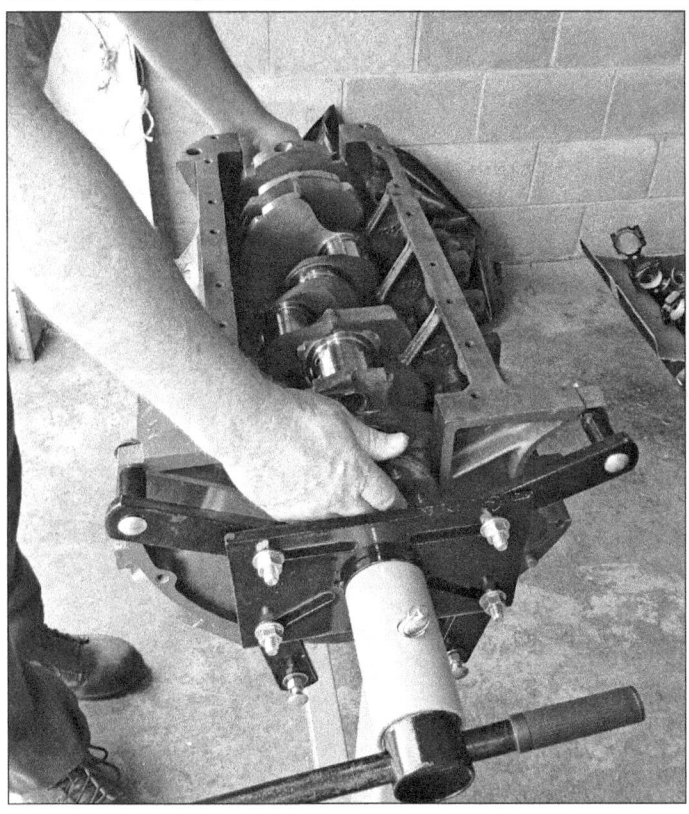

1 Drop in the crank and rotate it to make sure it spins freely. Watch for any catches or drag while turning the crank.

2 Begin to install each main bearing cap. They are numbered 1 through 5 with the number-1 bearing cap at the front of the engine. Be sure to install them in the right order.

3 The bearing caps are a tight fit; make sure to line them up evenly so that one side is not in farther than the other.

4 Sometimes you must tap the bearing caps with a hammer handle to make sure they fit properly. Do not use anything metal because it may damage the main bearing caps.

5 Snug all the bolts on the crankshaft in order. Again, make sure nothing is dragging and the crank turns smoothly. Torque all main bolts to specifications and check again to make sure that the crankshaft turns freely.

6 Begin to assemble the rod bearings. Pay careful attention to the chamfer on the edge of the bearing. Install the flat side of the bearing in the rod where number-1 and number-2 rods meet. The chamfered side of the bearing then matches the chamfer on the crank journal. This applies to the rest of the rods.

Piston and Rod Installation

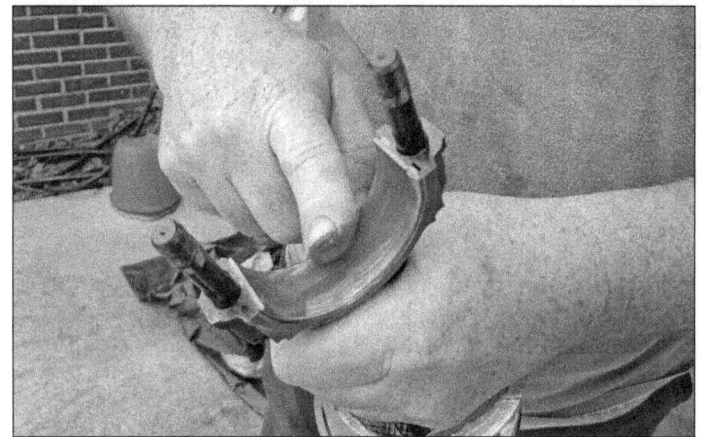

1 Pre-lube all of the rod bushings in preparation for assembly into the block.

2 Before inserting the pistons into each corresponding numbered hole, dip them into the assembly oil. This ensures that all of the rings are lubricated before assembly.

3 Wrap the spring compressor around the piston. Make sure that the rings have the proper staggered positions according to the instructions that came with the rings.

4 With the spring compressor tightened and in place, insert the assembly into the bore. Be careful not to scratch the cylinder.

5 Seat the ring compressor in the cylinder bore and tap the assembly into the bore, a little at a time, with a hammer handle. Never use anything metal or you may damage the piston.

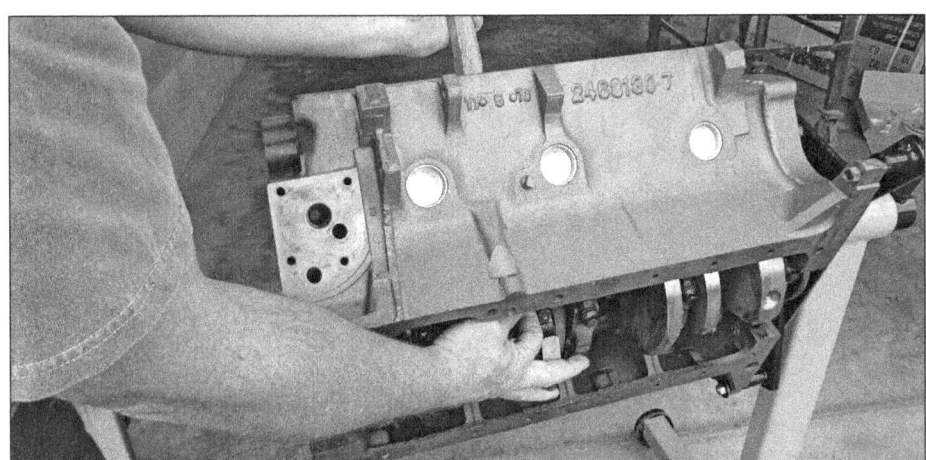

6 Make sure that the rod bolt does not scratch the bore or crankshaft. Install the correct rod cap and snug the nuts onto the rod bolt. Repeat this procedure until all pistons are installed. Torque the rod nuts to spec. Turn the crank and make sure that all of the pistons move freely in the engine bore.

Cam, Timing Chain and Rear Main Seal Installation

1 Clean and pre-lube all of the camshaft's lobes and the camshaft bearings in the block.

2 Install the camshaft; be sure that you do not nick any of the cam bearings. Work it in slowly, and clear each bearing as the camshaft goes into the block.

3 With the crank rotated so that the number-1 piston is at TDC, hold the timing chain and slide the crank sprocket on. At the same time, you can also line up the camshaft sprocket.

4 If the camshaft dot and the crank "0" are lined up, the cam installs without any advance or retard. Be sure to follow the instructions to set the cam because each manufacturer is different. Install with red thread lock and torque the cam bolt (or three bolts if it is a triple-bolt cam).

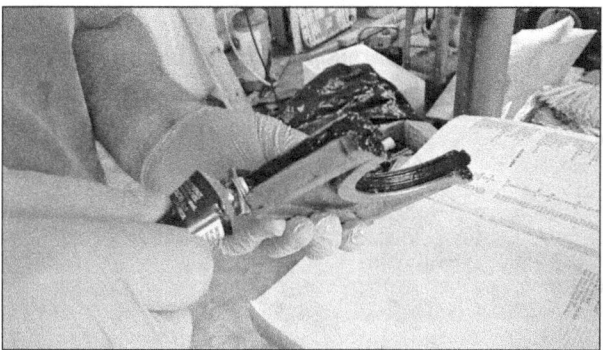

5 Install the rear main seal. Take every precaution to make sure the seal is installed correctly or it will leak. The rear main seal in a Mopar big-block is already prone to leaking. Two beveled "sticks" are located on each side of the aluminum seal retainer and the lower crank seal. Use plenty of silicone sealer on the side sticks. Do not use silicone on the rubber crank seal but dip it in assembly oil. Then, position the rubber crank seal so it is offset.

6 With the rubber crank seal offset, push in the already-installed upper crank seal to match the offset of the lower seal.

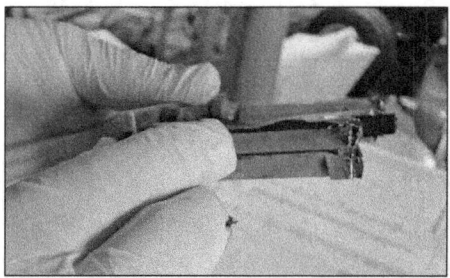

8 Work the seal retainer assembly into the block. Be sure that the sticks are all the way in the block as far as possible. Any gap and the seal will leak.

7 Push the side sticks into the recess in the seal retainer. Make sure that the wide part of the beveled stick is positioned to the outside.

9 Even when the seals are installed correctly sometimes a very small part of the stick seal needs to be trimmed off.

10 Fill the remaining recess with silicone to help ensure that you have no leaks after assembly. Torque the seal retainer bolts to spec. Do not use any extra silicone sealer inside the block.

Oil and Fuel Pump Installation

1 Install the oil pickup tube. If you are using the original be sure it is clean and the screen does not have any blockage. If you are using a new tube be very careful when starting it in the block or you may cross thread the fine threads. The pickup is very stubborn to get it all the way in place. You can use a pipe wrench to tighten it. Be careful not to bend or collapse the tube.

2 To test the tube's height and position, install and remove the windage tray and the oil pan as you go. The oil tube pickup cannot be flush against the pan bottom or oil starvation occurs. However, it only needs about 1/16-inch clearance.

3 Install the fuel pump pushrod. A plug is located just under the fuel pump opening on the block. Lube the rod with grease and insert it into the block. You see only a small portion of the rod when it is fully installed.

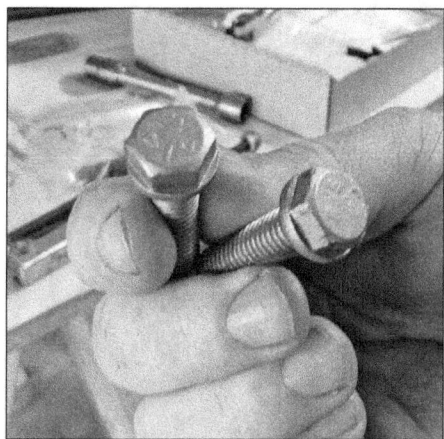

4 These are correct original fuel pump bolts; most engines have lost them over the years.

5 Coat the gasket with silicone on both sides to ensure no future leaks.

6 Position the fuel pump into the block. Make sure that the pump lever is seated correctly against the pump rod.

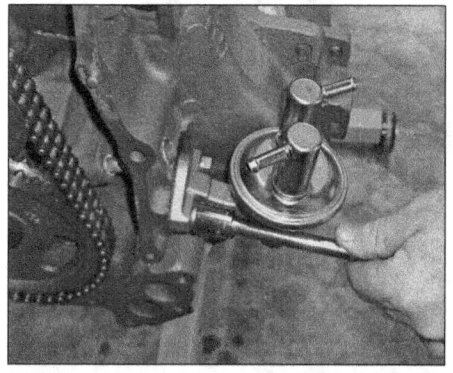

7 You feel some slight resistance from the pump lever when it is in the correct position. Install the bolts and torque to specifications.

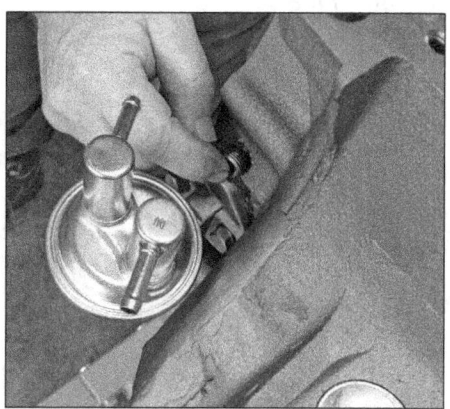

8 Apply silicone on the fuel pump pushrod access plug. Install it tightly.

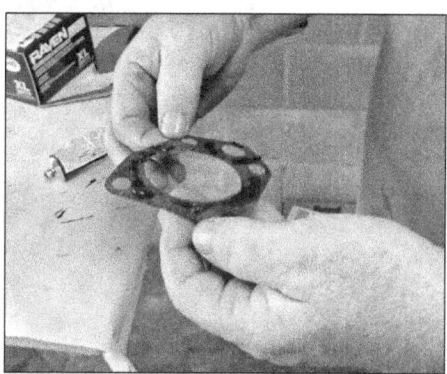

9 Always replace the original oil pump with a new high-volume pump. It looks the same and more oil flow in the engine is always a good thing.

10 Install the pump but don't tighten the bolts completely at this time. Install the oil pump driveshaft from the distributor. If you tighten the bolts now you will have difficulty positioning the rod in the pump.

11 The machine shop should have installed a new brass intermediate bushing in the block. Lube the oil pump driveshaft with assembly lube.

12 *Slide the shaft in and be sure that it seats in the oil pump.*

13 *The teeth of the shaft and the cam mesh together. To get the slot in the top of the shaft to the right position, hold the slot at about the 9:00 position to start.*

14 *Turn the shaft clockwise with a big screwdriver while supporting the shaft with the other hand. During insertion, the mesh of the teeth allows the shaft to turn to the desired 11:00 position. When the shaft is in position and seated in the oil pump, torque the oil pump bolts to spec.*

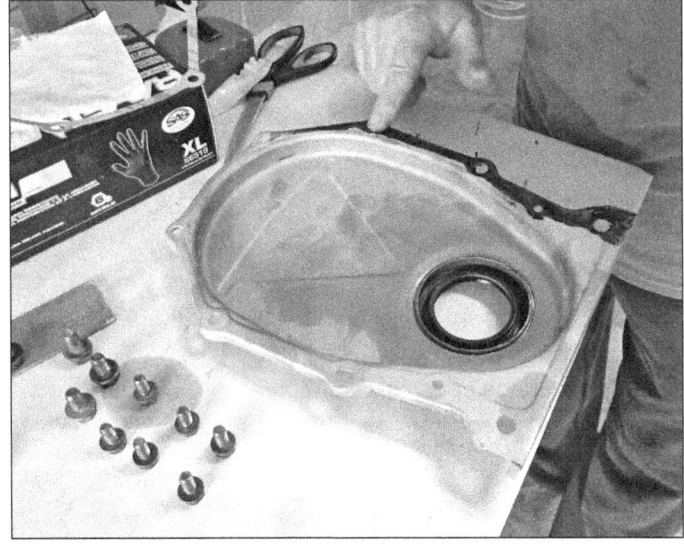

15 *Install the timing chain cover. It has a rubber seal mounted in a metal ring. The seal must be tapped into the cover. Again, make sure it is in the position shown here.*

16 *Install the oil slinger, which serves two purposes. It keeps the chain lubricated better and also keeps excessive oil off the crank seal.*

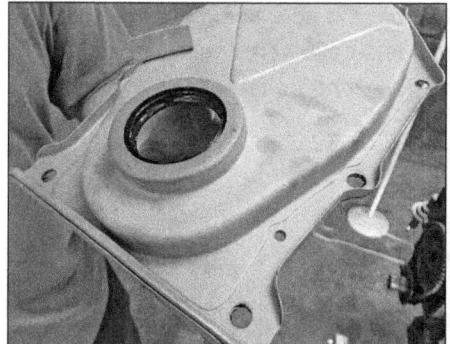

17 *The seal is installed correctly with a gasket and a thin coat of silicone and is ready to install on the block.*

18 *Always torque the front bolts to specifications. The timing chain cover has two different-size bolts.*

Oil Pan Installation

1 *You are now ready to install the oil pan and windage tray. This requires two cork pan gaskets. Apply high-temperature copper silicone on the oil pan. Coat both sides of the gasket with sealer and put the first gasket on the block.*

2 *Put the second cork gasket, with sealer, on the factory-correct 402 oil pan.*

3 *Position the windage tray on the block.*

4 This is an original, correct, pan bolt. Note the self-locking dot about halfway up the threads. Many enthusiasts have never seen this dot because, most of the time, the original bolts are long gone.

5 Finger-tighten the pan bolts all the way around. By doing this you don't flex the pan before you fasten them.

6 Snug the pan bolts with just enough pressure to have the equal pressure on the gaskets.

7 Tighten the bolts one by one while watching the two cork gaskets. Continue until you see the slightest movement of the gaskets and they start to bulge. Do not overtighten the cork or it will split and you will have leaks.

Head and Accessory Installation

8 Make sure all of the lifters are clean, even if they are right out of the box. Pre-lube all of the lifters with assembly lube and install them in the lifter bores. Be sure they move freely. Then install the head gasket. Some sets recommend not using any sealer.

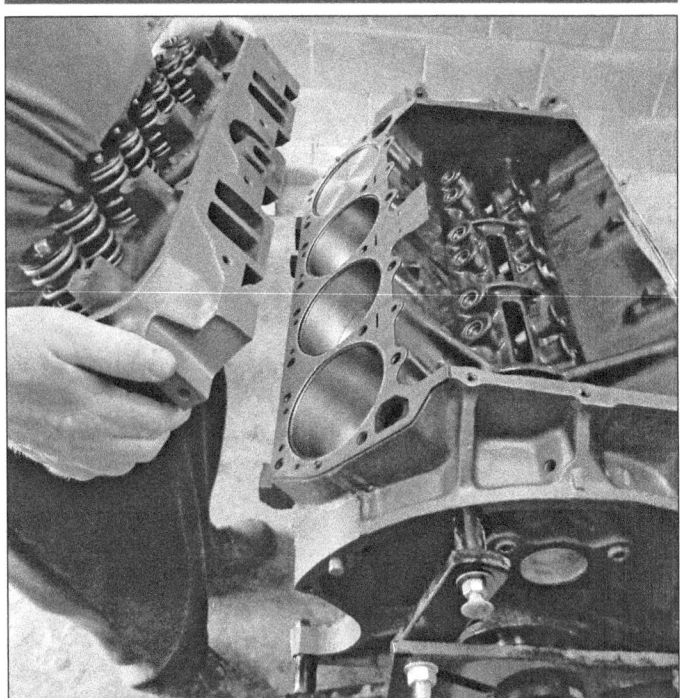

1 Place the already completely rebuilt and clean cylinder head on the block. Stock heads are identical so you don't have a left or right.

2 Once the head is in place positioning pins in the block keep it from falling off.

3 If you are using the original bolts make sure they are clean and then dip them in engine oil. If you are using new ARP bolts (shown) use the lube provided. If you are going to show the car in an OEM setting use only original-style head bolts. ARP bolts were used on this build because they are difficult to see and the new bolts do not have a chance to fail. Follow the tightening reference for the head bolts found in your factory service manual and torque all head bolts to spec.

4 Lube the ends of the pushrods and insert them into the lifters. Put some assembly lube on the ends of all the valves where they contact the original rocker arms.

5 You have a left and a right rocker, several spacers, different-size bolts with specific spacers, and a rocker shaft with oiling holes. If you have any doubt about how your rocker assembly goes together, you can use this picture as a reference.

6 Position the rocker assembly with all bolts in place.

7 Carefully line up each rocker, pushrod, and bolt with spacer as you set the assembly on the head.

8 It is good to have an extra pair of hands to hold the rockers and pushrods in position. Tighten the bolts slowly and equally. As you tighten, each rocker comes to rest at a different height based on the cam lobe's position. If you do not have everything in position you can bend a pushrod.

9 Torque the rocker assembly bolts to spec and repeat on the other side.

Intake Manifold Installation

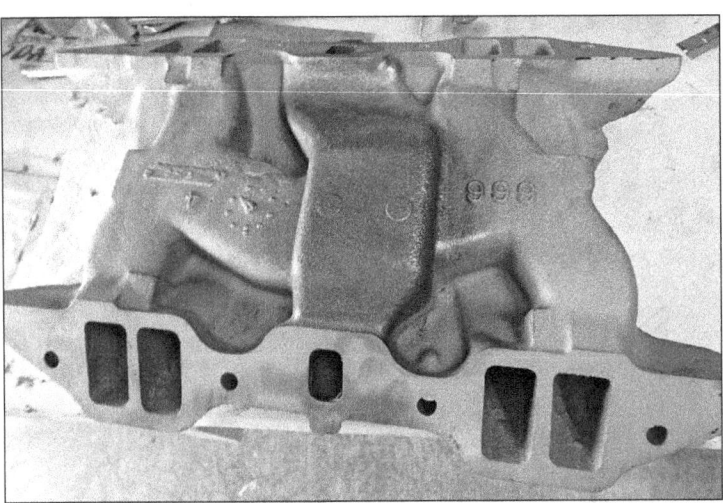

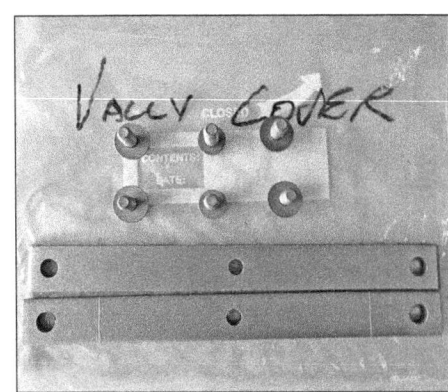

1 You are now ready to install the intake manifold. Even though this original intake was blasted you can see heat coloration of the metal. Unless you live in a cold area or you plan on driving this car every day, use the valley pan gasket that has the heat crossover blocked off. If you don't block the heat crossover with this gasket, all of your beautiful new paint burns off and discolors the intake.

2 These are the original valley pan bolts and bars. The washer indentions show where the two smaller bolts were. Not all engines have this; put it back the way you found it.

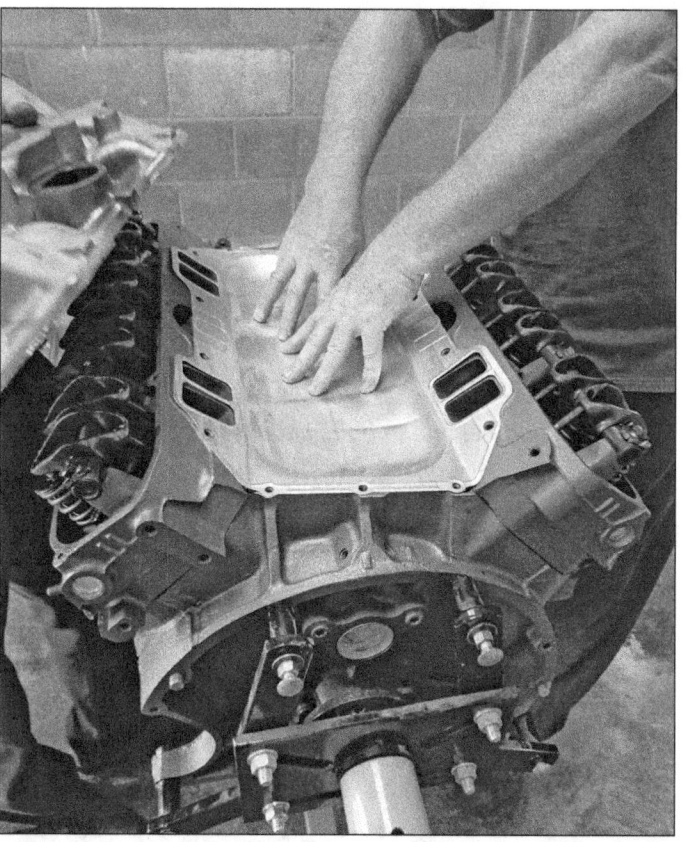

3 Before installing the valley pan gasket add some silicone on all four corners where the heads meet the block. No other sealer is needed on the mating surfaces of the valley pan gasket.

4 Press down the new metal gasket so it bends and conforms to the block and heads.

5 Again, an extra set of hands helps to hold the gasket in place while the intake is placed on the engine.

6 Place the retaining rails and bolts in the front and back of the valley pan and then tighten the bolts. A bevel is on each end of the rail; the longer side faces up.

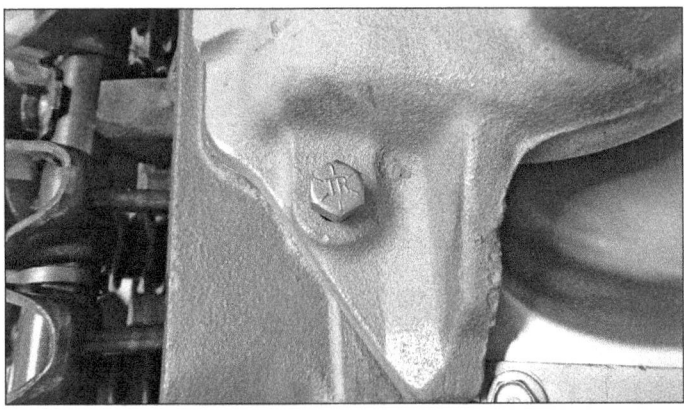

7 *The original intake bolts did not have any washers on the cast-iron intakes. The aluminum Dodge 1969½ 6-Pack and the Plymouth 1969½ 6-barrel intake originally had flat washers.*

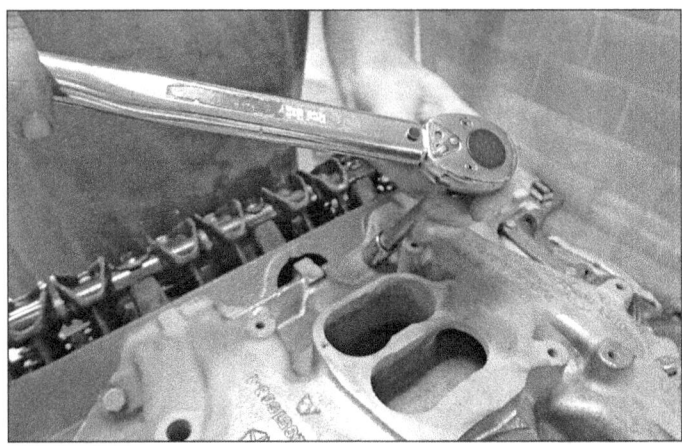

8 *Snug the intake bolts starting with the inner bolts, alternating from side to side, working toward the last outside bolts.*

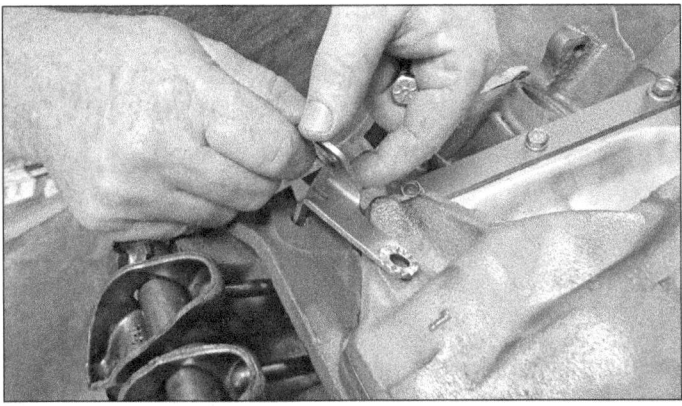

9 *The throttle-return bracket was mounted on the front driver-side intake bolt. They varied in style from year to year. This one is a 1971 type with serrations in the bracket. The 3 x 2 cars also had the serrations on the bracket. The negative battery cable is attached under the throttle return spring bracket. Attach it after the intake valley pan corner silicone seal has had a chance to dry.*

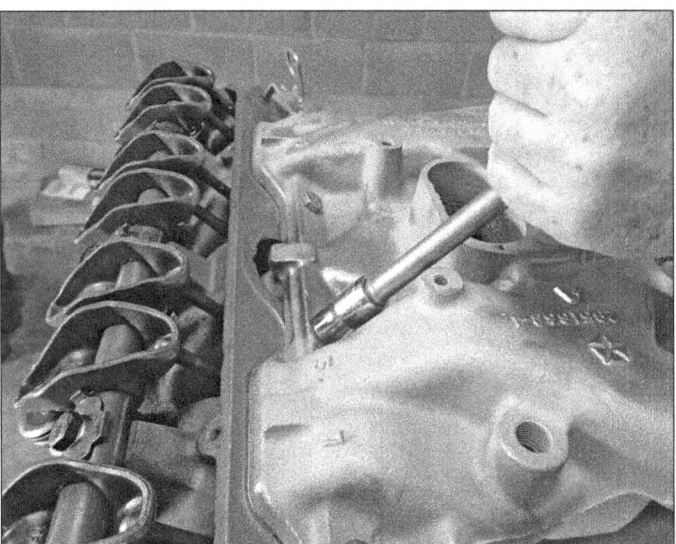

10 *After everything is in place and tightened equally, torque all the bolts to spec using the same inward-outward, side-to-side alternating pattern.*

Valvecover Installation

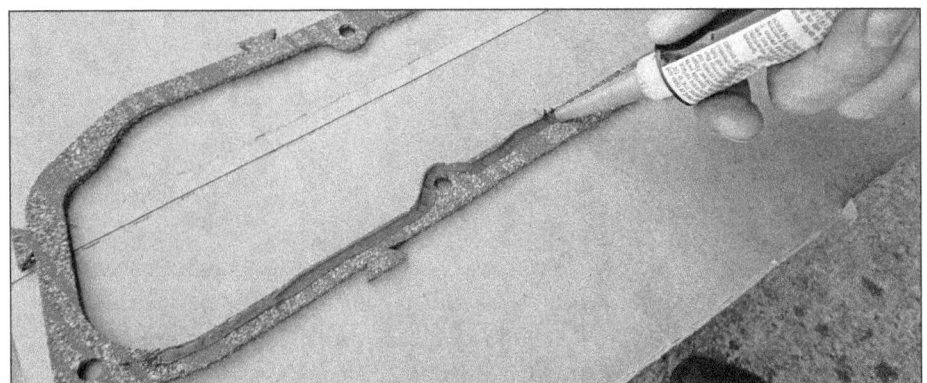

1 *Use cork gaskets because the engine originally used cork and the tabs of the valvecovers are visible. Use silicone sealer on both sides of the gaskets.*

2 Attach the gasket to the valve-cover first and then apply a thin coat of silicone sealer to the gasket.

3 Place the valvecovers on the heads and finger-tighten all the bolts. Then tighten each bolt 3/4 of a turn. Do not overtighten or the cork will split and the covers leak.

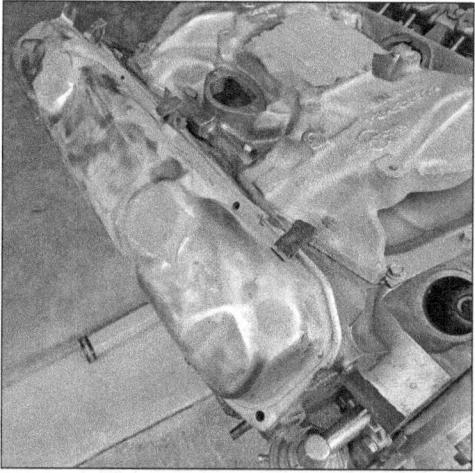

4 Tape off the oil filler hole and intake for paint.

Water Pump Installation

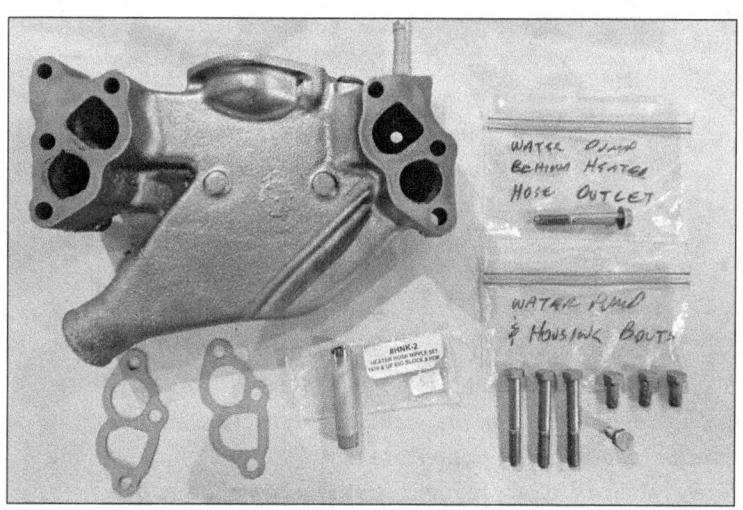

1 You install the water pump housing next. The only bolt that used a washer is the one behind the heater-hose nipple. Once the nipple is installed, you can loosen this bolt, but you cannot remove it. You can refer to this picture to identify the bolts on the water pump and water pump housing.

2 *After installing the water pump housing, put sealer on the threads of the heater-hose nipples. They must be tightened and not damaged. You can use this method to achieve flawless results.*

3 *Attach the negative battery cable and spark plug wire bracket.*

Engine Painting

1 *Use a grease and wax remover or a good grade thinner to clean everything that will be painted. Don't use any primer on the engine or the bellhousing.*

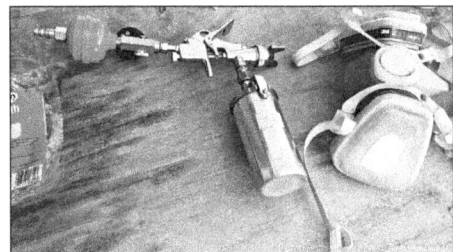

2 *You can use a touch-up gun to paint the engine. It makes it easy to get to all the little nooks and crannies.*

3 *The absolute best original paint match can be purchased from Frank Badalson. He sells pints of the single-stage enamel. It is reduced two parts paint to one part reducer. You should have enough paint for one good wet coat.*

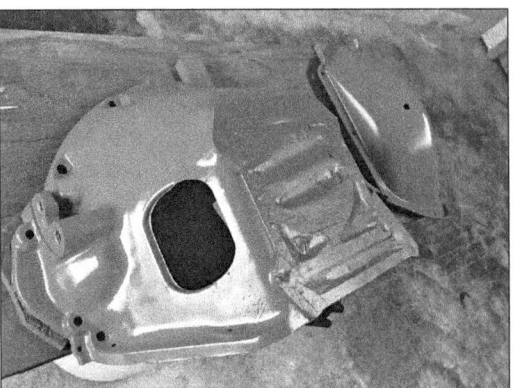

4 *Now it's decision time. Do you paint the engine the same way the factory did or do you paint it better than the factory? There is much discussion about how much paint actually went on the exhaust manifolds. The owner of this engine chose not to paint the exhaust manifold or the PCV valve, even though they were painted originally. The bellhousing and inspection cover were painted on the engine originally. Automatic transmissions were also installed on the engine during paint and only received overspray and some paint on the edges.*

6 *A full-size gun can be used to begin painting followed with a touch-up gun for tight spaces.*

7 *Your original negative battery cable may show paint all the way to the end of the cable. Paint the new one accordingly.*

5 Wet the floor (or ground) to reduce dust. A paint booth is preferable, but if you have a perfect day with no wind you can paint outside.

This fully assembled (minus the PCV valve and the exhaust manifolds) engine was painted better than factory. It is the correct color with not too much shine. It is correct with every bolt and part that originally came on it.

Engine Painting

You can paint an engine in two ways: with a paint gun or a spray can. Several brands and colors are marketed as the correct factory color. If your car is a 1966–1968 big-block it was painted Chrysler Blue. Many people refer to it as turquoise.

Also, if your car has air conditioning it was painted Chrysler Blue. All non-air cars in 1969–1970 were painted Street Hemi Orange. Chrysler produces spray cans of these paints, but they are not very close to the original color.

We highly recommend using a spray gun and acrylic enamel paint as was done at the factory. You get much more paint, a higher quality paint, and better coverage than with spray cans. If you cannot use a gun, use PlastiCoat Chrysler Orange. It has more gloss than original, but most people like its final results. It is very close to the original color and holds up well over time.

Frank Badalson paints are the closest in color and appearance to factory original. They can be purchased at Auto Restoration Parts Supply, along with many other factory-correct reproduction parts.

A pint of paint covers the engine. It is reduced as two parts paint and one part reducer. You do not use primer or hardener because the hardener adds gloss. You can use a touch-up gun or a high-volume/low-pressure (HVLP) gravity feed gun as we do.

Use short bursts and pay careful attention to keep runs to a minimum and still cover everything that needs paint. Always use a mask whether you paint outside or inside and have proper ventilation.

Wipe down the engine, blow off any dust with an air gun, and use a tack-cloth to be sure the engine is clean, clean, clean. Wet the floor to keep down the dust, and then shoot.

Remove the tape on the engine as soon as it is no longer tacky. You must be careful because you can still mess up the paint before it has a chance to dry overnight.

Engine Installation

The block should be factory correct in color, sheen, and painted components. By taking your time and paying attention to details, you can completely restore your engine and do most of the work yourself.

I suggest taking your engine to a dyno shop where they can break it in, tune it for maximum performance, and fix any problems before you install it in your ride. If that is not possible be sure to run the engine at startup at 2,000 rpm for 20 minutes to seat the rings and break in the cam.

Follow the steps in the factory service manual for installing the distributor, setting the firing order, routing the spark plug wires, setting up the carburetor and fuel lines, and installing the transmission on the engine.

After you restore the front suspension, as well as paint and assemble all of the parts, you can install the entire unit from the bottom of the car the same way you took it out. Do your best to have everything in the engine bay completely finished before you reinstall the assembly.

Transmission

You either have a manual or automatic transmission. You can change from one to the other, but may parts and an extensive amount of work are needed to accomplish the switch. The following is an explanation of the differences between the two types.

Manual Transmissions

Only a few transmissions were available in B-Body Chryslers during 1966–1970, which were all carry overs from earlier chassis. In the fall of 1963, Chrysler released an all-new transmission, the A-833, available in all B-Bodies ranging from vehicles equipped with slant-6s to those optioned with the legendary 426 Hemi. When introduced, the A-833 was equipped with a standard Hurst-Campbell Competition-Plus shifter and four fully synchronized forward speeds. It was built in Chrysler's Syracuse, New York, New Process Gear plant.

A-833 manual transmissions found in B-Bodies differed from those found in A-Bodies. The primary difference was in the extension housing and mainshaft length, low-gear ratio, and rear flange size. Although smaller, the manually shifted A-Bodies carried a stouter 3.09:1 low gear, which better assisted with initial acceleration, even when paired with a smaller-displacement engine.

In the following years, Chrysler improved on the A-833 in 1965 with an improved and redesigned 1-2 shifter fork to assist second-gear powershifts. More changes followed in 1966. The Hurst shifter went away, replaced by a hollow-shaft Inland unit. Then the ball-and-trunnion front U-joint was replaced with a more typical sliding-spline yoke.

Other improvements for 1966 included a new speedometer pinion setup (larger pinions and adapters) for more precise calibration, and a new gearset for the new Street Hemi models, featuring Oilitebushings lining each gear as well as new, stronger gear-tooth angles. Hemi cars with A-833 transmissions also featured a new, larger input shaft, with a larger (308) bearing and retainer and coarse-spline clutch disc.

Fatefully, in 1967, Chrysler redesigned the synchronizers. Brass stop rings were designed to eliminate stop ring breakage on hard shifts. A significant flaw was eliminated.

A-833 4-Speed

Be sure to have the correct parts for your specific bellhousing and flywheel for the year of your car. An 11-inch bell and 143-tooth flywheel that used an 11-inch clutch was common.

In 1970, Chrysler changed to a 10.5-inch bellhousing, 130-tooth flywheel, and 10.5-inch clutch. Again, have the entire unit rebuilt and all of the seals replaced. Inspect the clutch, replace the clutch plate, and refinish the flywheel. Replace the throw-out bearing and the clutch linkage hardware. The quality of your parts affects the quality of the operation and performance of your car.

The bellhousing and inspection cover were painted at the same time as the engine. Therefore, the bellhousing shows various amounts of paint coverage from total to just overlapping where it attaches to the engine. The transmission is natural as-cast and can also be painted.

This is also a great time to inspect and rebuild or replace the shifter, depending on its condition. Check the input shaft bearing and replace it if necessary. Also check the clutch boot condition; it almost always has to be replaced.

Automatic Transmissions

Of all of Chrysler's TorqueFlite models, the A-727 (which replaced the A-488 in 1962) is the most common among B-Body Chryslers. Once assigned to all V-8-equipped Chryslers until 1964, the A-727 was designed primarily for trucks and heavy-duty applications. Using an aluminum case rather than the outgoing A-488's cast-iron case (shaving off nearly 60 pounds), the A-727 previously used a pawl (lock) for parking. On some 1964-and-earlier models, a lever actuated it.

In 1966, the rear pump was eliminated, while the 1962–1965 A-727s had front and rear pumps, as did the 1960–1965 A-904. The differences among the 904, 998/999, and 727 were largely in the size of the transmission case and internal components, as well as the torque converters.

The A-904 and A-727 had virtually identical components, but in smaller scale for the 904.

A-727

Have the entire unit rebuilt. Now is a good time to have a shift kit installed, if you choose. You can upgrade the torque converter based on the final engine specs (that is, cam profile).

Inspect the transmission mount and replace as necessary.

The finish of this transmission body is aluminum. It can be soda blasted or cleaned and painted with high-quality aluminum-color paint or left natural. The transmission pan is natural steel and the bolts are black phosphate. The inspection cover is also natural.

Rear-End Rebuild

With limited space in this book we highly recommend purchasing a copy of *Jeep, Dana & Chrysler Differentials: How to Rebuild the 8¼, 8¾, Dana 44 & 60, & AMC 20*. It is a thorough guide to the rebuilding process of your B-Body rear end.

Rear Components Finishes

Here is a short list of the correct finishes for the various parts of the rear suspension.

Finish	Component
Semi-gloss black	Rear axle tube and brake backing plates, spring hangers (these can also be natural), shocks
Natural metal	Shock plates, shackles, U-bolts, rear brake hose bracket, center section, axles, brass distribution block, spring clamps, springs, spring hangers, emergency brake cables, drive shaft, brake drums
Gold cadmium	Front spring hanger bolts, vent tube on rear axle
Yellow	Rebound bumper straps
Black zinc	All attaching hardware nuts and bolts
Clear zinc (silver)	External tooth washer used with axle vent tube

MISCELLANEOUS MECHANICALS

When your powertrain is complete, you can add some functionality and some amenities to your B-Body. This chapter shows you how to incorporate some civility and creature comforts into your Mopar project.

Wiper Motor

As you restore the functionality of your B-Body, it's worth reviewing various accessories on your car, including the wiper motor, drive links, arms, and blades. An aged and discolored wiper motor can cost several points in judging and can otherwise detract from a clean and attractive engine compartment. Equally, a non-functioning wiper motor can be a safety hazard if ever caught in a sudden rainfall. The base trim–level B-Bodies typically came with a simple two-speed wiper motor; higher-optioned models came with the three-speed. For those cars equipped with a three-speed motor, the armature barrel came from the factory with dichromate zinc plating that can fade over the years.

A cursory search on eBay shows that similar motors in equally rough shape go for a few hundred dollars,

so it's worth having your motor properly restored. This is not the type of job for the everyday automotive enthusiast, so we strongly suggest having the motor professionally restored.

Disassembly

When you send a wiper motor to be restored, the motor is disassembled to assess the condition of all the internal components. For example, rust can collect on the rotator, as the factory shrink-wrapped wire sheathing can be cracked and/or non-existent.

Disassembling the motor starts with removing the plate covering the gear set. Inside of the housing, the lever attached under the cover fits into the mechanism operating the gear. The larger components (the armature barrel, aluminum motor gear body, end plate, and motor plate) must be sent to a plating shop.

A proper restoration shop uses both plastic shrink-wrap and factory-correct nylon sleeves on the wires. Even NOS shrink end caps were used to complete the wiring. Upon reassembly, new brushes, brush springs, wire insulation, shrink caps, and gaskets are needed to not

only restore the look but also the functionality of your wiper motor.

Reassembly

The wire windings must be cleaned and rewrapped in new cardboard sleeves. With the armature fully assembled, the two long screws that run the length of the barrel must be tightened. They are threaded into the aluminum motor body. The armature barrel, now freshly plated in dichromate zinc, is polished to remove any surface blemishes before being reinstalled.

The end plate, which was clear zinc plated, is outfitted with new brushes and new brush pressure springs. Before reattaching the rotator to the end plate, the windings are cleaned and wrapped in new wire sheaches. New short-circuit protective cardboard is slipped between the armature base and the rotator before seating the barrel.

With the head reinstalled with a new replacement worm gear and restored shaft (the gear requires a little wiggling to get it back on), all of the components are properly lubed and capped with a new switch plate gasket.

The switch plate, which was correctly plated, is rewired with each of the new wires soldered in their original factory locations.

New OEM-colored nylon and shrink-wrapped wires are installed, connected by NOS shrink cap connections. The plate is topped with a liberal dollop of ochre red sealant. This keeps the soldered wire points from the elements.

Wiper Motor Restoration

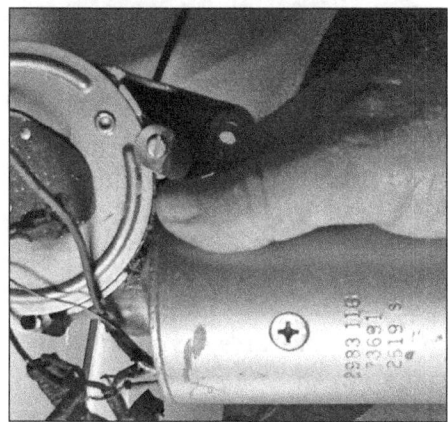

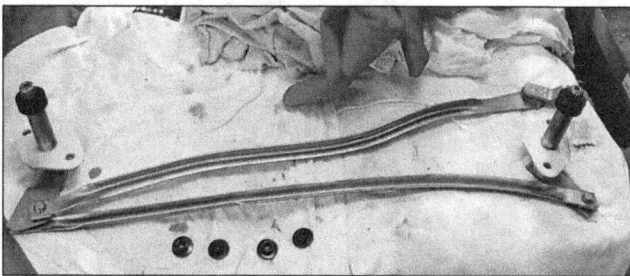

1 If your under-dash wiper assemblies need to be rebuilt they can be disassembled, cleaned or blasted, and painted with Seymour's Stainless Steel paint. Each pivot needs to be cleaned and lubricated so it turns back and forth freely. The nut that attaches the main pivot to the wiper motor is red.

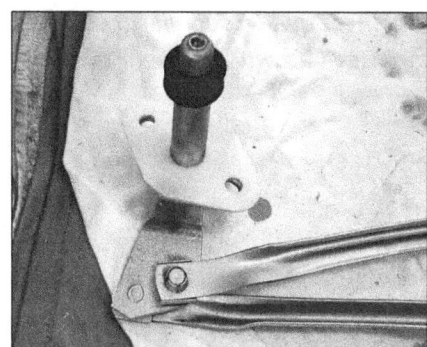

This wiper motor is a three-speed. Your car could also have a two-speed wiper motor that is black; instead of lying flat against the firewall it stands up. These motors are date coded and have the part numbers of the particular application. This motor has a date code of the 251st day of 1969 and came from a 1970 B-Body.

2 Purchase a wiper pivot seal kit and rebuild the pivots. This is the only way to ensure that you do not have water leaking onto your feet after the wipers are installed. Carefully install the linkage, making sure you have the correct positioning of both pivots and the linkage. Make sure it moves freely. Test the motor and the linkage for proper function before installing the dash.

3 Red paint remains on the ends of this three-speed wiper motor mounting studs. That is the way it came from the factory. The wiring pigtail plugs into the bulkhead connection box.

4 This is a correct reproduction wiper fluid bottle and pump. The forward opening of the cap is correct. Some bottles have the cap opening from the rear, which is incorrect. The body of the washer motor is white and cad plated and the ground wire goes toward the front of the bottle and is attached with the front screw. The attaching screws are black phosphate. The cap has the original recess and is not solid. Fluid has not been added and is blue.

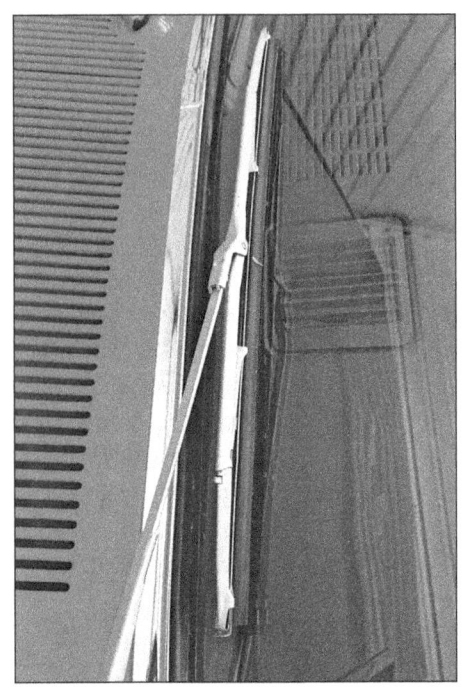

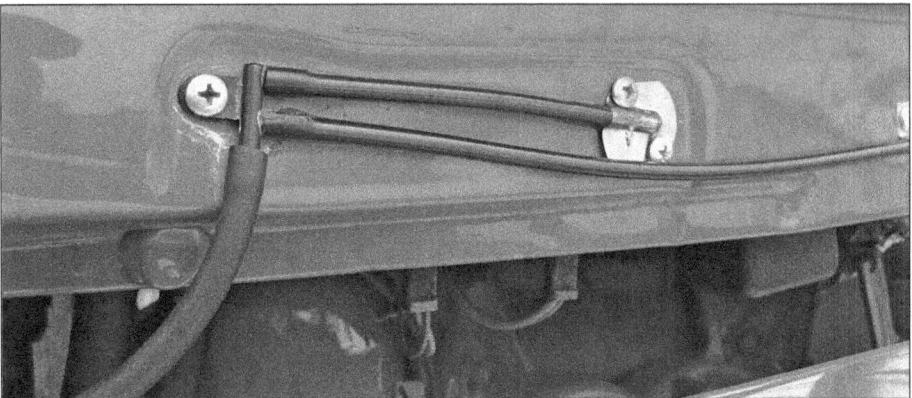

5 *Two styles of wiper blades are correct. The most popular is this Anco refill style. The wiper arms have "15B" stamped on them. The only exception is that those for convertibles do not have a stamp.*

6 *The correct washer hoses are ribbed and are available as reproduction. Replace the tee and the screws with the new kit. Make sure to seek out the highest quality supplier (such as YearOne or Classic Industries) that guarantees its products.*

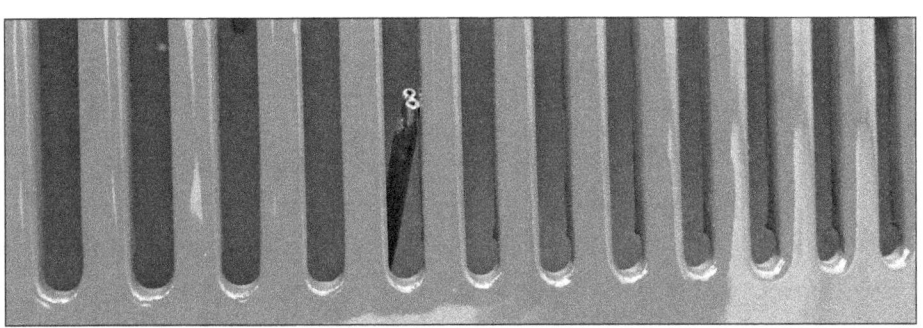

7 *The washer nozzles go down through the body and come out in the grid of this model. They can be bent so they spray the fluid on the windshield correctly.*

Grille

In less than a decade, a massive influx of aftermarket and restoration-grade parts have appeared, saving automotive enthusiasts thousands of dollars and hours spent hunting for original equipment. Only a few years earlier, finding replacement parts for an original grille required scouring forums, pages of eBay listings, and rifling through broken plastic and pitted and bent trim moldings at swap meets. Thankfully, companies such as YearOne and Classic Industries have helped to save you time and money.

Some models, including Road Runners and GTXs, benefit from readily available replacement grilles. Others, such as Dodge Chargers, Super Bees, and Coronets, are more difficult to come by. And while the metal frames are available, much of the molded plastic is rare. Because of this, consider purchasing several grilles so you can piece together one suitable grille. Cherry picking the pieces that are the easiest to clean, patch, and repaint can save valuable time and money.

Ranging from very basic to exceptionally complicated, Chrysler B-Body grilles can be as straightforward as a 1968 Road Runner or 1970 Super Bee, or as difficult as a 1969 Dodge Charger or a 1970 Superbird.

In the case of the Charger's grille, a metal frame features twin dual-headlight buckets with adjustable spring-loaded cups. Cleaning the frame requires not much more than a hammer and dolly to straighten up some bent edges and steel wool to scuff the surfaces in preparation for painting.

Plastic Repair

The key to repairing a split or break in the original plastic is to expose fresh material for the bonding agent. Because some plastic restoration sealants can be pretty pricey, many choose to use a two-part catalyst such as JB Weld to adhere and fill gaps.

Use an electric Dremel to clean up any open or jagged edges. If the cracks are too wide to simply fill in, use small patches of scrap metal to bridge the gaps, adhering them to the back of the plastic panel.

Because molded plastics have a tendency to return to their original shape and contour, much of the split and cracked plastic pieces only need to be coaxed into place before being permanently held back in form. With a pair of tin snips and some spare scraps of sheet metal, some small strips can act as a bridge holding two fractured pieces together.

Take care not to mix the two-part bonding agent too hot; a conservative amount can be applied into the crack itself. By holding the crack closed, a second more liberal amount can be added to the back (which remains unseen to most) where the small metal strip can be applied and eventually covered up. Applying the necessary pressure to close the gap until the compound cures can be done by hand (although that's pretty time consuming) or with a low-pressure C-clamp to avoid further cracking or damaging your original plastic.

Before the compound is fully cured and while it is still a bit pliable, use a razor blade to scrape off the excess from the visible side of the newly sealed crack. Be careful not to remove too much.

You can wrap a socket in sandpaper for the proper radius and start sanding the now fully cured sealing compound. Start with 60-grit and move to a finer 220-grit to knock down the cured compound. Continue sanding and filling any exposed pours and fissures, patching cracks, and filling in small holes where you find them.

Plastic and Frame Paint

Argent silver and semi-gloss black are the two most common colors found on Mopar B-Body grilles. Obviously, depending on your application, your needs change. A handful of different-widths and sizes of painter's tape are mandatory. It is much easier to paint each plastic piece individually, so start by coating everything with a spray adhesion promoter. This colorless spray helps bind paint to plastic and is a worthwhile extra step.

We know that it's difficult to wait for paint to dry, but don't peel off your tape too soon or you will have to repeat the process. While the chrome and stainless are off being refinished, you can take the opportunity to finish other parts of your grille. This includes cleaning and scuffing the frame before painting it.

If you're not too concerned with making a 100-point restoration, and really just want to freshen up an otherwise okay grille, spray can repaints can be effective. With a can of paint adhesion promoter, coat the scuffed and exposed plastic to help the paint bond better. Next, with a couple of cans of semi-gloss black and argent silver, mask off each piece in layers, which allows you to paint in stages.

Brightwork

With the entire grille repaired and painted, it is ready for its newly straightened and polished brightwork. Because most of the factory Mopar trim is made in stainless, be sure not to have your pieces chromed but merely polished.

Decorative emblems such as the "Charger" script or Super Bee emblems require a finer touch to clean, sand, and repaint. Replacement aftermarket pieces are eas-ily acquired from outlets such as YearOne or Classic Industries.

Trim Repair

Not all trim is created equal; aluminum sill plates, a pot-metal side-view mirror and gas cap, stainless door top trim, and die-cast stainless steel trim all require different types of restoration. With the variety of metals in a variety of conditions and lusters, you must evaluate which pieces are worth replacing, re-chroming, or re-polishing.

Counting from the front to the tail, the average B-Body can rack up nearly 40 individual brightwork items, including the front and rear bumpers, their accompanying pairs of bumper-ettes, multiple pieces of grille trim, windshield surround trim, side drip rails, side-view mirror, side-window

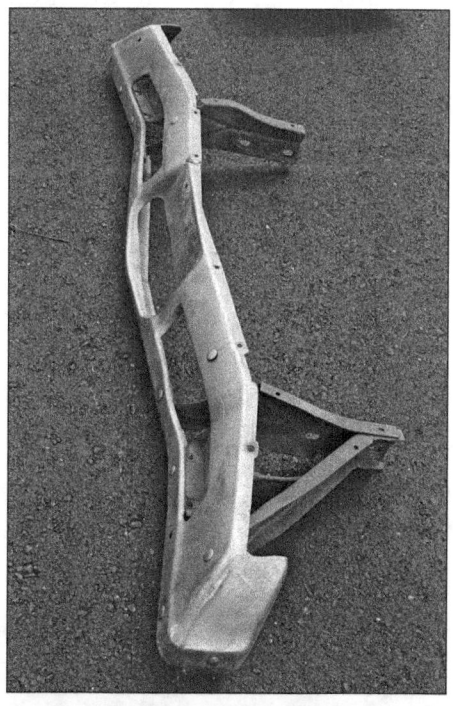

End-cap your B-Body Mopar with a set of bumpers. Outsource the chrome replating because the process is too environmentally hazardous to be handled at home.

moldings, vent-wing window frames, side-window seals, door handles, door locks, various emblems (grille, door, fender, quarter panel, rear), gas cap and its base plate, rear-window surround trim, taillight valance surround trim, and taillight lens trim.

Proper brightwork is like good movie special effects; if done right, nobody should notice. On Chrysler B-Bodies, there is far more chrome, stainless, aluminum, and pot-metal brightwork than you might realize.

Polishing and Buffing

Yet, with many original pieces, a Saturday morning spent with a clean rag and a small can of metal polish does the trick. Unfortunately, trying to hand polish the chrome plating on door handles or other pieces often can prove to be difficult or outright unsuccessful. Even passing over them with a buffing wheel on a two-speed electric drill sometimes does not remove the discoloration.

Most aftermarket outlets sell new door handles with chrome push buttons and not black buttons. Be sure you match what your car came with.

Items that do take well to some elbow grease are pieces made from harder materials such as stainless steel and the front and rear window reveals. Buffing these pieces can save a great deal of money and patience, as the front windshield trim (or "reveal") is currently on a pretty widespread back order, particularly as all bodies between 1968 and 1970 used the same trim.

Straightening

If they're in rough shape, it's worth having your bumpers straightened. Bumpers have a nasty way of rusting from the back if not properly treated. You notice this by a discolor-

ing or yellowing of the chrome from the front. Similar to rust bubbling up through the paint, the only way to remedy it is to strip the plating, address the cancer (media blasting or chemical dipping are good solutions), and replate. If you're not looking to replace your factory trim with aftermarket pieces, it's worth doing some due diligence to find a local chrome shop for straightening and buffing.

Most plating shops discount their rates depending on the size of the order. The more parts you bring in, the cheaper it becomes.

Re-Chroming

Although the aftermarket has grown exponentially over the past few years, particularly for Mopar lovers, enthusiasts have the tendency to think, "I'll just replace it." Although that might be a viable option nowadays, the cost can add up.

When tastefully done, brightwork can really make your paint pop. Re-chroming, can be pretty controversial, particularly if you plate items that weren't originally plated or getting a result that doesn't match the original product.

The down sides to re-chroming crop up particularly when considering textured surfaces. Original Charger and Challenger gas caps have a brushed surface that re-plating completely covers.

For many project cars, you simply don't have everything. The drip-rail trim may be gone, removed years ago; a replacement simply needed to be purchased. But that's not to say that it couldn't have been restored if necessary.

Drip-rail trim is often uncommonly expensive (about $250 per set). The stainless steel trim actually

rolls onto the B-Body's stamped railing deceptively easily. You can keep the protective blue film on the unit until it is fully installed. Then, when installed and the film removed, you attach the corner piece, connecting the two-part drip-rail trim together.

Reassembly proceeds a lot easier if each of your parts has been fitted beforehand. Re-plating has a nasty tendency to alter the close tolerances of smaller parts. Stainless steel items such as the belt line moldings and drip-rail trim are surprisingly durable and resist more pitting and aging than will softer components.

Many metal polishers can restore old emblems, smaller trim pieces, and taillights. When replacement taillights can cost $150 each, restoring the ones you have might be worth investigating.

Electroplating

The electroplating process has several steps and uses tanks full of caustic chemicals. Certain metals react better than others to the plating process, stainless being the most resistant due to its durability. Each piece is thoroughly washed in an electrified soap bath before being dipped in an acid bath.

Each piece is then submerged in nickel acid before soaking in nickel chloride. When washed, the part goes in a copper bath, and then a final round of washing before a chromium bath. Washing off the residue and passing the part under the buffing wheel, you can see the full luster of the newly plated part.

The pieces are passed under the buffing wheel before being cleaned in electrified baths. Because various metals react differently to the acid baths and bonding agents, each metal has a slightly different process.

Plating the pieces actually helps them stand up better than simply buffing them.

Phosphating

Phosphating (also called Parkerizing) can be done with zinc or manganese; both produce varying levels of gray to almost black (depending on the concentration, age of bath, length of time in the solution, and base material). The biggest difference between the two is the level of porosity at the microstructure level and depth of color.

Automotive hardware is generally made of zinc whereas many guns are made of manganese. Zinc also makes a good base for painted surfaces or can be oiled (sealed) for an attractive gray finish. As an alternative to oil, you can use a water-soluble sealer available from Caswell plating. This sealer can be left natural for a beautiful zinc finish or painted over at a later date.

Equipment

Phosphating requires a stainless steel or porcelain pot; it needs to be heated to approximately 180 to 200 degrees F. You need to season the bath prior to the first use (one time only as long as you continue to use a portion of your previously seasoned bath for future jobs). This is easily accomplished with iron filings or shavings and a coffee filter.

We first tried a propane camp stove for heating, but found it impossible to keep the temperature from creeping over the boiling point. Now we use a candy thermometer and double-boiler method with a large electric skillet from a garage sale. The skillet has water in it, and the solution is in a stainless pot sitting in the water. Temperature control is good. A Teflon skillet with water and a stainless pot inside works okay, too.

The average home user can accomplish phosphating pretty easily for a minimal investment. The process is convenient and the phosphate can be easily stored in plastic containers for long periods, making it easy to use later to freshen up details. (We tend to refinish even brand-new hardware if it doesn't have a good finish.) We don't recommend performing the process in your home; a garage is the better location, with an old stove or electric portable burner providing the heat.

Component preparation can vary but, in general, we blast first and often use a wire wheel for a nice finish prior to plating. The exception is that you may elect to skip the wire polish if you intend to paint the part.

Materials

Zinc phosphate is not a great corrosion protector; you may receive a box of new parts that already show corrosion. Zinc's ability to deter corrosion is largely dependent on the oil or sealer placed on the porous surface.

With the proper products you can replicate almost every finish and know that when you're done you have a good protective layer against corrosion, as well as a great base for painted items.

One source of phosphating solution is Shooter Solutions. This company claims that the solution is simply darker, but it's actually manganese. You can obtain zinc phosphate from Brownells. You can source electro deposited zinc with or without brighteners, yellow chromate, clear blue chromate, OD chromate, and black chromate from Caswell.

Prep Your Parts

It takes a little effort to prepare your fasteners, but it's worth the effort in the long run. Fasteners, such as body bolts, do not need to be restored if they are going to be painted. Just coat them with a phosphoric acid called Rust Cure. Then re-coat a week later, wipe, and they are ready for paint in one week.

Before tossing all of your fasteners in a bucket to get plated, take the time to document each one. You also have to separate the fasteners that are zinc clear, black, and yellow (gold) because they are barrel tumbled separately. Take a picture of each, along with markings on the head, and store in a Ziploc bag with the description written clearly on it. Also weigh each fastener on a digital scale and log it in a notebook. It does take time, but when you get everything back it is much easier to sort things out.

It's really not that difficult or horribly inconvenient, and this way you don't confuse yourself with what goes where. When you find a bolt or two that have been forgotten (maybe left on a sub-assembly) they are easy to plate at the same time as the parts that you've put in baggies.

The Process

Don't blast; just degrease and dunk your fasteners in vinegar for half-day periods to clean them. Then use a brass wire brush to chase the threads if necessary. Wear gloves to prevent fingerprints.

Because some time may pass between cleaning the fasteners and Parkerizing them, you need to re-clean them. Immediately before dunking in the Parkerizing solution, dunk in acid for a few seconds or minutes, spray with oven cleaner, and dunk in hot water.

Weatherstrip

Not everything on your classic muscle car is timeless. Sure, the long, sleek lines will survive the test of time, but certain things just are, well, pretty bad. Your original weatherstripping is likely to be very brittle, flaking, or just plain rotting apart. Obviously, it's high time to replace the old rubber with some new stuff.

Modern technologies offer far better replacement parts than what the original factory equipment could provide, namely in the way of electronics, plastics, and rubber compounds.

Today's plastic and rubber are embedded with new-age polymers that resist aging, cracking, and discoloring far longer than those from more than 40 years ago. These polymers also improve elasticity in softer contact points (including body bumpers and weatherstripping) and maintain that pliability over the years.

Sealing your cabin from the outside elements is easily done. Apart from insulating the cabin from road noise and debris, weatherstripping also acts as a vibrational buffer, keeping doors, windows, deck lid, and hood from rattling and chipping your paint.

Although most weatherstripping either comes with plastic clips or fits snuggly into channels to hold the rubber into place, a good bead of 3M Weather Stripping Adhesive keeps out moisture, dust, and debris.

Companies including B/E Parts, YearOne, and Classic Industries offer full sets of weatherstripping and body bumpers. A tube of 3M weatherstripping adhesive and a roll of narrow painter's tape (and some patience) are all you need to get the job done in a couple of hours. Proper weatherstrip adhesive is applied in a two-part process: Apply a thin bead on a clean surface and do the same to the mating surface of the backside of the weatherstripping.

The recommendation from 3M is to wait up to a minute before bonding the two together; the waiting period is to allow the oxygen-activated glue to "kick."

On the door rubber, the weatherstripping features a series of knurled plastic clips that lock the rubber in place. You can glue as you clip the weatherstripping in place. When finished, simply close the door to apply the pressure necessary to complete the bond. Applying the trunk lid weatherstripping requires a little more finesse, and painter's tape, to keep the rubber liner in line.

OEM-level restorers note that the seam for trunk weatherstripping is offset by 6 inches to the right from point of center. This was done to better seal from seepage.

When your weatherstripping dries, insert the body bumpers. These act as bump-stops for the doors, hood, and trunk to protect your car's paint from being chipped and damaged.

With a gentle cleaner, wipe down any excess glue and residue. The 3M adhesive requires a few hours to fully bond, so closing the hood, trunk, doors, and windows when you're done helps the glue dry faster.

Windows

The door glass, seals, window channels, and regulators must be carefully inspected and most of if not all the soft materials replaced. You must carefully inspect the door glass and quarter glass; if it is the original glass, it is in good enough shape to use. After a full restoration the original glass flaws are often magnified next to the fully restored paint and trim.

The two-door post, hardtop, and convertible side glass are all different. None of the convertible glass can be used in either the hardtop or the post cars. The hardtop glass has different trim where the door and quarter glass meet. However, the front door window actuator and glass channels are the same. The quarter glass actuator and window channels are very complicated. Inspect them closely to make sure all of the plastic rollers and guides are in good shape. If they are broken you must find replacements.

The door and quarter glass whiskers and seals must be replaced and are available through many sources. Take several pictures of how these mechanisms and channels are located in your car so that upon reassembly you can install the parts back in their general position, so that final adjustment is easier. Here too, the original factory service manual for your car is a must-have when adjusting your glass and doors. The manual devotes 50 to 100 pages to these installations and adjustments.

If you want date codes on your replacement glass various companies can apply your exact dates to the glass for you. Otherwise all new seals and plastic parts can be replaced with correct factory appearance from many reproduction part suppliers.

The best tip we can give you is to replace any questionable parts now. You do not want to have to do this again after you have completely restored your car.

Glass Restoration

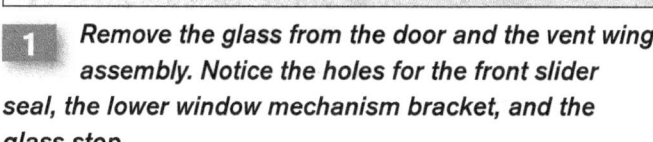

2 *The glass stop keeps the door glass from being raised too far and binding or, at worst, breaking when the door is closed. If it is missing it must be replaced.*

1 *Remove the glass from the door and the vent wing assembly. Notice the holes for the front slider seal, the lower window mechanism bracket, and the glass stop.*

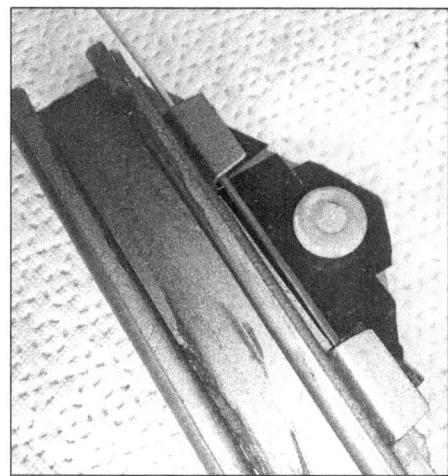

3 *This lower glass bracket has been fully restored. After blasting and painting the stainless steel, rest the glass against some glass-setting tape that has been glued in place so it does not break. Replace the clip and secure it by lightly driving the center pin into place, which spreads the clip and secures it to the bracket. Then lubricate the channel with grease.*

4 *Blast the window regular and paint with stainless steel paint. Lubricate and test it to make sure it functions smoothly and correctly. If needed, replace the plastic pivot wheel if it doesn't move freely in the slot of the lower glass bracket. Mount the device inside the door using three bolts. Make sure the threads for the handle are clean and in good shape. Chase it with a tap to make sure the handle screw fully seats.*

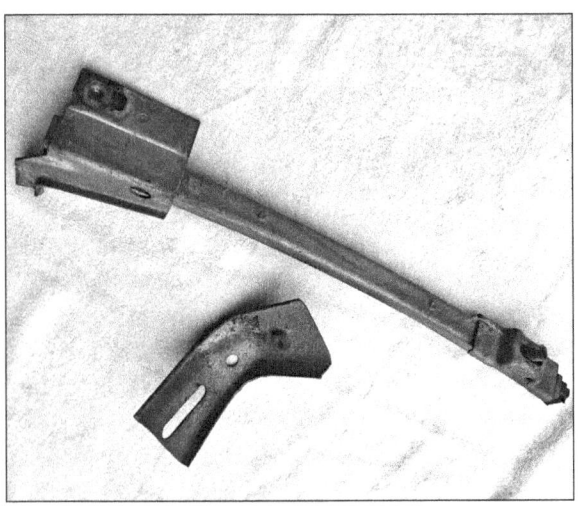

5 Inspect, blast, paint, and replace the felt used in the rear glass channel. The bolts that hold this in the door are black phosphate. (If you see them painted body color that is a dead giveaway that the car was painted without being disassembled.) Install them loosely in the door so the glass goes in easily. Adjust and tighten after the vent wing assembly and door glass are installed as one unit.

6 The rear door glass and mechanism in a hardtop and convertible has several adjustment points. If your glass is functioning well before disassembly take good pictures of these bolts and their position. They will prove to be very valuable upon reassembly.

7 The rear window glass actuator has many different metal and plastic parts. Inspect all of them for excessive wear and replace as necessary. The spring-loaded wheels that roll along the window guide are usually weak or worn. Hopefully yours are in good shape because they are not reproduced. If yours need to be replaced you must find good used or NOS ones. Again take pictures to aid in reassembly.

8 Replacement of broken rollers is necessary. Also replace any missing retaining clips. Even if the mechanism is in good condition, disassemble, clean, and lubricate before reinstalling.

9 Two-piece rollers must also be removed and the mechanism blasted, painted, lubricated, and reassembled. Do not take shortcuts when restoring these pieces.

Vent Wing Window

Often, when cars are entered for judging, judges go immediately to the doors and look at the vent wing assemblies. Just by looking at these assemblies, seasoned judges can tell, almost immediately, if the car was properly restored.

More often than not, cars that have been painted, the engine rebuilt, fitted with new tires, and a nice interior, have the original, but pitted chrome, bad glass, dry hard rubber seals, and scratched stainless. Ignorance about restoring these assemblies causes many to leave them in place and mask and paint around them.

Too often it is a telltale sign that shortcuts were taken, not only here, but in many other places in the car's restoration as well. Remember, there is a big difference between a restored car and a "perfumed pig."

The difference a brand-new vent wing assembly can make in a newly painted car is amazing! Here are the general procedures for restoration:

Phase 1: The Assembly

Before removing the vent wing assembly, remove the window lift mechanism, door handles, latches, and seals. Remove the bumpstop on the door glass and roll the window down completely. This exposes the window wipes and "fuzzies" for removal.

1 Loosen the rear window channel nuts, but do not remove the assembly. Label, bag, and tag all the hardware and store. Be mindful of the plastic plug that holds the bottom of the window to the bracket that engages with the roller lift mechanism.

2 After disengaging the lift mechanism from the window bracket, remove the bracket by tapping the center plastic plug out of the bracket mount.

3 You can remove the window with the bracket attached and then remove the mount. Inspect the lift mechanism; many of these are worn out or non-functional and must be replaced.

4 Taking the assembly out of the doorframe involves some hide-and-seek to find all the attaching points and adjustments. On the front of the doorframe two nuts hold a triangular mounting bracket inside the door.

Two large, plastic, flat plugs and one small plug are located on the inside of the doorframe toward the top. In addition another flat plug is located on the bottom of the door toward the front, to access the lower adjustment bracket.

The two nuts are 7/16 inch. The hidden two bolts are 1/2 inch; the small plug hides the Allen-head bolt. This bolt goes through the door inner frame into a small threaded rectangular keeper and is not attached. Under the door, the nut is 1/2 inch. Be sure to spray a lubricant on the bottom nut and threads, and take your time removing this stud. It turns loosely inside an angular bracket attached to the bottom of the vent assembly by two small welds. Often these welds are already broken and the bottom of the assembly is loose.

5 After removing all the attaching hardware the entire assembly comes out.

6 Remove the rear window channel, then inspect, blast, and paint it. You may need to replace the felt inside this bracket.

7 When you slide the door glass out of the vent wing assembly you see a plastic and felt slider seal on the front of the door glass. Most of the time this slider has deteriorated and must be replaced. Sliders are available through Chrysler and are reproduced. They are difficult to install correctly. Take your time.

Upon reassembly make sure the seal slides freely in the vent wing channel. You have to drill or punch out the holes for the pins to attach the slider. Using pliers squeeze the new plastic clips and pins through the hole in the glass and the slider. You have to trim the slider to length.

Phase 2: The Glass

Next you must remove the vent wing glass and chrome channel.

1 Drive the pin out of the shaft and loosen the screw. Disassemble the pivot; the glass and base easily comes out. You must cut out the old glass mounting tape that holds the glass in the base. Use a liberal amount of penetrating spray. Remove the catch lever by driving out the small pin.

Take care not to lose the special washer.

2 Have the base re-chromed.

3 Replace or clean the glass as necessary. Either use glass-setting tape from your local glass shop or use black silicone to secure the glass into the base, and trim when dry.

4 Buff and polish the pivot or replace as necessary. Be sure to use the round gaskets between the pivot and the glass or breakage may occur.

Phase 3: The Frame

The frame of the vent wing assembly is made up of two distinct units, the front chrome frame and the angled metal and stainless frame.

The rubber gasket can be reused or replaced depending on its condition. Three small posts that have been bent and spread secure the two frames together. Thankfully, there is a pair at each point and the factory only used one of them, leaving the other for you to use in reattaching the frames together.

1 With a Dremel or drill carefully grind the edges of the posts until the frames can be separated.

2 The chrome frame must be re-chromed and the stainless on the other frame buffed. Take care buffing the stainless because it is part of the frame and can be snagged by the fast-moving buffing wheel.

3 The lower adjusting/attaching mount is at the bottom of the frame. In most cases this bracket is busted or missing. Re-welding the bracket to the frame is tricky. If you re-weld it inside the channel it interferes with the sliding glass. So you

should spot weld it on the outside edges and dress with a grinder.

4 When you get the frames back from the chrome shop the process becomes more difficult. Protect the chrome at all costs. Position the two frames back in the original location.

5 With a sharp small chisel and hammer make an "X" on the unused post. Then with a punch spread each quarter-section of the post outward.

6 Reinstall all screws and hardware.

7 Install the rubber gasket and the vent glass assembly.

8 Blast and paint the triangular mounting bracket on the front of the door. Attach it loosely and put the Allen head and retainer in place.

9 Be sure to have the rear glass channel in place and attached loosely with the bolts.

10 Slide the door glass in the vent window frame and install it in the door as one unit.

11 Reassemble and adjust according to the factory service manual instructions.

Rear Window Trim 1968–1970

By Restorations by Rick

For 1968–1970 B-Bodies I highly recommend installing new molding clips. Because they are screwed in place they must be installed before the glass. Breaking a used clip while installing moldings can ruin your weekend! Be sure to carefully compare the new clips to your originals. It's vital that the catch edge of the clip is at the correct distance from the pinchweld.

Start with the lower strips: the one with the stepped end first and then the one that slides into it. The upper pieces are installed last in a

I made a special tool to reshape the edge of the molding grabbed by the clips. Often this edge becomes bent outward or otherwise mangled by impatient removal. The tool is made from ordinary vise grips and has 16-gauge 1¼ x 2½ "bills" welded to it. This is used to straighten the molding edge without damaging the outer visible area. Sometimes it helps to "tweak" the angle inward slightly too.

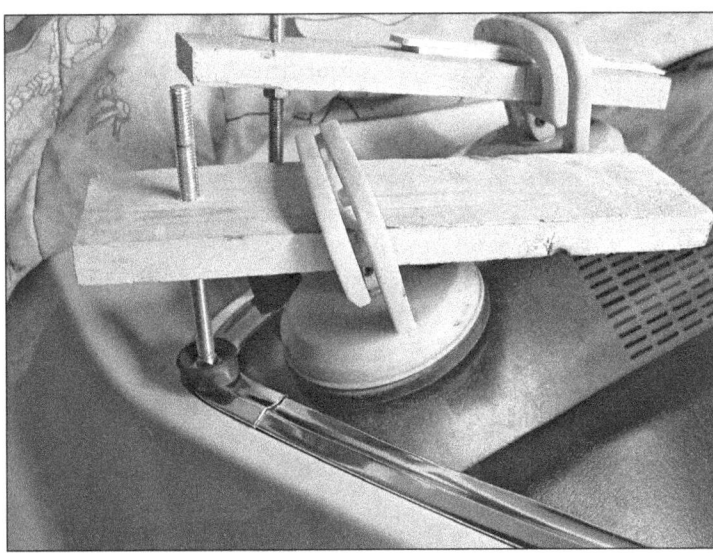

This simple tool helps apply pressure to a stubborn corner using a 1 x 4 pine board, a glass suction handle, a 3/8-inch carriage bolt, a hood rubber bumper, and a couple of nuts and washers. Apply a suitable dab of urethane window sealant first, and then clip the molding in place.

Another trick that can help install this trim is to give the molding a twist (while off the car). This creates a slight "preload" causing the corner to pull down and keeping it from popping up. This is especially helpful with manhandled molding that was difficult to get off because of Chrysler's sometimes-liberal use of sealer compound.

similar fashion, stepped one first. These can be a nightmare! The lower corners have a tendency to pop up.

Last, the tool is used to maintain pressure on the trim strip. After an overnight cure, the strip will stay put. Don't get carried away with the amount of urethane; if you ever need to get the trim off later you want to be able to saw it free without too much effort.

Be sure to tape a towel or thick blanket around the area just in case the suction cup comes loose.

Fresh-Air Induction

Hood scoops, scallops, and louvers were all used on these B-Bodies from 1966 to 1968. They had an aggressive "bad boy" look, and even when highlighted with chrome and contrasting stripes they were still just there for looks. In 1969 that all changed. On the Road Runner and GTX models Plymouth introduced a cable-operated fresh-air induction system aptly called the Air Grabber. Not to be outdone, Dodge introduced the same system for the Super Bee and the R/T models, in the same exact color, but labeled it the Ramcharger.

This is a 1969 Plymouth Air Grabber underhood box. It comes in three pieces. This box is being test fitted and does not have the rubber seal to the breather attached yet. You can see by looking at the holes in the left and right outer runners that the flaps are closed. The lever that the actuator cable attaches to is located at the back of the driver-side runner.

Interestingly, the Charger line never received the fresh-air option until 1971 when Dodge combined the Super Bee and Charger models.

The advantage of these fresh-air induction systems was that instead of the engine getting hot air from the engine compartment, it could now get cooler fresh air directly into the engine via a somewhat sealed outside source.

Now that the hoods were modified with the fresh-air induction boxes, the breathers had to also be modified to accept the additional fresh air and funnel it into the carburetor and intake. These breathers, filters, and their lids come in many combinations. Depending on the particular model, year, number of carburetors, and engine size, you could have a variety of air-breather styles.

The hood may or may not have a stripe with the 1969 Air Grabber. The

Air Grabber and Ramcharger

Here are some details about applications that use fresh-air induction systems:

- From 1966 to 1968 Plymouth and Dodge B-Bodies hood scoops were just for looks and they didn't have any fresh-air induction.
- In 1969, the Air Grabber for the Plymouth GTX and Road Runner, and the Ramcharger for the Dodge Coronet, R/T, and Super Bee, were both black.
- The 383 and 440 engines had different-height breather bases. The easiest way to identify whether you have a 440 or 383 baseplate is to lay it on a table; if it rocks it is a 383 base.
- In 1969½ the fresh-air fiberglass hood came only on A12 cars. The scoop had no way to open or close and therefore had a bathtub-style breather base with drains for water that may come in during operation in the rain. The drains had short sections of heater hose attached to the drain so the water could drip without wetting the engine. The hood was painted with Organisol and had either the

Dodge "SIX PACK" or the Plymouth "6BBL" decal.
- In 1970, the Plymouth Air Grabber became vacuum operated and was black and the Dodge Ramcharger became orange and remained cable operated.
- In 1969, the Air Grabber/Ramcharger breather lid for the 4-barrel and Hemi was the same large oval similar to the 1969½ Six-Pack breather lid. The bases were different for the 4-barrel 383 and the 4-barrel 440, and there was also the base with the three carburetor holes for the Six-Pack and 6-barrel Holley carburetors.
- In 1970, the N96 (fresh-air option code) 4-barrel breather had a large oval base but a small round filter and lid.
- In 1970, a new larger breather lid without a rain gutter was used on the Six-Pack and 6-barrel. The Hemi used the same lid as in 1969.
- The air dam is found only on 1970 Six-Pack and Hemi cars without fresh-air induction or California noise reduction (N97).
- Beginning in 1969, all Hemis (except 1969–1970 Charger or winged cars) had fresh-air induction. ∎

Here is a Ramcharger unit on a 1970 Dodge R/T. The units changed colors from black in 1969 to orange in 1970. Make sure you have the correct Ramcharger unit for your car.

Ramcharger had hood scoops with the size of the engine badge mounted on the side. If the hood had the V21 stripe option it was painted with Organisol. If the hood had the fresh-air option the screens that allowed the fresh air into the box were always Ralleye Red in color with or without a stripe. If the hood did not have the fresh-air package it had a solid ribbed plate painted semi-gloss black with or without a stripe.

In 1970 the Ramcharger remained manually operated by cable, but the color of the box was changed from black to orange. The Air Grabber changed completely in style and operation. It was no longer operated by a manual cable; it became vacuum operated and the scoop was flush with the hood. When the switch mounted on the lower dash was flipped, the vacuum from the engine went through a vacuum storage canister and caused the actuator to raise the scoop, exposing the menacing "shark" mouth and teeth proudly proclaiming "Air Grabber."

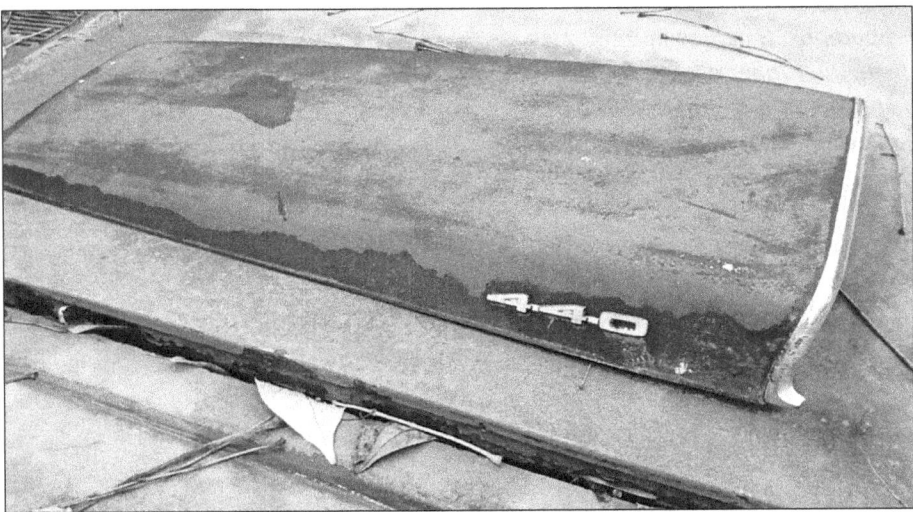

The Dodge Ramcharger hood came with two hood scoops. It has a chrome front bezel and the engine callouts mounted on the side. This one clearly lets everyone know about the big-block 440 that resides under the hood.

Thus the ultimate stoplight intimidator was ready to rear its head whenever an unsuspecting challenger revved its engine. In 1970 the V21 hood stripe changed from two equal stripes to three stripes with the middle stripe being the largest.

The rubber drain flaps have unique attaching clips. Notice that this runner is cracked. You could either repair this with fiberglass and paint or replace this side with a reproduction runner.

In 1969 the 4-barrel air breather on the Air Grabber was oval and included the iconic Coyote Duster decal. The 1969½ breather does not have this decal but only has two small rectangular decals with "DO NOT WASH OR OIL" care instructions on one and "SPECIAL INSTRUCTIONS" about subfreezing weather or heavy rainstorm warnings on the other.

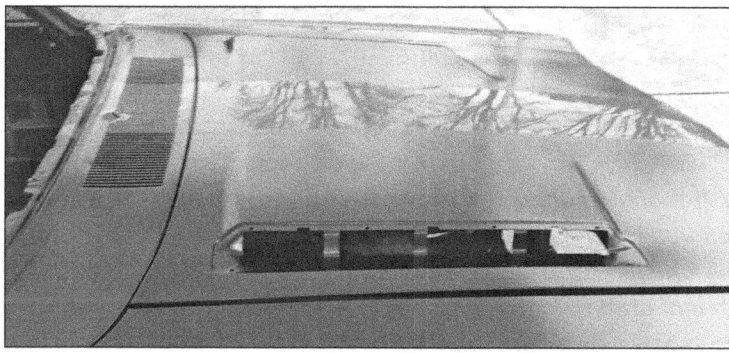

The hoods for the 1968 and 1969 Road Runners are the same basic structure. The slots in the hood in 1968 open toward the side of the hood and were solid. The 1969 inserts (shown) point upward. These hood stripes were a one-year-only style and were painted on with Organisol.

In mid-year 1969 the A12 cars were produced. These were Super Bees and Road Runners with the special option of A12. They received a full fiberglass hood attached with hood pins. The scoop was open all the time and required the development of a bathtub-style base that allowed the water to be diverted away from the three Holley 2-barrel carburetors. This hood was painted with Organisol and had either the "SIX PACK" or "6BBL" sticker applied to the hood scoop.

The hood inserts had Ralleye Red painted screens that allowed the air to flow into the Air Grabber box. These screens were painted red with or without hood stripes. Non–fresh-air hoods had ribbed solid plates mounted in the inserts. They were painted semi-gloss black with or without the hood stripes.

The breather changed from having a large oval top to a smaller round breather and filter. The base also changed in design but was still used to seal to the fresh-air box. It retained its iconic Coyote Duster decal but was modified to fit the smaller breather. Note that this engine has some performance modifications from original, but the fresh-air units are original.

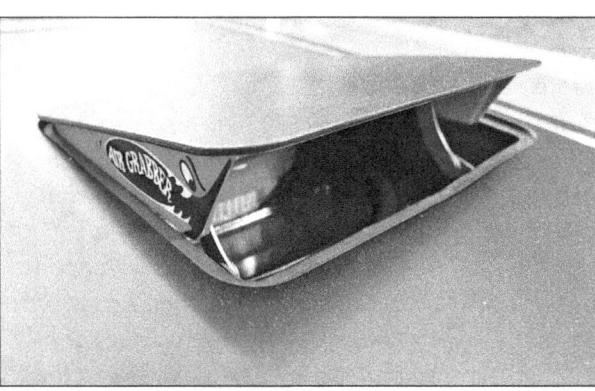

The passive inserts from 1969 gave way to a flush-mounted hood scoop that on command slowly opened revealing the bright orange and white "shark" teeth and mouth to let everyone know this car means business.

have a non-air unit, you can purchase a kit and do the work yourself. The following are general guidelines to restoring your non–air conditioning heater box.

Evaluate the Condition

The condition of your original box dictates the extent of repairs and the process for restoring the unit. It also helps you decide whether you can restore the unit yourself. The body of the unit is made of thermal plastic with sisal fiber added for strength and has a distinct finish.

If a repair to the box must be made you have to paint it. You can use a kit to refinish it, but only an original box without damage is able to keep the original unique finish. If your unit is damaged or missing parts, it is necessary to either purchase an original in better shape or send it to a professional to do the work. Even then, they cannot reproduce the original finish with paint. If your unit is in good shape you should able to achieve that goal.

Get Organized

Take as many pictures during the disassembly process as possible as reference for re-assembly. As always, clear a nice open work area with plastic baggies and small boxes to put the parts in as you go. You need basic tools, such as a nut driver, razor blade scraper, basic refinishing products (a paint stripper, fine steel wool, and lacquer thinner), and re-assembly products (spray adhesive from 3M).

The heater box kit has detailed step-by-step instructions for the foam installation. Some are pre-coated with adhesive and others need spray adhesive. You can purchase these kits from several sources.

A vacuum-release solenoid under the dash allows the scoop to always return to its flush-mounted position when the key is turned off. You can also use the toggle switch on the dash to lower the scoop on demand.

Non-A/C Heater Box

One of the important parts of an interior restoration is the heater box/ventilation system. Two systems are available in all cars: the non–air conditioning heater box and the air conditioning/heater system. They are very different and require many different parts to repair and restore.

Several businesses can perform high-level restorations on these units. You can expect to pay a minimum of $600 depending on the shape of your unit. Then, add to that another $100 or more for shipping and the risk of damage in transit.

If you have an air conditioning unit, we highly recommend you have a professional do the work. If you

Clean the Box

The box itself needs to be carefully cleaned. If it has been painted before, the paint can be removed by carefully spraying light coats of paint stripper, followed by cleaning with 0000 steel wool, rinsing with water, and then final detail cleaning with lacquer thinner and the 0000 steel wool.

If the box requires more cleaning, it can be blasted with very fine low-pressure glass beads. This also cleans all brackets and the center On/Off door. You can either mask off and paint these attached metal parts or remove them by grinding off the rivets.

However, if you remove the rivets you have to invest in a rivet gun and rivets that have the "peel type" or "banana peel" spread on the backside. Normal pop rivets do work, but are not original in appearance.

Process Overview

First you disassemble the rear blower plate. The squirrel cage is attached with an Allen head set screw. After removing the screw, coat the shaft with a penetrating lubricant and tap it off using a wooden hammer handle or dowel pin. Do not force it off or try to use a puller, it bends and ruins the balance of the unit.

Test the motor and refinish or replace as necessary. One wire is green and the ground wire is black.

Reassemble after blasting, painting, and testing.

We strongly recommend always replacing the heater core. They are available at your local parts store or online.

Inspect and test the resistor switch to make sure it is in good operating condition. It can also be cleaned with lacquer thinner and 0000 steel wool and painted with clear. It is attached with two small hex-head screws.

After blasting finish the front cover in a gloss or 30-percent-flattened gloss black. The back has a foam layer included in the kit.

Stamp the yellow part number on the cover. You can make your own stamp or purchase one online. Use water-based paint for the stamp.

After cleaning or blasting the case, paint it with a satin or gloss clear to return it to its original appearance.

After blasting all the metal parts, coat them with high-quality stainless steel paint. We recommend Seymour or Dupli-Color Stainless Steel paints. All moving parts, brackets, and both back covers are natural or stainless in appearance.

The finished box not only gives years of service but looks original and gains valuable points at high-level shows. It also sets your car apart from those that do not have this unit correctly restored. It also comes in handy when your windshield fogs up or on a cold night coming home from cruising!

Heater Box Restoration

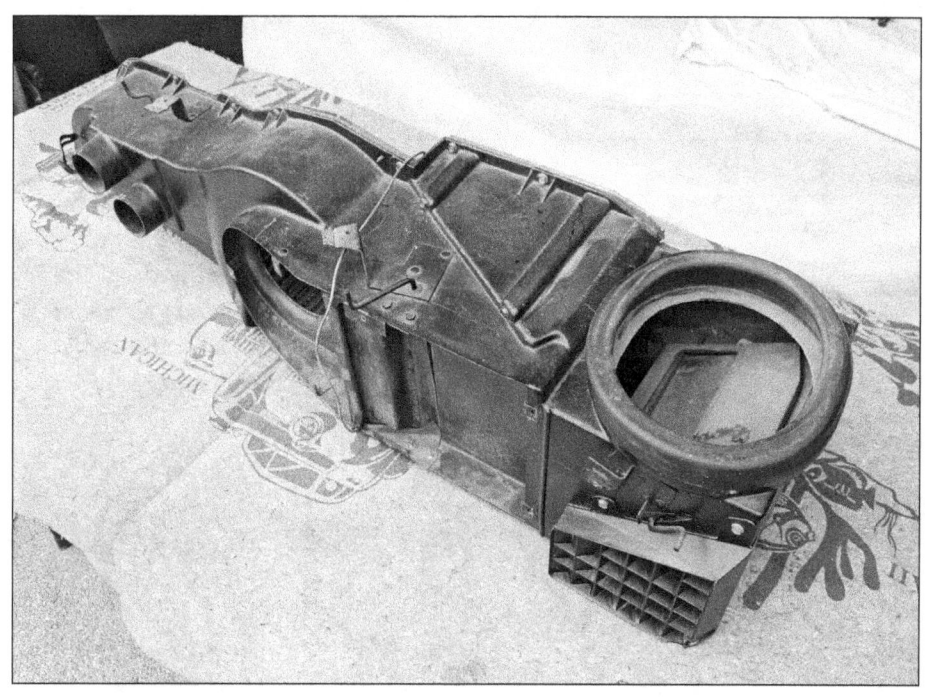

1 Many heater boxes are in poor shape. However, they can be restored and made to look brand new. The most important consideration before sinking a lot of time and money into one of these units is the condition of the body of the unit. If it is cracked and pieces are broken off get another core. Some people repair these flaws with fiberglass, but then they must be painted and therefore lose the original finish.

2 Disassemble your heater box. You can use this photo to account for all of your parts. (Photo Courtesy Chuck Buczeskie)

3 This engine plate will clean up nicely. Test your engine to make sure it operates correctly.

4 This heater core backing plate is in very good original condition. Notice that even the fan motor vent rubber hose can be salvaged.

5 It's a good idea to inspect the inside of the body of the unit. The distinctive fine white fibers have to be present for the original finish.

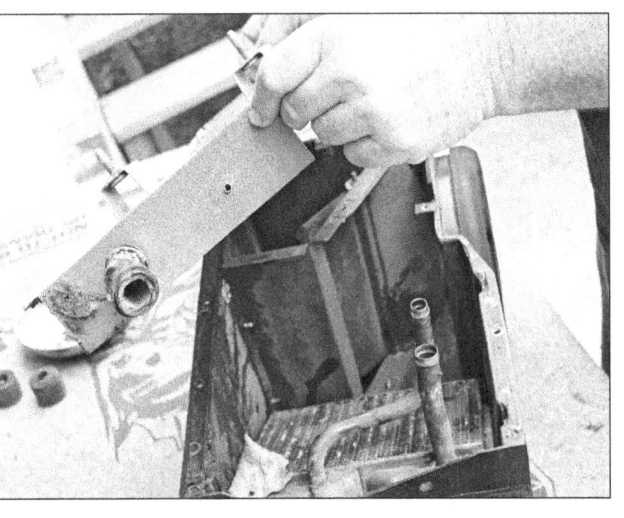

6 Always, always, always replace the heater core. The last thing you want is a leak after the car is completed.

7 The defrost/floor heat door is completely covered in foam, but is easily removed.

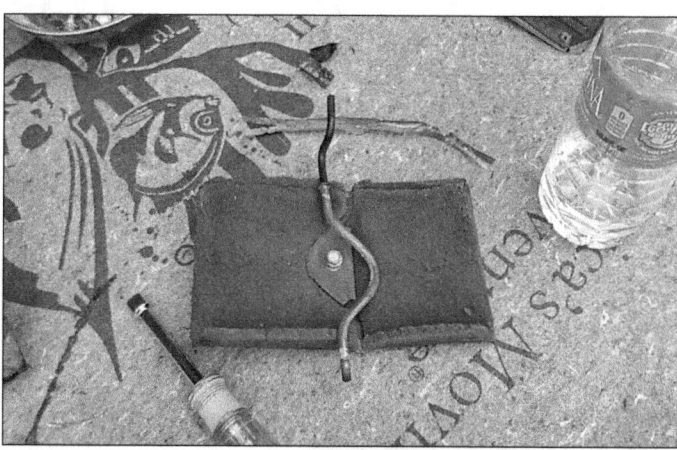

8 Remove the fresh-air vent control door as a unit. The two foam seals are very difficult to remove and replace. After the door has been removed it can be stripped, blasted, and painted natural metal.

9 After you remove the defrost/heat door you can strip, blast, and paint it natural metal.

10 You must bend the frame to remove and replace these foam seals. Take care so that the frame can return to its original shape. This one cleaned up well with a light blasting with soda.

11 A setscrew holds the fan cage on. Loosen it to remove the fan. Remove the fan motor from the plate, restore the motor, and blast with soda or glass beads.

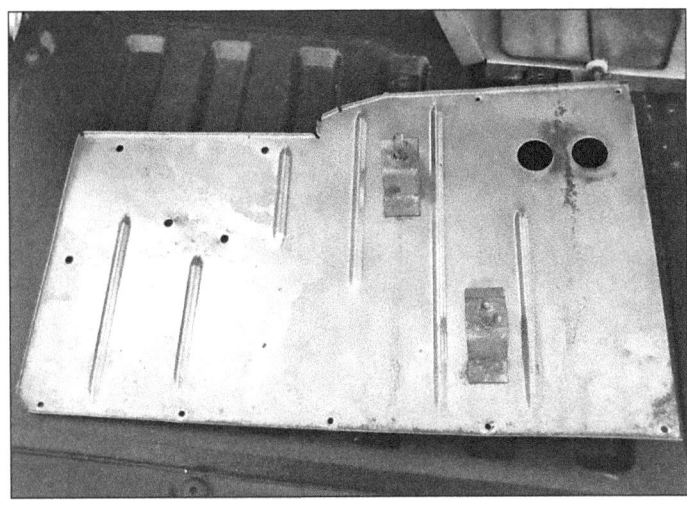

12 After everything has been removed from the body of the box it can be lightly blasted with soda. Don't worry that the color looks light after blasting. Spray it with a satin clear paint and it returns to its original finish, with light-colored fibers showing.

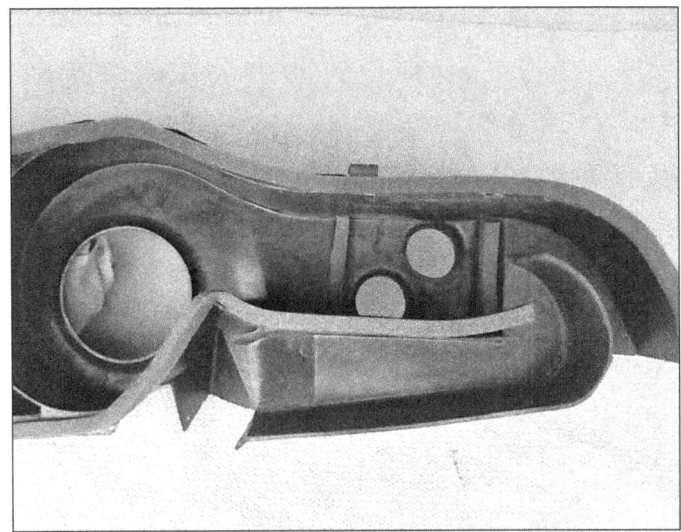

14 Using a foam kit, follow the directions to install all the foam seals. Some have a peal-and-stick design and others must be sprayed with glue and attached.

13 The blower fan can be blasted and painted. Be careful not to move any balancing clips if present. This one only had one clip and nothing was bent.

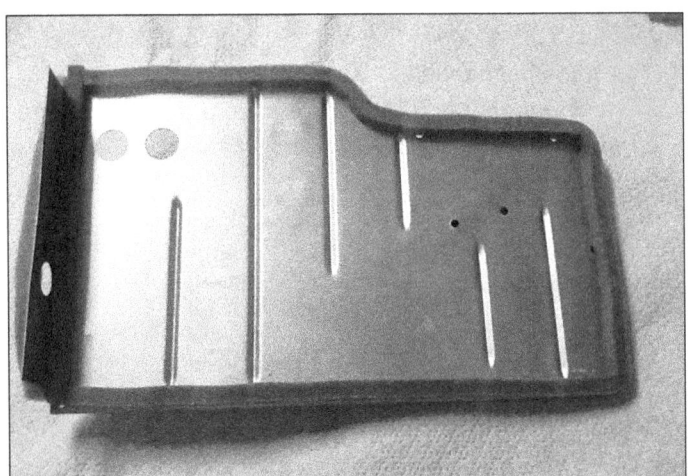

15 After blasting Seymour's Stainless Steel paint, install the peal-and-stick foam seal being careful to follow the edge of the plate so a tight seal is achieved after assembly.

16 Install the new heater core and secure it with the correct clear cad-plated screws.

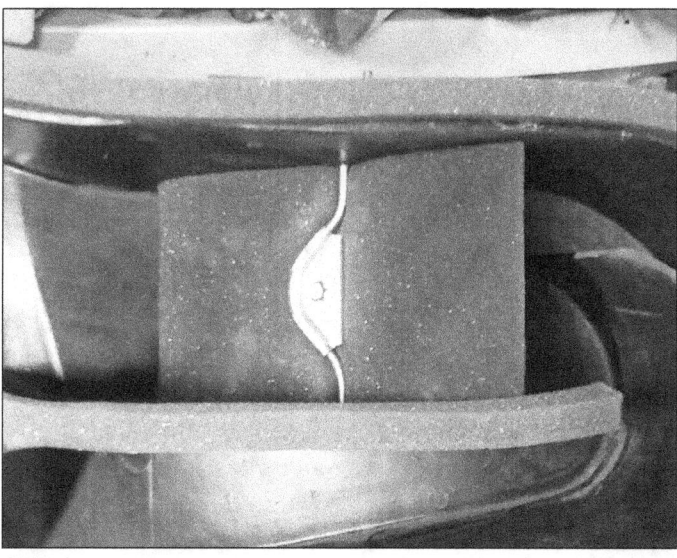

17 *Install the painted and foam-covered defrost/floor heat door.*

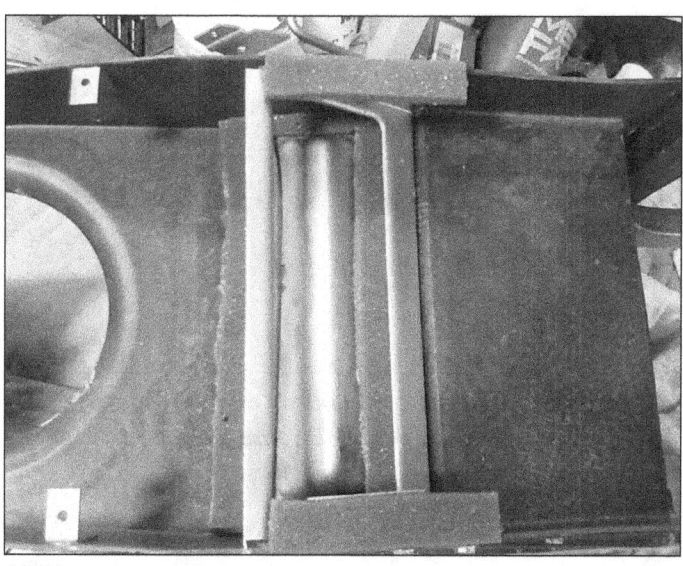

18 *Install the temperature control door frame and door.*

19 *Pay very close attention to the black phosphate tang that causes resistance when the vent door is opened. Without this tang the door is loose.*

20 *The back side of the fresh-air door is completely covered, unlike the front side that has the middle of the foam seal cut out.*

21 *Install the fresh-air door assembly with all the correct foam seals. Be sure to check for proper fit because the mounting holes have some play.*

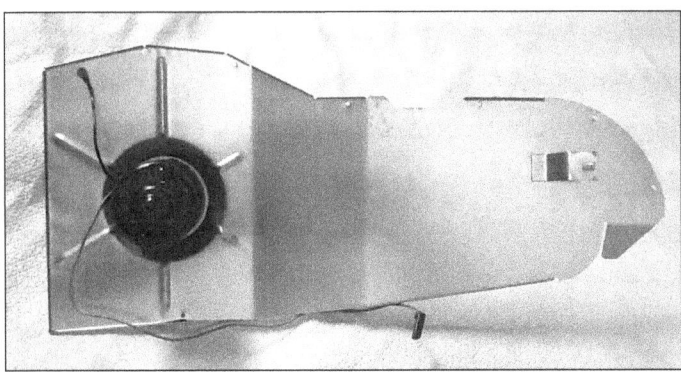

22 *Inspect your restored and assembled fan motor, blower cage, and plate. Be sure it has the correct wire colors, locations, and connectors.*

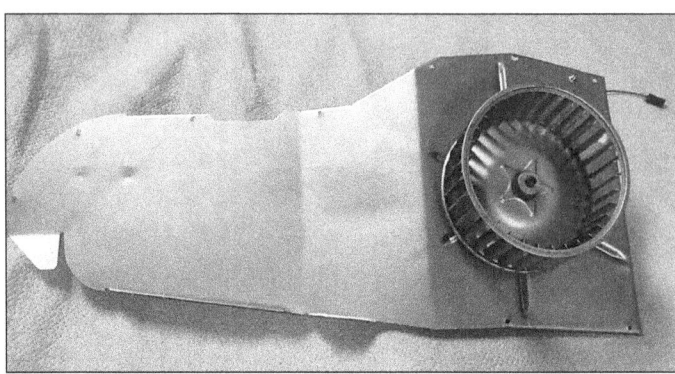

23 *Hook up a 12-volt power supply and test run the assembled motor and fan cage. If it is installed correctly it does not rub on the housing.*

24 *This is a correct heater box finished all the way down to the under-dash wiring clip with rubber-coated tips.*

25 *Be sure to use the correct clear cad-plated slotless screws to assemble the heater box.*

26 *The only thing left to complete the heater box restoration is the front cover. Mount the fan-speed resistor with special screws. It is made from a brown fiber; clean it lightly and test it to make sure it works.*

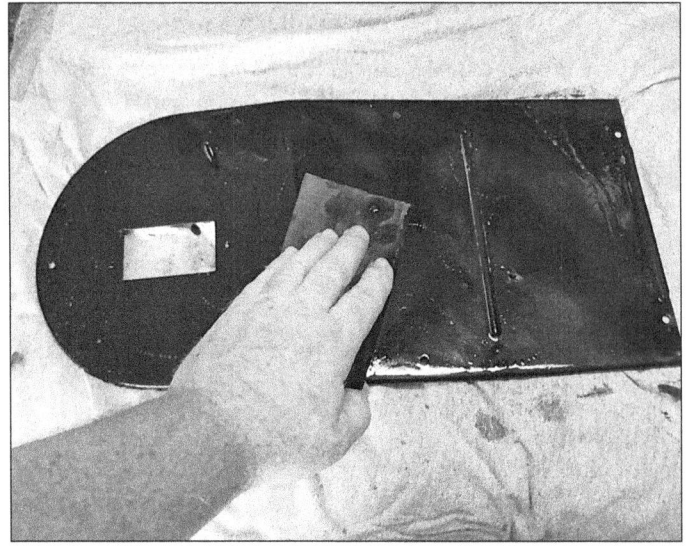

27 *Remove the resistor and sand the finish or completely strip it of paint if necessary.*

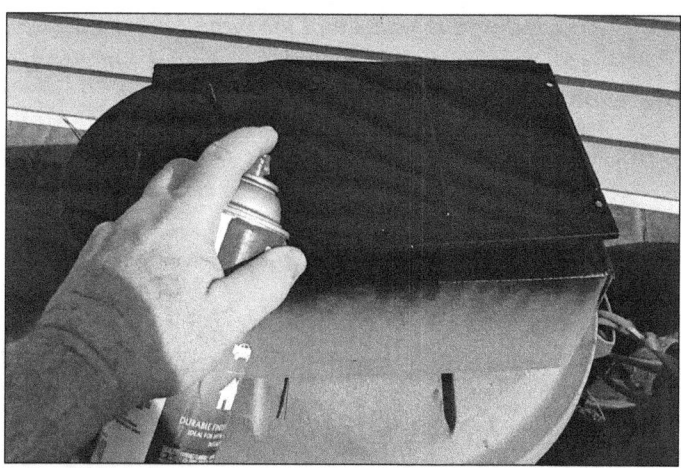

28 Paint the cover gloss black using single-stage enamel.

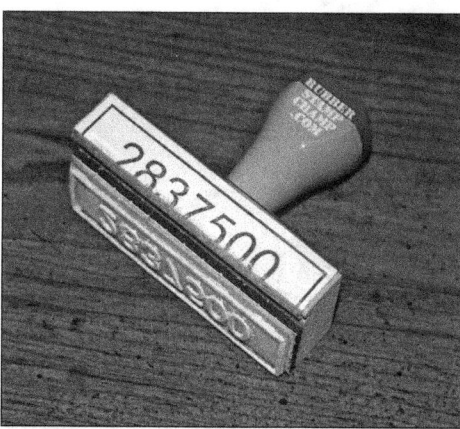

29 Every heater box had a part number stamped on it in yellow paint. Many heater boxes in restored cars are missing this stamp. It is located under the dash frame. You can take a picture of the original stamp and measure the height of the numbers and have a local stamp maker create the correct stamp.

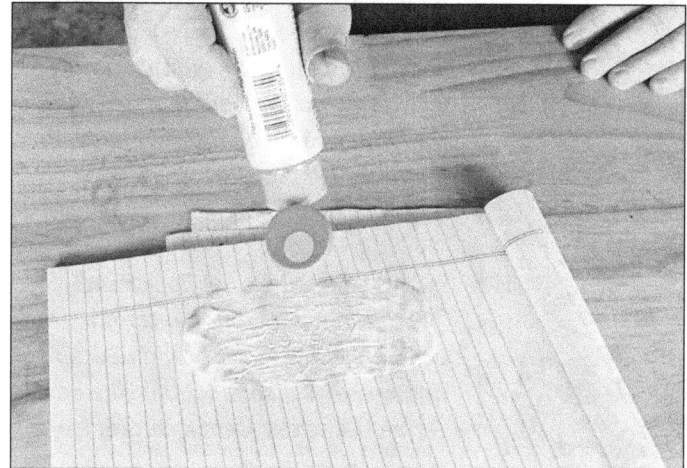

30 Apply a liberal amount of medium yellow water-based paint to a note pad.

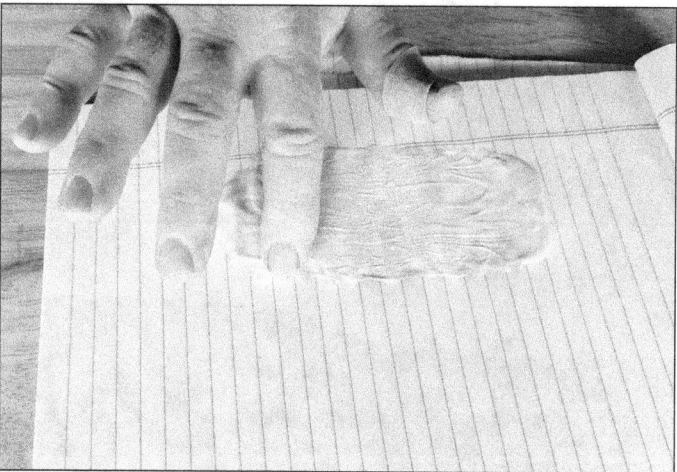

31 Spread the paint with your finger making sure you leave a layer on the pad.

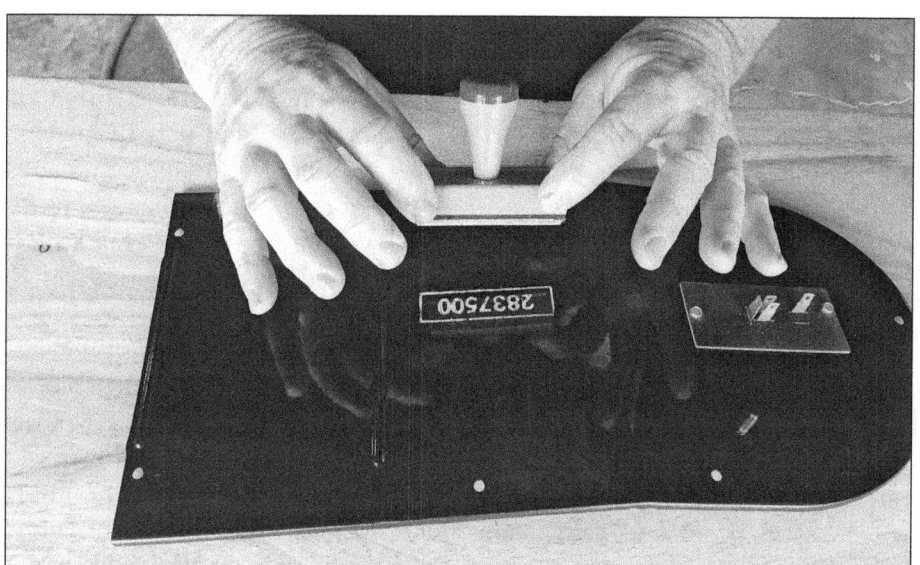

32 Using even pressure practice on the pad several times until you are comfortable with the feel and satisfied with the results. Too light a pressure and the stamp will not be uniform. Too heavy a pressure and the numbers will be hollow in the middle and heavy around the edges.

33 Attach the vent grilles and the large rubber vent seal. You now have a complete, original, functional heater box unit ready to install.

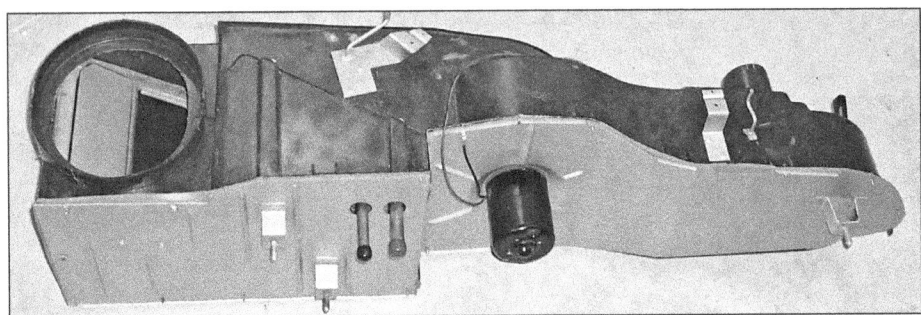

34 The back side of your heater box should have all the white foam seals, the thick rubber heater core seals, and the correct gold cad-plated attaching shoulder nuts with serrated washers that are seen from the engine compartment when installed. (Photo Courtesy Chuck Buczeskie)

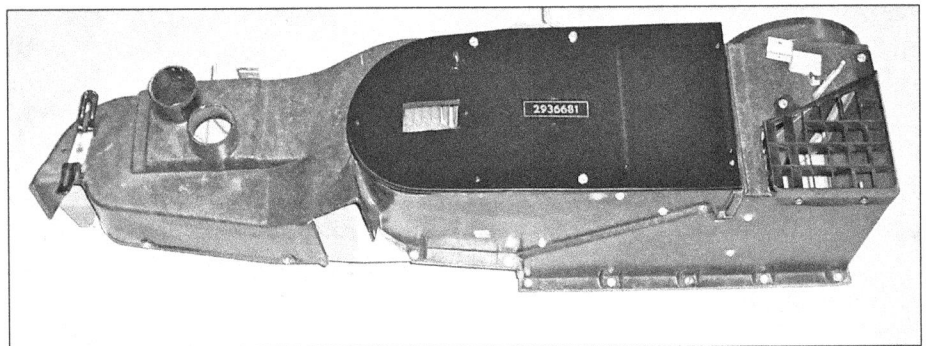

35 Install the final floor heat deflector. Your heater box assembly now looks brand new and original, and also functions like new. (Photo Courtesy Chuck Buczeskie)

Interior

In the same way that a different set of skills is required to restore the engine verses the paint, the restoration of your car's interior requires yet another set of skills. We have seen some fantastic mechanics absolutely butcher the interior of a car, while a talented painter may not be able to assemble an engine. By following the "how-to" guidelines and tips in this section, and with a little patience and a few basic tools, you can reproduce a factory-correct cockpit that is functional, comfortable, and beautiful.

Paint Color

Whether you painted your car body yourself using our guidelines or had a shop shoot the color, the interior has some special areas that need painting. Even though almost all the interior metal is covered with carpet, a headliner, or door panels, you must mask off and paint some areas. You may also have to use some vinyl dye on some soft parts that are not reproduced and may have come from another car that even had a different-color interior.

If you haven't already masked off and painted the door interior panels, now is the time to do it.

If you have a post car, the inside part of the post matches the color of the upper door panels. The A-pillars match the dash color. The rear seat upper panels also match the upper door panels. The metal and vinyl headliner trim matches the headliner

After removing all the seats, door panels, windows and mechanisms, and carpet, you can access any problems with rust-through or damage to the metal sub-structure. Luckily, we had no rust-through in the floorpans. If you have rust refer to "Floorpan Patch" in Chapter 4. If you find only minor rust-through and you can cut and butt weld a patch panel, refer to "Patch Installation" in Chapter 4. (Photo Courtesy Chuck Buczeskie)

With everything removed from the interior you can make a list of all the parts that need replacing. Just about any Mopar car show has good, reusable sets of rear armrests.

Even though things look pretty bad here, all of it can be salvaged and restored without purchasing all new parts. The seat rail needs to be completely disassembled, blasted, and painted before it can be used.

color. The package tray trim matches the headliner trim color.

Make sure you have done your research as to what is correct for your car's interior. The interior codes are on the build sheet and the data plate.

Kick Panels

You find a basic design of the kick panel in most of these 1966–1970 cars. They are all molded plastic with a grain on the surface. The original panels were plastic that was molded in the color of the interior. You have to be certain of the variation and color that were original to your car. All, no matter the color, have insulation behind them, lap over the door-jamb, and cover all the way down to the floor.

The sill plate then goes over the bottom tab of the kick panel. The kick panels have usually been scuffed over the years. If you only paint them you may still see the scuffs.

Reproduction panels are available for most cars, but to save money

You may find remnants of the original headliner still attached to the visor, indicating the original color and texture. Document this information about how your car was equipped.

Here is a great example of the door paint and where it is masked off from the contrasting body color. Paint the inside of the door with single-stage enamel.

they are all produced in black. You can paint them to match your original color. If possible, it is better to have panels that are molded in their original color (Such as OEM or from another car) because a black panel that is painted a lighter color appears black when scratched.

Door Panels

Behind the door panels is a plastic vapor barrier. This is a sheet of heavy plastic held in place with strip caulk. It served a very important purpose: It prevented water seepage into the cavity between the exterior body panel and the interior sub-structure.

Attached to the interior metal structure was the door panel with fiberboard backing. Without the plastic the door or interior panel became wet and warped.

Over the years door panels were often removed and the plastic tossed aside. During a certain period a favorite place to put additional speakers for the 8-track stereo was in the door panel. All of this means that you can very seldom use the original panels of the door and rear side panels. Fortunately, all of these panels are reproduced.

These models have different levels of trim so be sure to verify your car's original style. All the trim is attached with push-in clips and are easily removed and reinstalled.

If you don't have salvageable panels, sources such as Legendary Interiors restores original door panels and parts, saving enthusiasts from being "stuck" with old vinyl or padding. Simply ship your upper and lower door panels to their Newark, New York, facility where skilled craftsmen and women strip off the factory vinyl covers and yellowed, brittle foam and rebuild your panels

Install all the door plugs, door seals, window cranks, armrest, door handles, lock knob, and door panel. Be sure to polish the stainless trim to a high gloss. If your car is equipped with power windows your door panel is completely different.

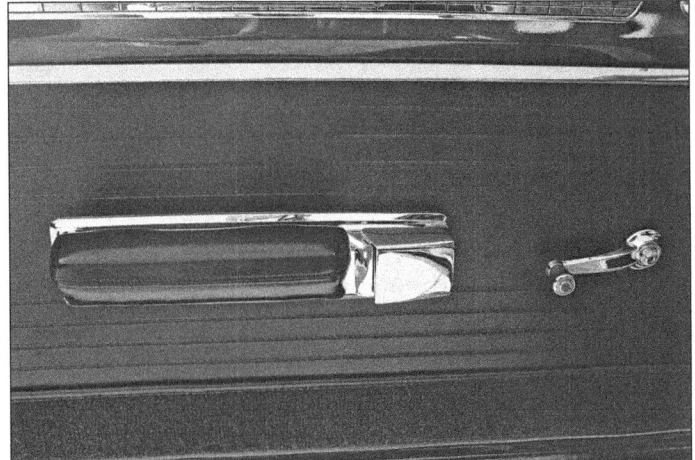

Your end goal is to have a perfect-appearing door panel with all the correct finishes, as seen here on the armrest base, molding, handle, and window crank.

from the ground up. Starting with the bare-metal base, Legendary's techs clean the surfaces and reapply a new coat of glue before attaching the pre-molded replacement foam.

Legendary already has replacement vinyl covers pre-molded to match pre-sculpted foam. They simply align the replacement cover with the base plate, glue the two surfaces together, and heat until they bond. It sounds a lot simpler than it looks, and it takes a skilled hand to do it right. The vinyl is stretched drum-tight and smoothed of any wrinkles before the edges are trimmed and glued down.

The final touches to the upper door panels retain the deluxe interior option's splendor, such as the chrome door lock ferrules and replacement "cat whiskers" window felts.

Although you might hope to have your originals restored, the factory cardboard panels are typically so aged that Legendary suggests replacing them completely and offers a variety of kits for DIYers.

New panels require popping open the holes for clips and cutting the vinyl for window regulators and armrests. The holes for them are perforated in the backing for easy removal with the small tool included in a Legendary kit. A skilled hand with an X-ACTO knife or razor blade can cut the holes in the vinyl from the backside with no problem.

Although our door panels lined up nicely in front, the rear quarters took some finagling to get aligned. Remember, these cars were built by hand, not by computer-controlled machines, so if it doesn't quite fit, it might just be the car.

Most Mopars came off the assembly line with a clear plastic covering that separated the exposed cardboard from moisture and the elements.

Carpet

The carpet on these cars almost always needs to be replaced. Many cars (and the majority of cars with 4-speeds) had black carpet, even with a different-color interior. A good rule of thumb is that a 4-speed car should have black carpet unless you can prove it came with carpet that matched the interior color.

Most reproduction carpet rolled up in a box for shipment. It is molded to fit the floor contours, so it must be laid out flat in the car as soon as possible. The rear section goes in first;

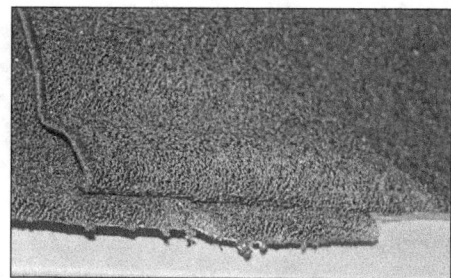

The carpet should lay out for a while so that the shipping folds and wrinkles relax. The rear carpet section goes in first, followed by the front section. Here the carpet is not in position, as evidenced by too much of the firewall showing between the carpet and the heater box and dash.

Before trimming in the carpet, find the holes for the accelerator pedal and mount the pedal. A foam gasket resides between the carpet and the pedal to keep any moisture from entering the interior. Place the carpet on the floor securing it in place with a brick or another heavy object. Use a punch or other sharp, pointed object to push it through the foam and carpet. Climb back into the cab and push a screwdriver through the hole that was just created to locate the holes for mounting the accelerator pedal.

Salt, grime, and dirt eventually tear up the fibers and create holes in your carpet. There are dozens of places to source carpet and prices vary. (Photo Courtesy Chuck Buczeskie)

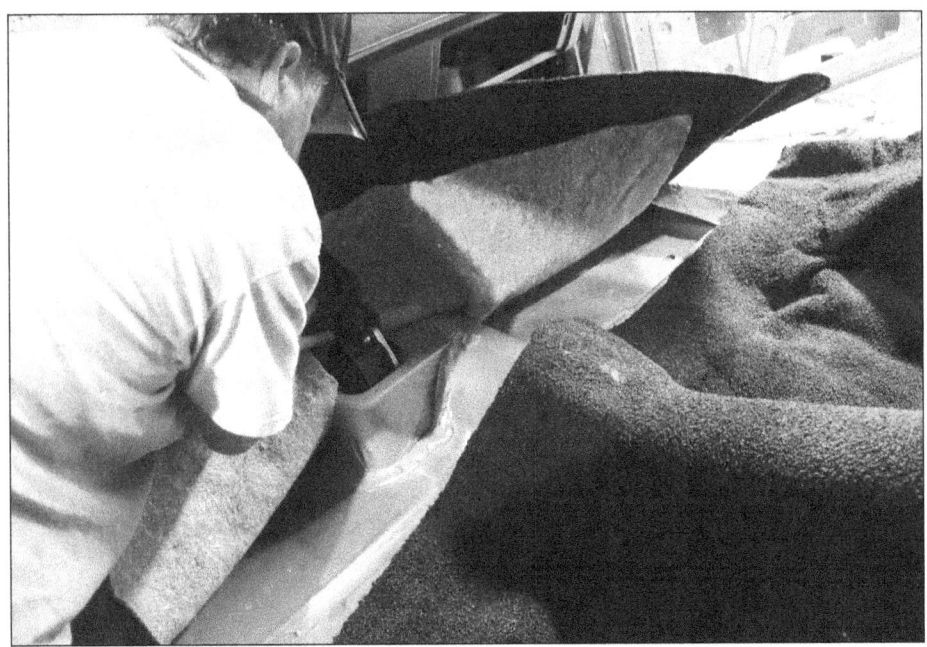

If your car is a 4-speed, or has a console, cut and install the carpet before you trim the outside edges of the carpet.

the front section is installed second and overlaps the rear piece. Some people install sound-deadening material first even though the factory did not. If you choose this sequence the sound deadening will be less visible after the carpet is installed.

When you have the carpet positioned correctly find the holes for the seat belts, the seat track holes, the 4-speed hole if equipped, and the dimmer switch hole. Use a soldering iron to sear the hole com-

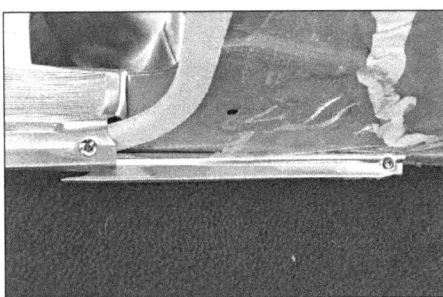

After everything is trimmed and installed, trim in the edges of the carpet. Install the door moisture barrier, wind lace, doorsill, and the often missing scuff plate.

pletely through the carpet. Then take a screwdriver and push it through every hole to hold the carpet in place. You can use a soldering iron to sear the holes for the belts and seats through the carpet as well.

Trim the sides near the kick panels, the front area where the pedal lever attaches to the firewall, and the rear floorpan area where it meets the side panel as necessary. Then wait until you have everything installed and bolted down before trimming the door opening. The dimmer switch has a plastic grommet provided with the carpet. The factory did not use one but instead cut the carpet and pushed the switch up through the hole.

Watch for the foam gasket that goes between the floor and the carpet under the base of the gas pedal. Sometimes the jute backing that is glued on the carpet must be trimmed so that this important seal fits and seals out any moisture from under the car. The carpet is never glued in

these cars. When everything fits, you can trim the door opening right to the raised edge of the pinch weld. It doesn't overlap this edge. Then install the doorsills.

Original doorsills are usually in bad shape and cannot be reused. New ones are available but be sure to buy the best ones you can find. Some are made very poorly. Also check to see if the sills you buy include the correct screws. If the screw holes in the new sill plate do not align exactly you may have to drill one or two new holes. A restorer often uses a larger screw to attach the plate when the hole is too large for the original screw. Because enough room is available to move the plate forward or back without causing any fitment problems, it is preferable to drill new correct holes.

A narrow carpet hold-down strip runs between the rear seat and the doorsill. It attaches with a screw in the front and one in the back. Many people do not have one and are not aware that it is missing. These strips are called two-door B-Body scuff plates. They help to hold the carpet down along the bottom edge of the rear side panel.

Carpet is one of the easiest interior projects you can do by yourself. Companies, such as Legendary Auto Interiors, offer molded carpet kits that are cut and patterned specifically after the factory floorpan and require minimal trimming, if any, to fit. You can use a clean soldering iron to burn the edges of your seat-belt holes so the loop carpet doesn't continue unraveling.

Seats

The seats for all four years and models share many identical parts and design aspects. You basically have the bench seat, bucket seats, buddy seats, and power seats. The convertible models feature unique rear seats.

Seats before January 1969 do not have headrests, but even the bench and bucket seats after January 1969 all have headrests.

You usually find two levels of interiors in each model. Be sure to research what your car came with on your data plate and make sure you purchase the correct style.

All these seats have a metal frame with S-springs that are almost always worn out or busted from years of abuse. Seat tracks bolt through the floor and "Fiber donuts" rest between the floor and the track.

The bench seat has a wire that goes from the driver-side release latch through an adjuster in the middle of the front seat frame. It then attaches to the passenger-side seat track.

Each bucket has its own release. The seat tracks are specific to the model and year and are difficult to tell apart. Most of these are rusted and supplies of them are becoming scarce. They are not reproduced, and even bench seats are harder and harder to find. This makes being able to restore what you have a necessary process to get your car back on the road.

Unless your car has low miles it is best to completely disassemble the seats. After removing the seat covers, the foam, and the burlap padding, examine the seat frame and springs. Replace any broken springs or parts of the frame that need more support. Your local upholstery shop can sell you springs and clamps. If your frames are in really bad shape it is best to strip and paint the frames and take them to a professional for repair.

Examine all the padding and replace as necessary. Foam kits are readily available for most bucket seats but few are available for bench seats. Again, unless your seats are in very good shape it may be best to take them to a good upholstery shop. If you only need to replace the seat covers and everything else is in good shape, almost anyone can install the covers with good results.

Seat covers are held in place by many hog (or pig) rings. Pay careful attention to where these are positioned so that you can correctly install your new covers. You need a good set of hog-ring pliers and at least one or two large boxes of rings.

New seat-foam kits include step-by-step instructions to install the seat foam correctly based on your particular seat. Be sure to have some new razor blades and spray adhesive handy.

When you receive your new seat covers lay them out in the sun or in a warm room. This helps relax the shipping folds and wrinkles before you install the covers.

Seat and Seat Cover Restoration

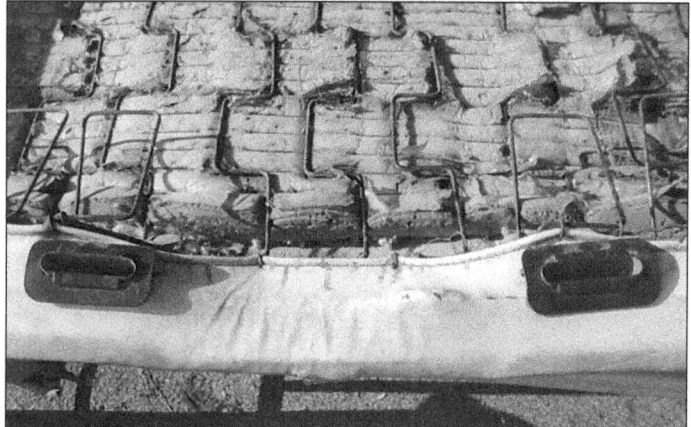

1 *During disassembly carefully document all parts. Here is an example of a seat belt guide in a 1970 Plymouth bench seat. This feature is unique to this B-Body and care must be taken to remove it without damaging the part. If your plastic seat belt guides are still flexible and not brittle they can be disassembled without breaking. Notice the location of the hog rings that hold the seat cover to the frame.*

2 *After removing the back of the front seat examine the pivot to see if it is in good enough shape to support the new seat or if it needs to be replaced. This is a big stress point and vital to the operation of the seat when accessing the backseat area.*

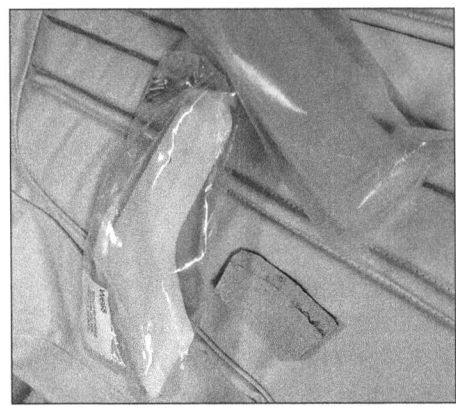

4 *An original swatch of seat material confirms the color of the new seat covers from Legendary. Unless you have a black interior the colors of the different parts of the interior vary. This hinge cover is whiter and the armrest is a bit darker than the seat cover.*

3 *After removing all vinyl, foam, and padding and any old hog rings, blast and paint the seat frames semi-gloss black. You can then install new padding and foam, followed by new seat covers.*

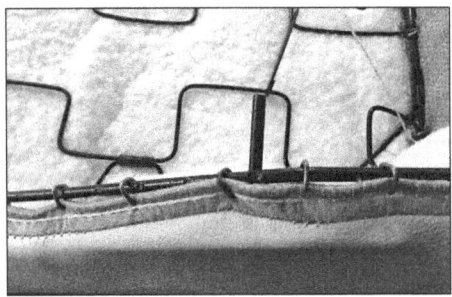

6 *Here are the new seat covers using the new hog rings to attach the covers to the restored seat frame.*

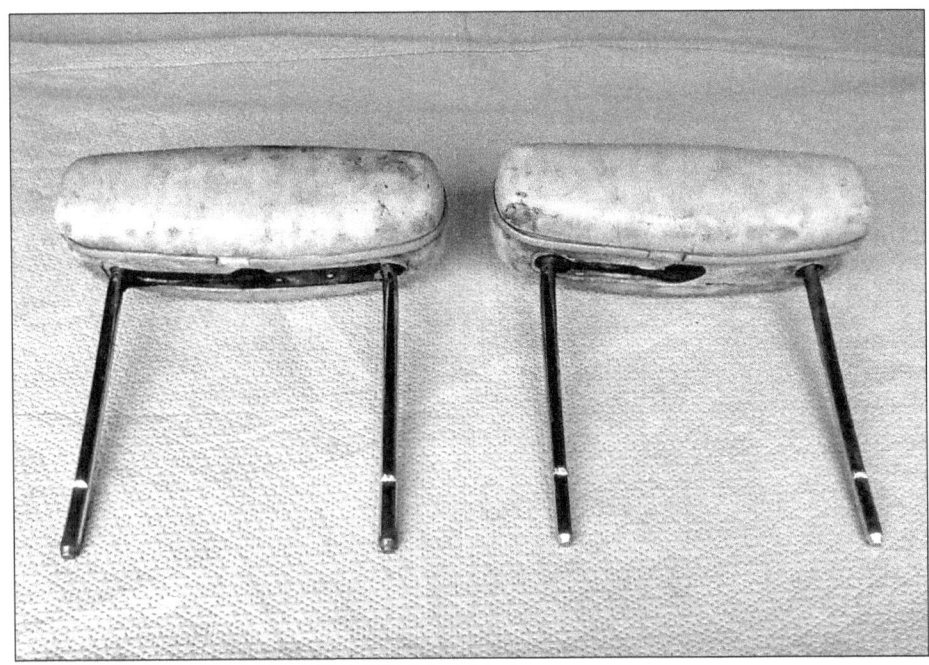

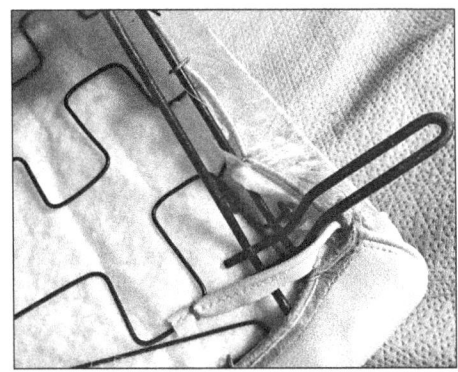

5 *If your headrests are in similar shape as these you can restore them: Replate the posts, replace the chrome trim strip, and clean and re-dye the vinyl. If your vinyl is damaged or cracked you have to buy new ones. Fortunately they are now reproduced and can be purchased on eBay or from several distributors, including P.G. Classics.*

7 *Stretch the covers and attach them from the inside out. Atttach the corners like this. Notice that only a foam pad base appears on the rear seat back.*

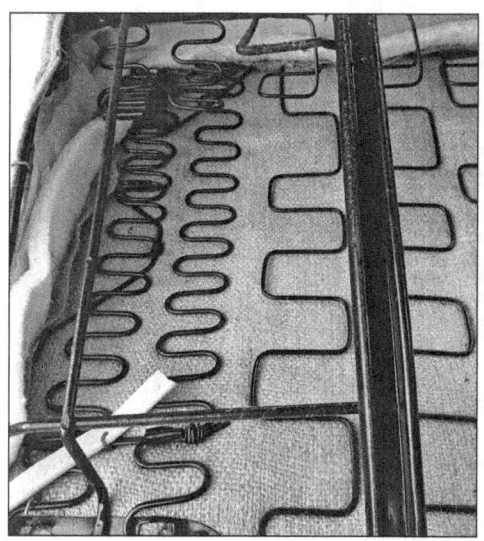

8 Use burlap to reinforce the seat bottom. The springs should have been restored and replaced so you have a comfortable seat that supports your body weight.

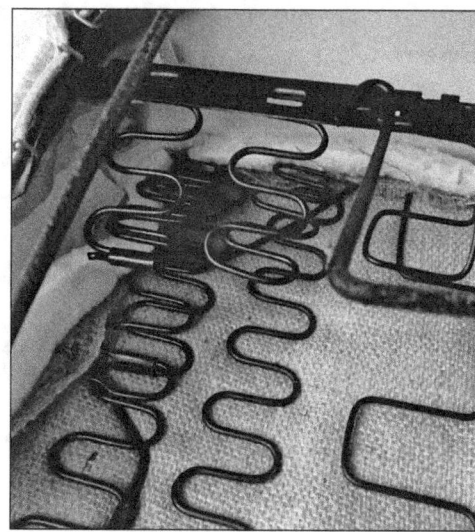

9 The sides of the seat frame have extra springs that support the seat and keeps it from collapsing under the weight of the occupant.

10 The back upper and lower seats are the easiest ones to re-cover. If you have never done any upholstery work before start with these. Notice the hog rings along the bottom holding the cover in place attached to the seat frame.

11 The upper and lower front seats are more difficult to re-cover because of the latches and headrests. Lay out the new covers so that all the piping follows the edges to end up with seats that are not only functional but beautiful.

12 The rear seat mounting clips must be in good shape. They are reproduced and available from many sources. To remove or install the seat bottom you must press the seat inward and either lift upward or apply downward pressure.

13 Do not forget to replace the fiber seat divider that goes between the trunk and the rear seat. It hangs on the upper seatback hooks. The bottom is not secured but hangs freely.

Seat Belts

Most of the time the seat belts and shoulder belts in original cars have been completely neglected. They are either missing or have been lying on the floor or underneath the rear seat. The chrome is rusty and the webbing is hard and faded, and the clips and retractors barely function. The date code and part number tag are also missing, or torn and faded.

Shoulder belts were not even installed in many of these cars, and because they are difficult to remove from the clips over the door, were seldom used. The restoration and replacement of this life-saving equipment is very important.

The first thing to do is inspect the belts and decide if you are missing any of them. The rear seat should have enough belts for three people. If you have a bench seat or buddy seat with buckets in the front, you should also have belts for three people. If your car is a 1969 or 1970 shoulder belts are standard. The shoulder belt configuration is different for 1969 and 1970.

In 1969 cars the buckle is on the shoulder belt and snaps into the tang that is mounted with the sun visor for storage. The rest of the belt is held into place with an elastic band with a snap. In 1970 cars the buckle is on the seat and the tang and belt rest in two clips above the door.

If your car has all of the belts and they are in good shape you can clean them with Simple Green. You can then use 0000 fine steel wool to shine the chrome pieces and remove any grime. You can also repaint the buckle and re-dye the webbing if needed.

If you are missing a few belts you can find them at swap meets, at online "for sale" locations, or at online auction sites. The belts can be

No clips are used on the backseat of convertibles, yet the belts lay nicely.

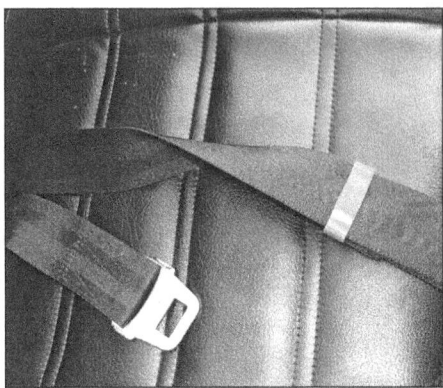

The belts for convertibles are unique because they have a clear plastic strap that keeps the loose part of the belt in place.

re-dyed if you find the missing ones in a different color.

If you do not have any seat belts or shoulder belts you can find complete original sets for sale. Just be sure to check your factory service manual so you know which belts your car originally came with from the factory.

If you have all the original belts, you can have them rebuilt to origi-

nal appearance, even down to the correct date/part number tags. One source that provides all the necessary services is Ssnake-Oyl. Their standard of work is on the highest level and if you are serious about showing your car they are the best way to go. They also have complete sets that are already restored ready to ship if you are missing your originals and all you have to do is install them.

Here is an example of a bench seat with a 4-speed. The seat belts are clipped into the seat belt clips that are mounted to the lower edge of the front seat. When completed, the interior of your B-Body will look and feel the way Chrysler originally built it. Don't cut corners by not replacing the necessary clips and hardware.

Of course, you can always buy a complete reproduction set of belts for your car from suppliers such as P.G. Classics. They have many sets for many applications in stock and ready to ship. These belts are not exactly like your originals and they do not have the date/part number tag, but they are very similar and are much less expensive than sourcing an original set.

The bolts used to secure the seat and shoulder belts are gold cad in finish and come in various shoulder depths depending on where and how many belts are mounted to the bolt. Originals are usually rusted and must be replaced.

Door Latches

A car that has been repainted with the door latches and catches on tells you if a true nut-and-bolt full restoration was performed on the car. If the person who restored the car did not take the time and expense to remove and replate these parts you can count on find corner cutting elsewhere.

The door striker plate on the doorjamb has as few as one and as many as three plates between the striker and the doorjamb. These help with striker and door-latch fit. It also has nuts that float in metal pockets inside the quarter panel. This also helps with correct adjustment of the door. Sometimes these areas are cracked from years of door slamming.

The best way to repair the door latch body-mount panel is to cut it out and butt weld in a replacement. The striker and attaching screws are silver cad plated. The latch is gold cad plated. Convertible models have an upper latch that is spring-loaded and helps to reinforce the door-to–quarter panel fit.

Inside the door several rods connect the door latch to the door lock knob, the door key, and the interior and exterior door handles. These are passenger-side and driver-side specific. The clips for these are also specific, are plastic, and are often broken. A hook mounted inside the door is for the rod from the interior door handle to the latch. This rod has a sleeve so that it does not rattle.

Unless your door latches are in great original shape we recommend you have a professional shop rebuild and replate all of the latches and strikers.

Headliner

Hanging a headliner in a Mopar is as easy as counting to six. A sequence of six metal bows stretch across the width of the ceiling, helping the soft material keep its arced shape.

Two smaller bows do likewise for the massive C-pillars, while serrated teeth at the windshield and snap-in retainers on each side keep the headliner taut.

For cars such as the Dodge Charger, Daytona, and Superbird with long, rakish C-pillars, the headliner requires that special triangular panels glued directly to the headliner or a clip installed into the inner roof liner. You can also use pre-wrapped panels that attach to the inner liner over the headliner, both securing the headliner and looking great.

Trim for the hardtop and the post car is completely different. You need a notch in the trim so that it fits against the post. To help find all the screw holes in your new headliner simply install them before you glue it in. Just slit the material with a

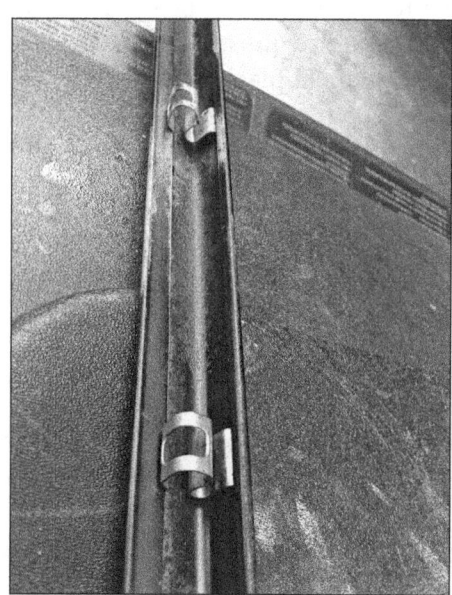

The headliner side trim snaps into place with these unique clips. There are about seven per side and they can become weak over the years. Replace them if necessary from any major aftermarket supplier.

When you have completed restoring the seats it is time to focus on the headliner. On all hardtops and sedans you find insulation that has to be glued to the roof. Without this insulation the car is much hotter because the roof becomes warm from the sun.

razor blade so the screw head comes through the material.

Of course, the C-pillar cardboard plates are available two ways: bare or covered to match the headliner.

Installation in a Nutshell

With a few tricks of the trade and a fair share of patience, headliner installation is a job that can be done by an amateur with professional results.

The first step is to make a sketch of the positioning of everything fastened to the headliner. This includes items such as the rearview mirror, visors, seat belt clips, coat hooks, shoulder belts, dome lamp, etc. Several pictures can be very helpful, too.

Take your time and use the following guidelines. We haven't scrapped one yet, but we've come close!

1 After removing the original headliner, be sure to note the correct order of the bows. They are different and must be reinstalled in their original place. If they were previously removed and mixed up, they can be laid out side-by-side and sorted for position. Your A-pillar cover and front windshield trim should match the color of your dash, whereas the headliner trim matches your headliner color.

2 If the car already had the headliner removed, be sure that the dome-lamp wiring is in place correctly, and if your model has brackets for the shoulder belt clips check that they are present as well. The visors should match the color of the headliner. The shoulder belts and belt holder clip normally matches the interior color. However, in the case of a white-interior car, the seat belts and shoulder belts are black; the shoulder belt clips are also black.

3 The new headliner comes folded in a small box. The headliner may be laid out and warmed in the sun to relax out wrinkles, but it is not absolutely necessary.

4 Slide the bows into the listing pockets and center them. Carefully trim the listings so that about 1 inch of the bow is exposed. (Do this step outside of the car.)

5 Now move the headliner with bows into the car. Place the rear-most bow into the hanger clips. The rear bow has two small wires with hooks on the ends. One end hooks on the bow and the other presses into a small hole in the rear-most roof crossmember. One wire retainer is used per side. We like to hook them slightly inboard so that as the headliner is stretched to the sides it pulls them straight.

6 Continue placing the rest of the bows, working forward.

7 Use about a dozen or so small spring clamps to secure the headliner edges without stabbing it onto the gripper teeth. (Some refer to these as pony clamps, the ones with the orange-dip coating on the tips and handles.) These clamps allow you to work your way around the headliner gradually pulling it tight and eliminating the wrinkles.

Start in the rear by verifying that the centerline marked on the headliner is lined up with center of the rear window opening. Pull the headliner rearward and clamp it in place. Do not press it into the gripper teeth yet.

At the front verify the centering and pull the headliner forward and clamp it in place. Again, don't press it into the gripper teeth yet.

Now work down the sides, pulling the headliner gradually from each side, clamping it along the way. As the headliner is pulled outboard, the listing pockets need to be re-trimmed. Approximately 3/4 inch of bow should be exposed up to the roof-side crossmember. Be consistent with this dimension so that the point where the side-to-side stitch seam curves is the same down the whole side. Continue pulling and clamping around the perimeter until the headliner is taught.

8 When the entire headliner is tight check that the front and rear side-to-side seams are straight. Unequal pulling can make them uneven; this is easily corrected by readjusting.

9 Small tight creases from packing folds come out easily with careful heating. Overheating melts the material. Practice on a scrap piece if you're unsure how hot you can make it. It's also important to keep moving around with the heat to prevent overheating any spot. Time in the sun also relaxes these packing folds.

10 Starting at the rear, pull slightly and press the headliner material onto the gripper teeth. Start in the center and work toward the outsides.

11 Repeat this step on the front edge.

12 The sides must be glued with trim adhesive. You can brush on the glue or use a special glue gun with a pinpoint spray pattern. Glue between the clamps and install headliner clips at each seam. Trim the edges to approximately 5/8 inch.

13 Remove the clamps as each section is dry enough to hold the headliner in place.

14 Trim and glue down areas in front next to the visors. Pull out any soft wrinkles by the visor corners as you glue.

15 Tug on the headliner to eliminate wrinkles and push it down onto the gripper teeth in the sail panel areas. Additional glue along the bottom may be needed.

16 Trim around all edges, being careful not to cut too close to the teeth.

17 Refer to your drawings and pictures to locate the dome-lamp position. On many cars, the dome lamp can be attached at the front or the rear of the center roof crossmember. Be sure you have the right place, then make a small slice for the wiring and socket to pop through. Only trim the slice large enough to allow the lamp to be screwed on without distorting the headliner.

18 Cutting a large opening is not necessary or recommended.

19 The visors, mirror, etc. can be located by feeling through the material to find the indents for the screws. A small needle can also be used to locate the screws. If you put the screws in before you installed the liner, they are easy to find.

Electrical

All electrical components are important and cannot be ignored. Any issues must be addressed, and items repaired or replaced with quality replacement parts that are similar to the originals in appearance and function. More cars are destroyed by re-using old, faulty wiring, gauges, relays, and fuse boxes than anything else.

And that brings up a good point. *Always* carry a good fire extinguisher in your car. It can mean the difference between replacing wires in a small section of the car and a total loss of the car due to a catastrophic fire.

Exterior Lights

Headlights on these cars were never Halogen-style bulbs. They were sealed-beams, either made by Westinghouse or General Electric. Actual date codes are stamped in ink on the backside of these bulbs. Working original bulbs are hard to find but are worth the effort. The wrong headlight bulbs can easily cost you four points in a judged show.

Taillights are also important and must function in the running light, turn signal, and stop light mode.

Parking lights or front turn signal light also must function and have the correct color lens and bulbs. Some have clear bulbs with colored lenses while others have clear lenses with colored bulbs.

Side-marker lights must also function correctly. The exception was in 1969 when Dodge and Plymouth were able to get around federal requirements by using front and rear reflector lenses. The government quickly put a stop to that in 1970.

Interior Lights

Dome lights, map lights, glove box lights, console lights, under-dash lights, and rear seat lights must function correctly. Tracking down all these wires and getting them to work can prove to be a frustrating and time-consuming effort.

You must be able to read a wiring diagram and have an ohmmeter and a test light to work on them. If you have power to the socket you must also have a good ground. Often the lack of a good ground keeps these small but important lights from working.

Wiring Harness

It is best to replace all wiring, wire looms, and connections with new reproduction wiring. The old wires in these cars have deteriorated over the past 40-plus years. With age these wires develop additional resistance; when they are again used in the operation of the vehicle they can heat up and cause a fire.

The new reproduction wiring harnesses are well constructed and look exactly like the originals. They have new connectors that save you hours of frustration trying to track down a bad connection. When they are replaced you never have to deal with them again; you can spend your time enjoying the car and have peace of mind knowing it's safe from potentially dangerous wiring problems.

Dashboard

Dash restoration should be done right the first time because lying on the floor with a droplight trying to fix an under-dash problem is no fun. And having to do it more than once is just plain torture.

Removal

The following general steps are a good reference for this important process.

1 Remove the windshield and steering column.

2 Unplug the wiring harness that runs alongside the driver's kick panel to the rear of the car.

3 Five special bolts hold the upper part of the dash and two hold the lower part. Loosen the two lower bolts but leave them in place. They help to support the dash until you are ready to remove the unit from the car.

4 Remove the upper bolts and use a 3-foot piece of heavy wire to keep the dash from falling into your lap as you disconnect the remaining wiring. The support wire can be threaded through the bolt holes in the dash and the body where the dash attaches, then twisted together, leaving an access space between the dash and the car.

5 The engine wiring harness should already be free of the bulkhead connector. Clips hold the bulkhead connector to the firewall; they must be compressed from the engine's side of the car. Then the connector releases to the inside of the car.

6 Disconnect the heater and vent control cables from the heater box. As always, save, bag, and tag all the attaching clips and screws. They really slow you down if you lose them on re-assembly.

7 Make sure everything is disconnected from the dash assembly including small items such as the antenna cable from the radio.

8 When the dash unit has been disconnected, you can remove it in one piece. Lay it aside on a work table with a blanket for protection (or fashion a jig to mount it) while you disassemble, replace, repair, and reassemble the dash.

Now everything under the dash can be evaluated, cleaned, stripped, and replaced. Remember, this is probably the first time these areas have seen the light of day in many years.

Evaluate your skill level, time, and the financial resources you have to completely restore this unit. Some shops test and replace any non-functional gauges, wiring, and components, and return them to you completed and ready to install. However, this process is not cheap, but you have a guaranteed, fully restored unit.

Depending on your car's options you have several areas to address during the restoration of the dash unit.

Wiring

The wires and connections of the under-dash unit are, without a doubt, the most important wiring in the entire car. A short in the under-dash wiring is the easiest way to burn your car to the ground.

For safety's sake, do not ever bypass the fusible link with a hard wire. It is the main connection between the battery and the dash. Many car fires are caused by owners who removed or bypassed the fusible link, or by faulty dash wiring.

The aftermarket offers many reproduction under-dash wiring harnesses, all with the correct wires and plugs. Replace it now and never have to worry about it again.

Gauges, Switches, and Control Panels

We suggest having your dash cluster and switch panel bench tested and cosmetically restored. These gauges are usually yellowed with the plastic faded, and the chrome is almost always pitted.

Send these components to a professional shop that restores these gauges. Replace any switch that does not work. Nine out of ten times you have to replace the headlamp switch because the dimmer coils are bad.

The lettering on the switch panel can be restored by painting it with semi-gloss paint. Separate a brand-new eraser from a number 2 pencil, dip it into some water-base white paint, and dab it on the raised lettering.

With a little practice you can have a professional-looking panel with correct lettering. This technique can also be used on the heater controls.

Radio

Now is the time to decide whether or not to restore your original radio, upgrade it to modern components with original appearance, or replace with a new unit. The original radio is often long gone and the radio dash plate has been cut to mount a cheap aftermarket unit. Because this is about restoring your car to original appearance, the best answer is to either purchase a new unit or have your original radio upgraded with modern components.

Another popular option is to have your original unit rebuilt and then wire in a removable modern

Tired from years and years of weathering and sunshine, the cluster must be removed and sent to a gauge restoration specialist. (Photo Courtesy Chuck Buczeskie)

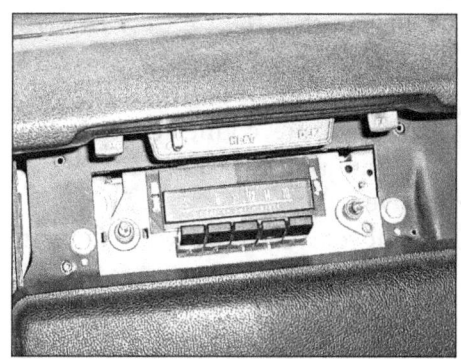

Missing knobs, stuck buttons, and sheared wires are just some of the fun associated with your stock radio. Check first to see if it works, then decide which direction you want to take in restoring the unit. (Photo Courtesy Chuck Buczeskie)

unit with CD or MP3 capabilities. No matter what you decide you must replace the speaker and make sure the radio receives and changes channels as it did originally.

Reproduction antennas are available through many online sources.

Each year from 1966 to 1970, changes were introduced in the face and the knobs of the radios. The 1968–1969 thumbwheel units are interchangeable. The Plymouth radio says "Chrysler" on it and the Dodges specifically say "Dodge."

Dash Pads

You find variations in the style and type of dash pads each year of the 1966–1970 Plymouth and Dodge B-Body. Some of these pads interchange from one year to the next (as with the 1968 and 1969 Plymouth models). However, be aware that even if the dashes appear to be the same, some differences can catch you off guard. A good example is the ignition switch and hole in the dash of a 1968 Plymouth B-Body; it is smaller than the same part and hole in the dash of the 1969 Plymouth.

Different models of the same line of cars featured different levels of dashes as well, such as a standard dash versus a Rallye dash.

Dash pads are often cracked. If that is the case, they must be restored or replaced with originals. Reproduction pads are available, but most of them have small differences, such as in thickness or finish that set them apart from original parts. Whenever possible use original parts and refinish them.

All of the years of grime come off with a thorough cleaning with lacquer thinner. Repair any problems in the back of the pad with black silicone. Check for any scratches and scrapes and smooth them out with a fine file or sandpaper. Then, for a black dash pad use SEM Landau Black. It correctly duplicates any interior black vinyl parts. Spray several light coats and let them dry.

SEM offers other colors in their line so you can match the color of your original parts. If you do have to buy reproduction parts most of them only come in black or white. We suggest starting with white if you want to match a light interior color and black for all dark colors.

Heater and Vent Controls

Every car, no matter the year, has the same basic layout of the heater and vent controls. Bench test the unit to make sure all of the controls function normally. The tabs and faceplates are reproduced, but the original can also be restored.

If you have extra units to use for parts you can almost always restore one unit to full function. Verify that the switches work and that the cables move freely.

Vent controls are under the dash; reproductions of these are available

as well. They must be replaced if they're not in good condition.

Glove Box

Most models feature a fiber insert that has an access flap to the fuse box. These are reproduced and are easily replaced. Some models have a glove box light; it must function normally. The inside of the glove box door's appearance is as important as the exterior.

Also, now is a good time to mention that if you do not have the original owner's manual, get one. If you show the car at a high level the judges will look for it.

Dash Paint

The dash's metal frame, unless in pristine condition, should either be sanded or cleaned, or better yet, dipped and stripped. One of the most difficult steps in the restoration of the dash frame is identifying the holes that were originally in the dash and the ones that have been drilled over the years. The best way to tell which type you have is to look at the backside of each hole. Most factory holes are finished, whereas owner-drilled holes have a rough back edge.

If your car has a 4-speed the dash has a reverse light. The same goes for an Air Grabber car. Depending on the year, an under-dash cable or a vacuum switch actuates the Air Grabber. All other holes must be welded up and finished for paint.

Painting the dash is very straightforward, except for the specialized finish that all dashes had from the factory. The steering column and the ashtray cover is also painted with the same finish. All colors of dash paint included an additive for a suede finish to eliminate any reflective glare from the sun.

The original paint formula and additive is hard to find so sometimes you have to settle for a close match. It resembles the feel of 100-grit wet/ dry paper. The dash vents are painted with regular semi-gloss enamel.

Installation

Either tape off the tag if it is in really good shape or remove it by grinding off the rosette rivets from the backside. Strip the tag and repaint with semi-gloss black. ECS has the dry transfer Chrysler logo, and the original-style rivets are available online from many different resources. After the dash is painted reattach the VIN. It will look incredible!

When the dash is out is the time to completely replace and restore all the insulation, heater box, emergency brake assembly, brake and clutch assemblies, and wiper assembly. Everything is accessible and easy to work on. Several types of insulation is used under the dash. The glue on upper pad insulation and the fiberboard-backed insulation are all available as reproductions; not all of it is. Save what you can't find as a reproduction and reuse if possible.

When everything has been restored and all the under-dash assemblies installed, it is time to install the restored dash assembly. We suggest that the same techniques used to remove the dash be used to

reinstall it: Set the unit on the two lower bolts; use a heavy wire to hold the dash in place until all the wires and cables are connected. Lift and push the unit into place and attach the five bolts.

The dash, along with all parts of this assembly, is the command center for your car. In addition, it is the focal point for your eyes from the moment you slide into the driver's seat. I cannot stress enough the importance of thoroughly detailing this vital assembly. Make sure every part of every area works as originally intended. Not only is it a thing of beauty, but all operational aspects of the car flow through this central command center.

Dashboard Restoration

1 Remove and disassemble the pedal assembly (if you have an automatic transmission) or the clutch and pedal (if you have a manual transmission). Blast and replace the bushings. Test the taillight switch and replace it if necessary. The pedals are natural metal with semi-gloss black paint three-fourths of the way up the shaft.

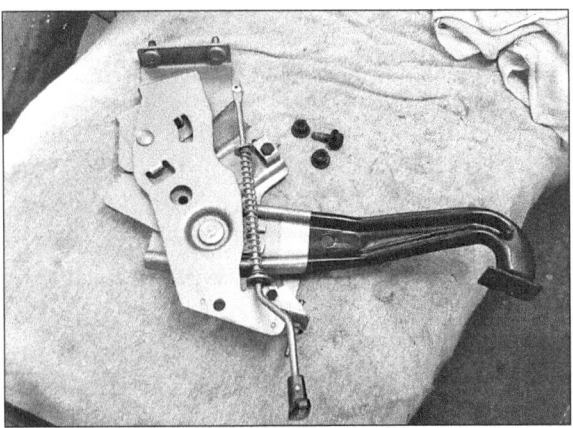

2 The emergency brake assembly is attached with two bolts from the inner wheelwell. Remove it and the cable. Blast and refinish the entire brake assembly.

3 The area behind the emergency brake assembly needs to be stripped. A plastic retainer and metal clip dipped in rubber holds the taillight-wiring bundle away from the dash. Unfortunately, no reproduction clips are available currently from the aftermarket, so you must seek out original parts.

5 *Access to the wiper linkage enables you to replace the seals and end link. This is a good time to send your wiper motor off to be restored.*

4 *You may have several types of insulation under the dash. The glue on upper pad insulation and the fiberboard-backed insulation are all reproduced. This insulation is original; save it if possible.*

6 *Remove the fuse box and clean all the connections with a wire brush. NOS fuse boxes are available if yours is too far gone to reuse.*

7 *After removing everything from the dash either blast or dip strip the frame. The paint for these dashes is unique in finish and in color. It is a low-gloss black with a suede additive and best results are achieved with a spray gun. Dashes of another color also have the low-gloss finish. This finish correctly reproduces the OEM finish.*

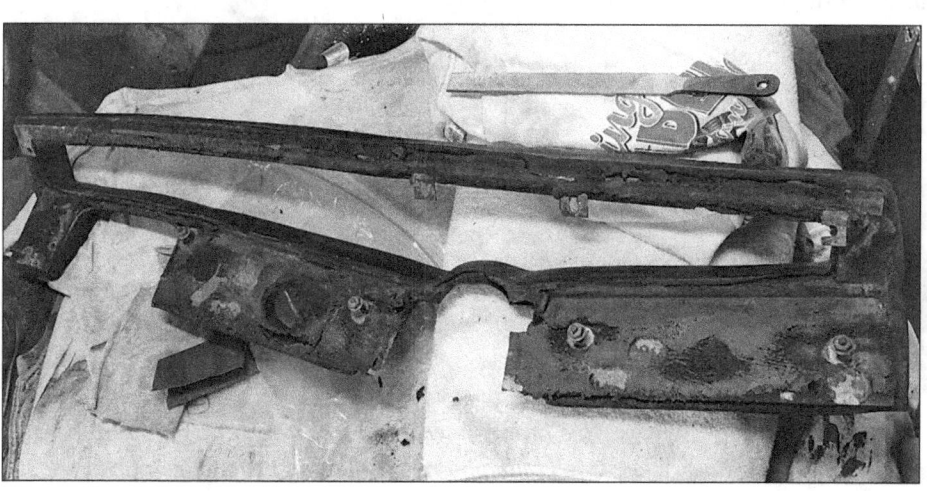

8 *Each year of Plymouth and Dodge models has a different dash pad. Inspect your originals and if at all possible restore them. Reproduction pads are often different from originals. This pad could be trashed, but with patience and the correct products it can be saved. You can repair the backside with black silicone.*

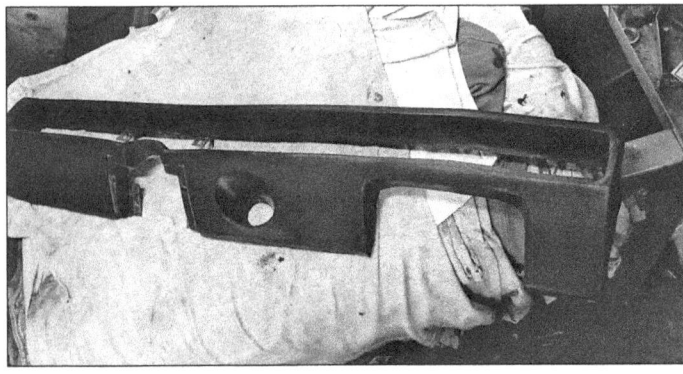

9 *If your pad has no cracks it can be restored. Clean with lacquer thinner and remove any small imperfections with a fine file or sandpaper.*

10 *Years of use leave some very tough stains. Use lacquer to remove them; they must come off for the paint to stick.*

11 *This is the best dye/paint to match the original finish of a black dash pad. Spray several light coats to produce a show-quality result.*

12 *After cleaning and painting, the dash pad looks fantasic.*

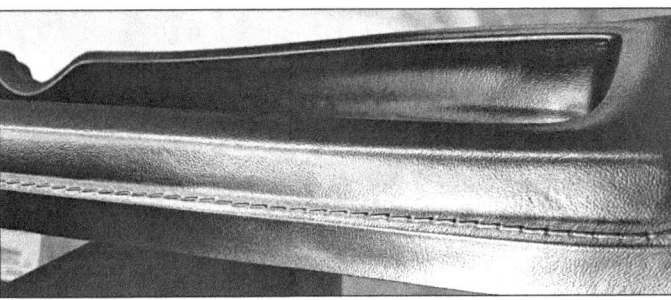

13 *The detail and appearance of an original unit cannot be found in a reproduction pad. With the correct process and product it is better than new.*

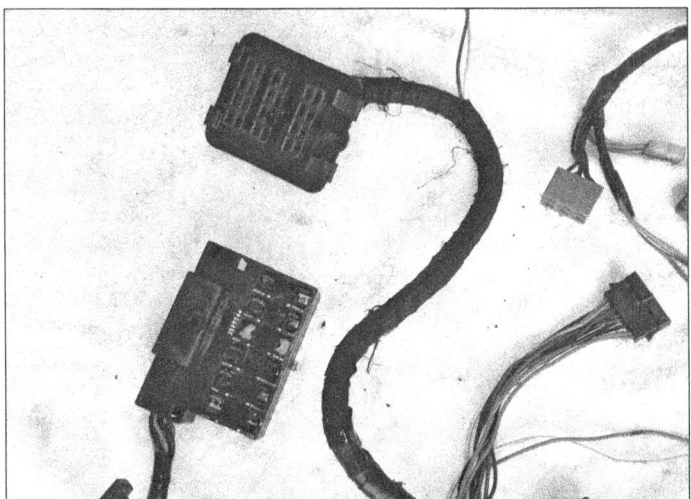

14 *You can splice and repair the original harness, but we recommend replacing all under-dash wiring of these cars.*

15 *This brand-new, tested, correct, and complete under-dash wiring harness will never have to be touched again.*

16 *You can make a homemade jig to mount your dash and be able to access the front and back. You can work on a table, but only on one side at a time. Also, with your dash mounted you do not have to worry about scratching or marring it.*

17 *Your new, working, reliable, tested dash is now ready to go back in the car. ESE and Associates can rebuild your dash to completely original specs.*

18 *This is a rare B-Body convertible switch. Notice the added label from the factory. The other lettering was done with a fresh pencil eraser and white paint and looks factory original. Always replace the switches if their finish or function is not correct.*

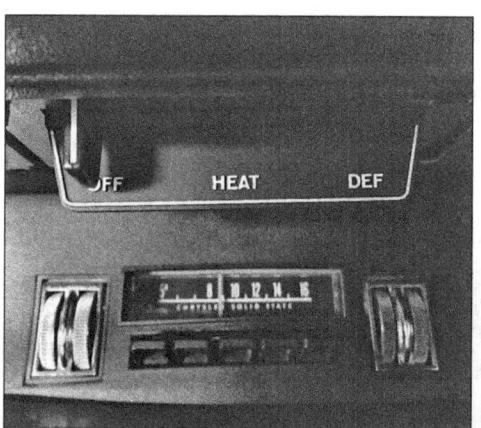

19 *Radios varied from year to year and must be restored along with the heater controls. The heater control buttons are reproduced and match the originals exactly. That is great because most of the time they are worn from years of use and are not restorable. This is a Plymouth 1968–1969 thumbwheel radio; it reads "Chrysler" on the dial. The Dodge version says "Dodge."*

20 *This is a 1970 Plymouth radio. It was a one-year-only style and very difficult to find in working condition.*

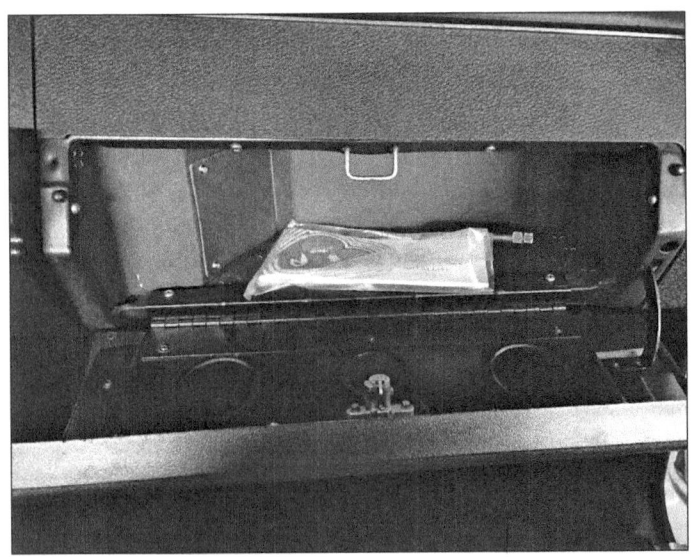

21 This 1970 glove box has an owner's manual. The door opens downward and is brittle plastic instead of durable vinyl. From year to year, the latches are different and cannot be used interchangeably.

22 Don't forget to restore the brake backing plate inside the engine compartment. It is painted semi-gloss black no matter the car color. The foam seals are white and are installed after paint.

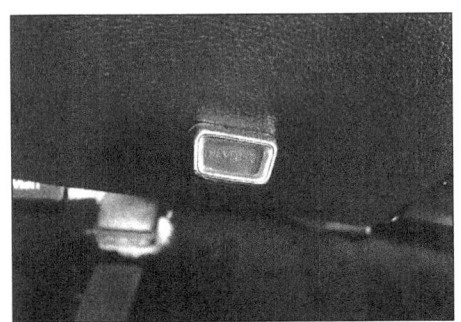

23 The manual reverse light is mounted on the dash and must be in working order.

24 Manually operated fresh-air systems were available on 1968–1969 Dodges and Plymouths. The red handle to open and close them is mounted under the dash beside the vent cables.

In 1970 a vacuum-operated fresh-air system was available. It has several lines running from the canister in the engine compartment to the relief valve, then to the switch, and back to the engine compartment. Make sure this all works before installing the windshield.

25 The Rallye dash was an option on some Plymouth and Dodge models and came standard on other models. (Photo Courtesy Chuck Buczeskie)

DETAILING AND SHOWING YOUR CAR

After you have spent literally thousands of hours building and restoring your car, a final and very important part of showing your car and winning first place is in the final details. These cars have sometimes cost six figures to build. Only one or two points may separate first from second and often it comes down to the finest details. Where the average enthusiast cleans his car with a sponge and bucket of water, when you are detailing for show you have to use a toothbrush and cotton swab.

Whether you are getting your car ready to show at the local cruise-in or the Mopar Nationals, the goal is the same: to present your car in the very best condition possible. No one area of your car is more important than any other. Although most people spend all of their effort making the paint and interior shine, the undercarriage and trunk are just as important for a car to truly be show ready.

We have a rule of thumb when going over our cars: "If I see it, I assume everyone sees it." We have heard car owners say, "The judge won't see that, only I will know." Wrong! The only way to show your car is with your best possible effort, especially in the area of cleaning and detailing.

A Detail Job Worthy of Judging

You can choose from literally thousands of products to clean and detail your car. Almost everyone has his or her own group of favorite products. Do not be afraid of trying new products, especially if you like the results you see on someone else's car. It's great to check out everyone's detail basket and see what he or she uses.

The best detailing is done in your garage, before you take the car to a show. Never wait until you get on the show field. That is where you do the final touch-up and cleaning.

We always recommend that you wear soft cotton sweat pants or shorts

This is the moment you've been waiting for, when it's time to finally unveil your project to the world. It can be a nerve-racking experience if you're not prepared.

and a tee shirt. No buttons, belts, jewelry, or key chains. Wear nothing that can scratch your car. You may not look cool, but it isn't about you; it's about your car! Detailing can be a hot job so you may also want to wear a sweatband or hat. You don't want that sweat from your head to drip on a seat or fender.

Some basic items you need include microfiber cloths, cotton baby diapers, hand towels, bath towels, shop paper towels, a California duster, a soft toothbrush, cotton-tipped swabs, newspaper, detail fine paint brushes, canned air, 0000 steel wool, masking tape, a hand brush with soft bristles, round toothpicks, and a sealable jar for touch-up paint and another one for lacquer thinner.

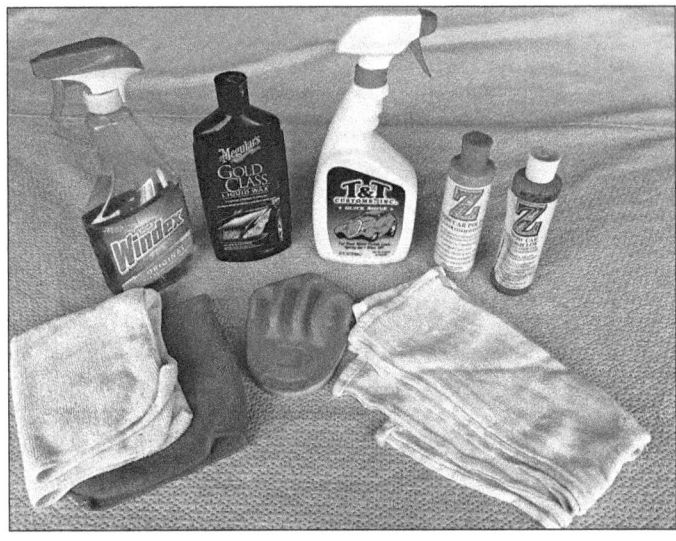

Windex is a great cleaner than can be used on all surfaces. The Zaino polish system includes some of the best products for a show-car finish. A good detailer works well at the show for a last minute cleanup and shine boost.

Interior

Always start with the interior so that any dust or dirt that brushes up while cleaning does not settle on the exterior of the car. Vacuum all the carpet, and move the front seat up and back to make sure you remove everything under the seat. Vacuum the package tray carefully with the brush attachment; the fiber finish can be marred with a hard attachment. Also vacuum in the seat cracks where the seat back and bottom meet.

Wipe down all the hard surfaces in the interior with a damp cotton cloth such as a baby diaper or hand towel. Use any all-purpose cleaner. Many use Windex to clean all of these surfaces including the glass.

Using a small duster that has been treated so the dust clings to the duster, dust all the dash, bezels, and instruments.

Then we wipe all of the soft upholstery with the Meguiar's Natural Shine. We never use any treatment that makes everything so slick and shiny that it looks wet.

Do not forget to clean above the sun visors, in the glove box, in the ashtrays, and the kick panels.

If you have leather use a high-quality leather conditioner. Do not use any product designed for vinyl on leather because it dries it out.

You can use canned air to blow any dust from areas you cannot reach with a rag, such as vents.

If you have wood grain you can bring back its shine with Lemon Pledge. Also use Lemon Pledge on the Organisol exterior stripes. Use the natural shine on all rubber seals, pedals, and rubber heel pad. Remove any mats for final showing.

On the show field you can use a long piece of masking tape, wrapped around your hand with the sticky side out, to remove any small bits of trash or grass from the carpet.

After cleaning all the interior surfaces it is time to clean the interior

Detail Supplies

As you detail your car more often you will try various items. Here is a list of our favorite brand-name products:

- Windex original formula
- Zaino Brothers polish
- Meguiar's quick detailer, natural shine for vinyl and rubber, Gold Class Liquid Wax
- Wolfgang's tire cleaner
- Bleche-Wite white wall and letter tire cleaner
- Dupli-Color paint in aerosol cans. Flat black, semi-gloss black, gloss black, engine color
- Seymour's Stainless Steel paint
- Wenol chrome and stainless polish
- Pinnacle Natural Brilliance Black Onyx Tire Gel and foam applicator
- Sheen Genie All Metal Polish and Cleaner, Sealer and Repellent

Lemon Pledge is great for detailing any Organisol-painted stripes or panels. Use steel wool on any flash rust or for polishing chrome with very tiny pits. You can also use it on glass to remove dirt from difficult areas. Be sure you have various chrome polishes in your detail pack. Cotton swabs help to detail even the smallest crevasses and microfiber cloths are a must! Use masking tape to pick up any last minute debris by wrapping it around your hand with the sticky side out.

A California duster must be used to remove any fine particulates from the paint surface before wiping. Tire cleaners and treatments make the tires look perfect. You can clean with Meguiar's Natural Shine. It leaves a natural, non-greasy shine on important rubber and vinyl areas.

side of the glass. Again use Windex but change to a microfiber rag. Use one rag with the Windex and then follow up with a fresh, clean and dry rag. After this you can take a wadded-up piece of newspaper and wipe the glass. This removes the last bit of streaks so often found on glass.

If your glass has any difficult dirt that does not come off with a rag and cleaner you can use 0000 steel wool or a razor blade to remove it.

Clean all of the dash plastic bezels with the Windex and rag. In tight spots you may have to use the cotton-tipped swab.

Finally, using artist-quality fine-detail paintbrushes touch up any chips in your interior painted surfaces. No matter how hard you try to avoid them, chips and scratches get into the interior painted hard surfaces. As is the case anytime you touch-up paint, apply new paint only to the part of the chip or scratch that is missing. If you paint outside the chip you will always be able to spot the repair.

Engine and Engine Bay

After the interior turn your attention to the engine and engine bay. Use a soft cotton rag and take your time; wipe every area with the Windex so it is clean. Windex dries without leaving a residue.

Apply Meguiar's Natural shine to a small rag and wipe all rubber parts. It looks clean and natural and not greasy as are other rubber treatments.

Clean the fins of the radiator with a soft-bristle brush. Also have a pair of radiator fin pliers to straighten any fins that may have been bent.

Next, blow any dirt or dust out of the lower radiator support and K-member with canned air.

Touch up any body color, engine color, or painted surfaces with touch-up brushes. Spray some paint into the top from an aerosol paint can. Make all the touch-ups then clean the brush with lacquer thinner.

Do not forget to clean the edges of the hood and the bottom of the hood hinges where fine residue appears from opening and closing the hood.

Tires and Wheels

When preparing a car for a show you should remove the wheels and tires to clean them. This way you can also detail the wheelwells and front and rear suspension while the tires are off the car.

Wet the wheels and tires with water before applying Bleche-Wite white-wall cleaner. Try not to get this cleaner on the wheels because it can stain polished aluminum; if you do, wipe it off immediately. Use a steel-wool or stiff brush to scrub the

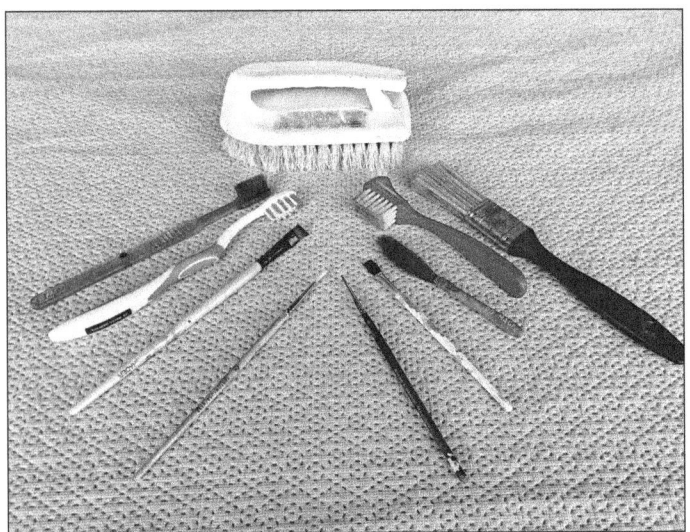

Brushes for different areas of cleaning and for small paint touch-ups are a must-have in everyone's detail kit.

A wide array of paints can be used to detail these cars. Here are some of the best I have found to duplicate original finishes; they can be sprayed into their tops for small last-minute touch-ups at the show.

white/red wall or raised letters on the tires. Rinse with water.

If your tires do not have any white/red walls or white letters just skip this step and use Wolfgang's tire cleaner. Then wipe the tire and wheel dry with a large soft towel.

Polish the wheel with a cotton cloth using Sheen Genie All Metal Polish and Cleaner. This product cleans chrome and polished aluminum very well. Follow this with Sheen Genie sealer and repellant. This is an amazing product that keeps your wheels looking great and stops any future oxidizing.

Now that the tires and wheels are completely clean and polished apply Pinnacle Natural Brilliance Black Onyx Tire Gel with a foam applicator. Many tire treatments leave your tires much too glossy and looking greasy. This gel treats the tire and leaves it looking really clean and with a natural look. You can also reapply this gel on the show field because it isn't a spray.

Hand polish all the lug nuts, check the air pressure and adjust as necessary, and install all the tires and wheels back onto the car.

Now your tires and wheels are ready to show and only a quick wipe down to remove any grass or slight residue may be needed when you arrive at your spot on the show field.

Trunk

Detailing the trunk is often overlooked and left until the last. Many points are lost in this neglected area. The trunk paint, mat, spare tire, jack assembly, wiring, trunk latch, trunk seal, and light bezels need to be in correct and original condition. Clean and treat everything in the trunk the same as you would the exterior.

Judges always lift the trunk mat to inspect the condition of the paint and the body plugs. Many check the ribs in the trunk floor to watch for "puddle" primer painted over with body color. They also look for correct sound deadener patterns.

All the attaching bolts that attach the trunk lid are painted body color along with the catch. Even the trunk slider is greased and then painted before installation on the tension trunk bars.

Be sure to follow the jack instructions. They tell you how to mount the jack, spare, and hold-downs.

Unless the car was special ordered with a "styled" wheel the spare is a plain steel wheel painted gloss black with about 10 to 15 percent flattener added. Some cars have the size of the spare written on the inside of the trunk lid with a grease/paint marker.

In addition to having everything correct and as clean as possible, *always* remove everything from the trunk before your car is judged.

Paint

The exterior paint of the car is the first thing everyone notices on a car. Good paint can make or break a restoration. Here are several things you should do to get the best out of your car's paint. Seldom "wash" a restored car. The best way to detail your car for show is to clean it completely before it leaves your garage or shop. If you trailer your car or if you drive it, it needs to leave your garage as clean as possible. The first thing to do before touching the car with a rag is to use a California duster. Even if the car had a cover, use the duster as soon as you remove the cover and again before you put it back on. Be sure to invest in the best car cover possible. Any fine dust creates "spider swirls" in the paint unless they are removed with a duster.

After dusting the car it is time to clean the car by using microfiber cloths and Windex. Spray a fine mist over a section at a time and wipe with a cloth that has Windex sprayed on it and is damp, followed by wiping with a clean dry cloth. Do this on all the painted exterior surfaces, the stainless, the chrome, and the glass.

After the car is clean use a high-quality show car polish system from Zaino Brothers. It really is worth the investment and makes even the best paint job look deeper and the shine fantastic. Good results also come from Meguiar's Gold Class Liquid Wax and quick detailer.

No matter what products you use, the basics are the same. The paint must be wet sanded and buffed correctly. It must be clean from any contaminants, and it must have quality products applied correctly.

Undercarriage

Clean, clean, and clean. The undercarriage must have all of the correct finishes and be completely clean before you leave the garage. A car that follows the steps for correctly painting the undercarriage the way the factory did always outscores someone who paints it with body color or all black. Inspection marks on the suspension go a long way in separating you from the rest of the pack.

If you drive your car you must really spend a large amount of time under it compared to a car that was brought on a trailer. If the show field is on grass and it has rained your work doubles. No matter the conditions, many first- and second-place cars are separated by the level of detail to the undercarriage. So spend time to make the bottom as good as the top!

Stainless and Chrome

The last areas to be detailed for show are the stainless, light bezels, emblems, and chrome. This is where even the smallest details make a big difference.

Many use a toothbrush to remove polish residue from around emblems and cotton swabs around turn signal bezels and grilles. Wenol chrome and stainless polish is a great product and you only need to use a very little to get the desired results.

Be sure to polish between, over, and under all trim. The same basic rule for the paint also goes for the chrome and stainless. Polish does not make poor paint, chrome, or stainless with scratches better. It only makes the good finishes better!

Touch up

Now that you have cleaned, polished, and detailed all areas of the car you can see where to touch up the paint and parts. Use the very best fine artist brushes to make these touch-ups.

Have a can or a small bottle of every color used on the car in your kit along with a small bottle of lacquer thinner. Several soft cloths or shop towels come in handy for cleanup during this process.

Always be aware of other cars around you when using touch-up paint sprayed into the cap of the aerosol can. Any breeze at all can spread your color to the car next to you. Something no one wants to have to deal with is overspray from a neighbor!

Show Venues

Now that you have your car finished, detailed, and ready to show, you can enjoy several aspects and show levels. There are as many different shows as there are cities, including cruise-ins, local weekend shows, regional and state shows, and national shows. These shows can have no judging, drive by judging, participant judging, and points judging. No matter what the venue it helps you to enjoy the show more if you understand the process of the specific show.

No matter where you show your car it is important to remember to enjoy the experience. It really is not about a piece of plastic or a plaque, but it is about enjoying your car as you strive to make it the best it can possibly be. By showing your car you can learn where it needs to be improved. In the process you make some wonderful memories and get to know many great people who love these cars as much as you do.

Local Cruise-Ins

This type of show is so popular that literally thousands if not tens of thousands of these venues have them on Friday, Saturday, and every other night of the week. You will enjoy the laid-back atmosphere of everyone driving their car and wiping it down and setting up your lawn chair and talking with all the friendly people who also love and enjoy their car just like you do.

No real judging goes on at these venues, but many give away a trophy of the week. This is completely subjective and frequently does not go

Driving and showing your B-Body can become one of the most satisfying moments in car ownership. Take satisfaction in the fact that others now get to see your work of art. (Photo Courtesy Rick Pawlenty)

to the best or most correctly restored car in the lot. This is a good place to get to know other owners with similar cars and develop friendships that can last a lifetime.

Local Weekend Shows

A group usually sponsors this type of show to raise money for a charity or club. A small entry fee is standard, music and food are available, and a trophy is presented at the close of the day. The classes for different years and makes of cars are broad in scope. They may have only one class for Mopars that includes all years, models, modified, and original cars.

This type of event can have participant judging, which is really just a popularity contest, or a count of who has the most friends in attendance that day.

These shows may instead use drive-by judging, where several people take a quick look at your car and score it with a general judging sheet.

Or they can have true points judging in which experienced, trained judges look at each car and score it according to a detailed judging sheet. They total the points in each class and award trophies based on points.

Regional and State Shows

These are usually organized on a much larger scale and draw participants from more than one area or state. The Antique Automobile Club of America (AACA) hosts these type of events all around the country. These shows are for original cars only and their goal is the preservation of great cars 25 years or older of all models. Members of the AACA that attend these events can be assured that their car is fairly judged and can receive judging sheets that show how the car can be improved.

The first year you can achieve Junior First or Senior First if you score well enough according to their guidelines. The next year you can show at a Grand National event and receive Grand National First. The third year you can attend a Grand National event and receive Senior Grand National First. If you have a Senior Grand National car you really have one of the finest examples of an original car.

Many shows fit into this level of competition and most of them have qualified judges who judge according to a points sheet. That way all cars have a fair chance and stand on their merits.

National Shows

For Mopars several shows in various parts of the country meet the standards of this show level. The basic requirements are clearly defined classes, separating cars by years, and specifying whether modified and original.

Experienced, qualified judges spend at least 30 minutes with each car examining every aspect and part of the car to determine whether it is truly original, according to the standard of the way it left the factory. They check any original paperwork or documentation you have for the car.

The event usually lasts for more than one day and the reputation of the cars that win at these shows increases the value of the cars. This is where magazines find cars they are impressed with and do full features, including a photo shoot and article in their publication. To have your car featured in one of these magazines is an experience of a lifetime.

At national shows you may find an even higher level of judging for only a few cars. That is called OEM level. These cars are judged to the highest standards and each car can be evaluated for three hours or more.

SOURCE GUIDE

440 Source
3680 Research Way
Carson City, NV 89706
775-883-2590
440source.com

Accurate Muffler
541-672-2661
accurateltd.com

ARP
1863 Eastman Ave.
Ventura, CA 93003
800-826-3045
arp-bolts.net

Auto Metal Direct
940 Sherwin Pkwy., Ste. 180
Buford, GA 30518
866-591-8309
autometaldirect.com

Auto Restoration Parts Supply
P.O. Box 35300
Richmond, VA 23235
804-743-0570

B/E&A Restoration Parts
8801 Norwalk Rd.
Litchfield, OH 44253
330-725-3990
beaparts.com

Brewer's Performance
10510 St. Rte. 571
Laura, OH 45337
937-947-4416
brewersperformance.com

Champion Spark Plugs
federalmogul.com

Classic Industries
18460 Gothard St.
Huntington Beach, CA 92648
800-854-1280
classicindustries.com

Coker Tire
866-513-2744
cokertire.com

Dante's Mopar Parts
19 Turtle Creek Dr.
Mullica Hill, NJ 08062
609-332-4194
dantesparts.com

Detroit Muscle Technologies
23624 Roseberry Ave.
Warren, MI 48089
586-777-7167
detroitmuscletechnologies.com

Dixie Restoration Parts
605 Harmony Grove Rd.
Ball Ground, GA 30107
770-975-9898
dixierestorationparts.com

Eastwood
263 Shoemaker Rd.
Pottstown, PA 19464
eastwood.com

ESPO Springs 'n Things
75 Pine Tree Rd.
Danville, PA 17821
800-903-9019
springnthings.com

Edelbrock
2700 California St.
Torrance, CA 90503
310-781-2222
edelbrock.com

Fine Lines
127 Hartman Rd.
Wadsworth, OH 44281
finelinesinc.com

The Finer Details Restorations
2001 E. Main St.
Danville, TN 46122
317-745-2124
thefinerdetails-1.com

Griot's Garage
3333 S. 38th St.
Tacoma, WA 98409
800-345-5789
griotsgarage.com

Hardcore Horsepower
109 Beasley Dr.
Franklin, TN 37064
615-595-0060
hardcorehorsepower.net

Holley
866-464-6553
holley.com

Hotchkis Performance
12035 Burke St., Ste. 13
Sante Fe Springs, CA 90670
888-735-6425
hotchkis.net

Just Dashes
5941 Lemona Ave.
Van Nuys, CA 91411
818-780-9005
justdashes.com

Keisler Automotive Engineering
2250 Stock Creek Blvd.
Rockford, TN 37853
keislerauto.com

Kelsey Tire
800-325-0091
www.kelseytire.com

Legendary Auto Interiors
121 W. Shore Blvd.
Newark, NY 14513
800-363-8804
legendaryautointeriors.com

Mancini Racing Enterprises
33524 Kelly Rd.
Clinton Twp., MI 48035
www.manciniracing.com

Original Car Radios
originalcarradios.com

Passion4Mopars
363 E. Lansdowne Ave.
Orange City, FL 32763
865-365-5833
passion4mopars.com

Promax Carbs & Performance
30 Gasoline Alley, Ste. A
Indianapolis, IN 46222
317-484-1451
promaxcarbs.com

Ray Barton Racing Engines
224 E. Penn Ave.
Robesonia, PA 19551
610- 693-5700
raybarton.com

Restorations by Rick
Rick Kreuziger
608-697-0994
restorick.com

R/T Specialties
2156 E. St. Rte. 292
Falls, PA 18615
570-388-1082
rtspecialties.net

Spicer Automotive and
    Four-Wheel Drive
8613 N. Hwy. 27
Rock Springs, GA 30739
709-375-5000

Steer and Gear
1000 Barnett Rd.
Columbus, OH 43227
800-253-4327
steerandgear.com

Stephens Performance
9321 Hwy. 207
Anderson, AL 35610
888-466-7276
stephensperformance.com

Ssnake-Oyl Seat Belt Restoration
114 N. Glenwood Blvd.
Tyler, TX 75702
800-284-7777
ssnake-oyl.com

Totally Auto
337 Philmont Ave.
Feasterville, PA 19053
215-322-2277
totallyautoinc.com

YearOne
P.O. Box 521
Braselton, GA 30517
800-932-7663
yearone.com